D1042379

Greenhill Books

ACES OF THE REICH

ACES OF THE REICH

The Making of a Luftwaffe Fighter-Pilot

Mike Spick

Greenhill Books, London
MBI Publishing, St Paul

Greenhill Books

Aces of the Reich
The Making of a Luftwaffe Fighter-Pilot

First published in 2006 by Greenhill Books/Lionel Leventhal Ltd, Park House,
1 Russell Gardens, London N11 9NN
www.greenhillbooks.com
and
MBI Publishing Co., Galtier Plaza, Suite 200, 380 Jackson Street,
St Paul, MN 55101-3885, USA

British Library Cataloguing-in Publication Data
Spick, Mike
Aces of the Reich : the making of a Luftwaffe fighter-pilot
1. Germany. Luftwaffe – History – World War, 1939–1945
2. Fighter pilots – Germany – History
3. World War, 1939–1945 – Aerial operations, German
I. Title
940.5'44943

ISBN 1-85367-675-6

Library of Congress Cataloging-in Publication Data available

For more information on our books, please visit www.greenhillbooks.com, email
sales@greenhillbooks.com, or telephone us within the UK on 020 8458 6314. You can
also write to us at the above London address.

Edited and typeset by Palindrome
Printed and bound by Creative Print and Design (Wales), Ebbw Vale

CONTENTS

List of Illustrations   7
Prologue   9
1   The Richthofen Legacy   17
2   The Commanders   25
3   The Fledglings   39
4   The Fighter Force   51
5   Victory by Day   73
6   The Conflict Widens   94
7   Strategic Defence   126
8   The Net Closes   147
9   New Weapons, Old Errors   161
10   Five Minutes to Midnight   175
11   The *Experten* (1)   192
12   The *Experten* (2)   208
13   The *Experten* (3)   223
References   235
Index   237

ILLUSTRATIONS

Photographs

Alfred Galland	97
Hermann Graf with Willi Messerschmitt	98
Walter Nowotny	99
Heinz-Wolfgang Schnaufer with Helmut Lent	100
'Franzl' Lützow with Wilhelm Balthasar	101
'Jochen' Müncheberg with film star Carola Höhn	102
Herbert Ihlefeld with RAF pilot Howard Squire	103
Otto Schulz	103
Günther Rall with Walter 'Graf Punski' Krupinski	104
Wilhelm Batz with Gerd Barkhorn and Otto Fönnekold	105
Werner Streib	106
Erich Hohagen	106
Johannes 'Macky' Steinhoff	107
Horst 'Jakob' Tietzen	107
Kurt Bühligen with Adolf Dickfeld and Erich Rudorffer	108
Otto Kittel	109
Theodor Weißenberger	110
Dietrich Hrabak	111
Hannes Trautloft	111
Helmut Lipfert	112
Walter 'Gulle' Oesau	112

Graphs and Diagrams

The Break	52
The Sandwich	54
The *Abschwung*	56
Aircraft Guns: projectile weight/rate of fire	60
Second World War Fighters: comparative weights of fire	64

Aircraft Guns: weight of fire/muzzle velocity   66

Angle-off Shooting   68

Variations on a *Staffel* Formation   70

Comparison of Bf 109E vs Spitfire IA and Hurricane I:
maximum level speed/altitude   74

Comparison of Bf 109E vs Spitfire IA and Hurricane I:
sustained rate of climb/altitude   76

Comparison of Bf 109E vs Spitfire IA: Acceleration/CL_{max} 78

Deflection Shooting   80

Gun Attack Angles   85

Comparison of Bf 109E vs Spitfire IA: Minimum radius sustained
turn   86

The Effect of Speed on Turn Radius   114

Boxing   116

Radar Interpretation   132

Limiting Mach Numbers: Me 262 vs Allied Fighters   165

The Roller-Coaster   185

The Up-and-Under Attack   209

PROLOGUE

'I started a wide left-hand turn, handling the controls of the sensitive high-speed aircraft carefully so as not to lose any of its momentum. The engines were humming evenly and without vibration. Just at that moment a swarm of Lightnings – American twin-boom fighters – shot across beneath us...

'With a shout of "Lightnings down to port!" I found myself in a steep curving climb, partly to avoid the possibility of any others that might be above us taking us by surprise, and partly to get into position to attack. Fährmann (my wingman) had tried in vain to stay with me, but was now hopelessly left behind some 1,000 metres (more than 3,000 feet) below, undoubtedly looking all over the place for me...

'It all happened very fast. I could not worry about Fährmann; I had so much excess speed (and was gaining more the longer I dived) that I had my hands full looking after myself. The safety catch on my weapons had to be released. I uncaged the reflex sight – a luminous area on the windshield in front of me – and it promptly began to wander all over the place. We were trying for the first time to fire with a gyroscopic sight that allowed for lead and obliged the pilot to line the sight up with the target... Then the Lightnings loomed up terrifyingly fast in front of me, and it was only for the space of seconds that I was able to get into firing position behind one of the machines on the outside of the formation. And as if they had received prior warning, they swung round smartly as soon as I opened fire. Pop, pop, pop, went my cannon in furious succession. I tried to follow a Lightning's tight turn but the gravity pressed me down on my parachute with such force that I had trouble keeping my head in position to line the sight up with him. The sight was still wandering all over the windscreen and I shot too short; I thought I could see the acceleration drag the shells down to pass harmlessly below the Lightning's fuselages. Then a shudder went through my aircraft as my leading-edge flaps sprang out: I had exceeded the permissible gravity load.

'The Lightnings made for the ground in tight spirals. No use trying to follow them: the Me 262 had no dive brakes. It was agony every time, losing height without picking up so much speed that the aircraft became uncontrollable.'

Oberst Johannes Steinhoff, 176 victories

It was April 1945. The very experienced Steinhoff had opened his account as long ago as 1939. Since then, he had flown in the West, against Britain, and in the Soviet Union, North Africa and the Mediterranean, then on home defence against the American bomber fleets. Now he flew the world's most advanced fighter, the Messerschmitt Me 262. He commenced the combat with the classic air combat advantages of height and position. His opponents were Lockheed P-38 Lightnings of the USAAF, a type widely regarded as a turkey. He was never at any point on the defensive. While the Lightnings were more numerous, this did little more than to provide the German Experte with a target-rich environment. And yet he failed to score.

In fact, this combat was a throwback to a design controversy dating from 1916. The question was: which is the most desirable quality for a fighter; performance or manoeuvrability? Both had their advocates. Performance consisted of three elements; speed, ceiling, and rate of climb. Manoeuvrability was basically the ability to out-turn one's opponent.

A speed advantage allowed a fighter to overhaul a slower opponent and attack it. By allowing an attacker to close quickly from visual distance to guns range, it made a surprise attack easier to achieve. Finally, it made disengagement easier if circumstances were not propitious. A higher ceiling potentially gave an altitude advantage which in a dive could be traded for speed. Rate of climb allowed an altitude advantage to be obtained; it also allowed a pilot to remove himself vertically from a dogfight if things got too hot.

Manoeuvre gave fewer advantages, although these were often regarded as critical. On the defensive, it allowed a rapid turn out of the line of fire which a faster, if less manoeuvrable attacker, was unable to follow. On the attack, the ability to turn inside an opponent allowed the sights to be held on target for longer.

Ideally, a fighter needed performance and manoeuvrability advantages, but as turning rate and radius are functions of speed, for a variety of reasons, this was not possible.

In the combat described, the turbojet-powered Me 262 was more than 120 mph (190 kph) faster than the propeller-driven Lightning in level flight, and could outclimb it with ease. When sighted, the Lightnings were probably at combat cruise, and a reasonable assumption of the speed differential would be about 200 mph (320 kph). So there was Steinhoff, with both speed and altitude advantage.

But he did not attack straightaway. Instead he pulled high, suspecting a trap. It is axiomatic that for any high-scoring fighter ace, the first priority is survival. The logic is simple. If you don't survive, you don't build up a score. By the seventh year of the war, Steinhoff's survival instincts were finely honed. And by April 1945, only a rump of the Jagdwaffe was left to face hordes of Allied fighters. For nearly three years, being increasingly heavily outnumbered had become a way of life.

On spotting the Lightnings below, his instinctive reaction was to assume that there might be others above and behind. So he pulled high to clear his tail. As Steinhoff himself commented, '…years of practice at sneaking up on the enemy, dodging out of his way, and hiding in the infinity of sky, had developed new and unknown instincts in the few who had survived.'

So quickly did he react that his regular *Kacmarek* (wingman) Leutnant Fährmann, who was probably searching the sky astern for danger, was caught flat-footed and left trailing far below. Given the outstanding performance of the Me 262, this was no big deal. Even if attacked, Fährmann could probably look after himself. More importantly Steinhoff now had an altitude advantage over the American fighters.

In a conventional propeller-driven fighter, this would have been no great problem. Steinhoff would have nosed down, selected a target, and quickly closed to guns range. In the Me 262, things were not so simple. Aerodynamically clean, it accelerated rapidly in a dive. As it approached its limiting Mach number, heavy buffeting would start, making accurate aiming impossible. Then when the limit was exceeded, the aircraft became uncontrollable. The problem was compressibility, then very much an imperfectly understood phenomenon. The Me 262 was red-lined at 595 mph (957 kph), and to exceed this was to court disaster.

Too great an altitude advantage was therefore potentially embarrassing. Matters were not helped by a lack of speed brakes; Willi Messerschmitt had designed his fighter to go fast; he had not foreseen the need to slow it. Nor, with the immature Jumo 004 turbojets, was throttling back a practical proposition. Unless done very gently, this would result in a compressor stall (the jet equivalent of a backfire), followed by the engine flaming out.

Neither was slowing down a viable option for the Me 262. Wing loading for both types was very similar, as was turning ability co-speed. Even worse, the Lightning could tighten its turn significantly by using combat flaps and throttling back its inside engine; a facility not available to the Me 262.

The heart of the matter is that while the Lightning was not a dogfighter, the Me 262 was even worse. Disturbed airflow caused by hard manoeuvring could result in compressor stalling and flameout. Even when this did not happen, hard manoeuvring bled off speed at an alarming rate as the angle of attack, and with it, drag, was increased.

But whereas the Allison engines of the Lightning provided good acceleration from low speeds, this was not the case with the Jumo turbojets. Although these ran at high revs, typically 8,000, the acceleration they provided was very poor compared to that of a propeller-driven aircraft. Once lost, speed was only slowly regained, and until it was, the Me 262 was vulnerable.

The Me 262 handled nicely, but it was no aircraft for a novice. In combat, events happened so fast that even experienced flyers had difficulty in keeping track. Then the turbine inlet temperatures (TITs) of the engines had to be monitored continually. If these were allowed to rise above a certain level, fire was inevitable. And with an engine out, as happened all too often, asymmetric handling was far from easy.

It must of course be said that the Lightning, which featured a yoke rather than the typical fighter control column, was also a very busy aircraft to fly. Engine temperatures and oil pressure all had to be checked regularly. The Jagdwaffe rightly regarded it as inferior to the single engined P-47 Thunderbolt and the P-51 Mustang.

If this was not enough, Steinhoff had a further problem to deal with. The new reflex sight, which required the target to be tracked for a second or two to allow it to compute the necessary aim-off for shooting, was not working properly, owing to faulty installation.

We are left with Steinhoff on a high perch, accelerating rapidly downhill, trying hard not to reach the compressibility region, and seeking a target. His next problem was rate of overtake. With what was probably a closure rate exceeding 300 ft/sec (90 m/sec) and a maximum effective firing range of about 1,000 ft (300 m), time available to line up and shoot was marginal.

Under normal circumstances, an overtake speed of about 200 mph (360 kph) would have allowed a fair chance of surprise. But with a dozen or so pairs of American eyes, all on the *qui vive* for German fighters, there was little chance of surprise being achieved. When Steinhoff finally arrived within shooting distance, the by now alerted Americans took evasive action.

As Steinhoff recorded; 'I thought I could see the acceleration (g) drag the shells down to pass harmlessly below the Lightning's fuselages!' This was quite possible. The 30-mm Mauser MK 108 cannon carried by the German jet were designed to destroy heavy bombers, needing an average of three hits. Against small manoeuvring targets they were less effective, as the low muzzle velocity resulted in quite severe projectile drop over any distance. Even worse was the effect known as bullet trail, caused by firing during hard manoeuvring. As the shells left the muzzles of the cannon, the g-forces (acceleration) imparted caused them to deviate from a straight path. Almost certainly this is what Steinhoff observed. One final point: a higher muzzle velocity would have minimised the deviation and improved accuracy. Neither were matters helped by the failings of the reflex sight.

But whatever the shortcomings of the weaponry and sighting system, the real reason that 'Macky' Steinhoff had failed to add to his score was a huge performance mismatch. The new German jet was the first of a whole new fighter generation. For the entire period of the war, new fighter aircraft and variants had been continually introduced by all combatant nations. The improvements had largely concentrated on performance, and with the exception of rate of roll, manoeuvrability had suffered. The performance increments were generally small, and had seen the advantage pass from one type to another; from one air force to another, with none able to establish a commanding lead for long.

The dominant factor in air combat had always been pilot quality. The more experienced or better-trained fighter pilots were able to take full advantage of superior performance when they had it, and to minimise the effects when the enemy held the upper hand. Of course, this was modified to a degree by the local situation, such as heavy odds, or who had the initiative. But by and large the steps were small.

Then in late 1944 the Me 262 made its combat debut. This was a huge step by any reckoning. What it produced was a situation where all enemy fighters were totally outclassed in terms of performance, but were far superior in manoeuvrability. In fact, the overwhelming speed advantage was a mixed blessing. In fighter versus fighter combat, the vast majority of victories were scored using the surprise bounce from above and astern, which gave an easy no-deflection shot at a non-manoeuvring target. Even if the attack was spotted at the last moment, it was usually too late for the victim to do much about it.

At the outbreak of war some sixty-eight months earlier, effective guns range, i.e. the maximum distance at which the average pilot could realistically expect to hit something, was about 1,000 feet (300 metres). The ideal closing speed was about 50 mph (80 kph); not too fast; but not too slow. Once guns range was reached, the attacker had to decide: open fire at once, or keep closing, thus risking the chance of detection to get a better shot.

Only one thing was certain. Once fire was opened, unless the first burst was fatal, the victim would not sit quietly and wait to be finished off. Instead he would take violent evasive action, making himself a very difficult target. The attacker would then have to decide whether to follow, or disengage. The latter was the percentage option, with an overtake margin sufficient to allow it. To continue the attack was to risk being forced to fly through and end up in front. And almost certainly, the victim had friends at hand.

Aircraft guns had made considerable strides since 1939. The newer 20-mm cannon had a higher muzzle velocity and rate of fire than before, and in theory could be used at much longer ranges – but only by a tiny minority of exceptionally gifted marksmen. But with the EZ 42 reflex sight a failure, the pre-war Revi reflector sight remained standard. Therefore for the average pilot, maximum effective gunnery distance remained unchanged.

Unlike propeller-driven fighters, cruising speed for the early jets was very near their maximum speed. The overall result was that when using a surprise bounce, closure was rarely less than 200 mph (320 kph), and sometimes a good deal more. Travelling at nearly 300 feet (90 m/sec), the time available to aim and shoot was very brief – little more than one second. As Steinhoff recalled, '...the Lightnings loomed up terrifyingly fast in front of me'. Overshooting was impossible to avoid, but in the normal way of things, the Me 262 would be out of range before its opponents could react. Mid-air collisions in the new jet were all too possible. Disengagement downwards was not a good idea; the Mach limit would be reached all too quickly. Upwards was a better option, but gently. Too hard a pull and speed would be dumped; never a good idea in fighter combat, and even worse given the poor acceleration of the jet.

The Me 262 was designed as a bomber destroyer. It could penetrate the screen of escort fighters with ease, thanks to its speed, but then had to get well within the reach of the bomber's defensive fire in order to attack. This weakness was addressed by using a battery of twenty-four R4M rockets carried underwing, but as the effective range of these was only about 1,800 feet (550 metres), this was not enough to keep them out of the danger area. In any case, it was too little, too late.

In 1939, the Jagdwaffe had started the war with an excellent single-engined fighter, and the best tactical system in the world. They had swept the skies clean over Poland, Norway, France and the Low Countries. Only over Britain in 1940 did they have a setback, which they regarded as temporary. In 1941, they not only held their own over France, but cut a deadly swathe through the Soviet Air Force. They were also successful in the Balkans, over Malta, and in the Western Desert.

The tide turned against them in 1943, from which time they were too overstretched and outnumbered to be really effective. A shining example in a tarnished cause, the Jagdwaffe *Experten* set victory scores that will never be beaten, fighting on until exhaustion claimed them. For them, the Me 262 was the last throw of the dice. This is their story.

CHAPTER I

THE RICHTHOFEN LEGACY

The Treaty of Versailles in 1919 had dealt harshly with the defeated Germany, and one of its provisions was to proscribe all forms of military aviation. Humiliated but determined, Germany sought to circumvent the ban. Fortunately for them, the victorious Allies had not occupied the country, which meant that they could make a small clandestine start. As early as 1920, the Defence Ministry connived at the formation of the Deutscher Luftsportverband. This unique organisation, which provided free or heavily subsidised flying and gliding for the masses, had no counterpart anywhere else in the world.

The bold investment paid off. By 1930, Germany had a large reservoir of air-minded youth with elementary flying skills. This could be drawn upon when the time came, as it certainly would, to rearm. Behind the scenes, other plans were brewing. Civil aviation, and in particular the national airline Deutsche Lufthansa, was being developed with military needs in mind. Then with the full co-operation of the Soviet Union, a clandestine military aviation school and weapons-testing area was set up at Lipetsk, south of Moscow.

At home, civilian flying schools provided a covert nucleus of trainees for the military; then with the advent in 1933 of Adolf Hitler as Chancellor, aircraft factories and airfields were built; modern military aircraft were developed (some Second World War bombers started life as airliners or fast mailplanes), and the cloak of secrecy became ever harder to maintain. It was finally dropped on 1 March 1935, when the Luftwaffe was officially revealed.

In any fighting service, tradition looms large. In the First World War, the Luftstreitkräfte had been the aviation branch of the army. To a degree this was also the case with the new Luftwaffe; its pilots were regarded, and referred to themselves, as soldiers of the Reich. For tradition, all they had to do was to hark back to the previous conflict. As well as tradition, they needed heroes, role models. These abounded: not a few unit leaders at this time were distinguished flyers from the earlier conflict, as was the Commander-in-Chief, Hermann Göring. But the influence of one man stood head and shoulders above the others.

The Red Baron Legend

Rittmeister (cavalry captain) Manfred Freiherr von Richthofen, better known as the Red Baron, is still, almost a century later, a name to conjure with. He was not actually a baron, although the soubriquet has stuck, but a slightly lesser Freiherr, nevertheless a minor aristocrat. The scion of Prussian landed gentry, he commenced the war as an officer in a Uhlan (lancer) regiment, but after an undistinguished career with the cavalry became bogged down behind the Western Front trenches. Bored beyond belief, he transferred to the fledgling German air service, the Luftstreit-kräfte, first as an observer, then as a pilot. Then in just twenty-one months, from September 1916 until his death in action in April 1918, he was credited with shooting down eighty enemy aircraft, to become the top scoring fighter-pilot of the war. His all-red fighter had become almost as well-known to his mainly British foes as to his friends.

In 1914, warfare was regarded as a glamorous occupation. The public perception was waving banners, headlong cavalry charges, the sun spark-ling on swords and bayonets, deeds of outstanding heroism, brilliant victories in double-quick time, medals and above all glory. But when in early 1915 the front lines stretched unbroken from the Alps to the North Sea, with no gaps or open flanks to exploit, the illusion was shattered. Battlefields became moonscapes of mud and shell craters, bounded by elaborate trench systems protected by barbed-wire hedgerows that sprouted almost overnight. Not only was the slaughter on an unimagin-able scale; it was almost completely anonymous. Artillery was by far the biggest killer. The big guns sited behind the lines lobbed shells at targets which for the most part they never saw, killing men by tens of thousands. Infantry, attacking across open ground, were mown down by faceless machine-gunners. Cavalry lurked impotently in the rear areas, awaiting a call to exploit a breakthrough which never came. Any heroic deeds were too often overshadowed by the enormity of the general carnage in what had become a war of attrition. Of glory there was little trace.

Except in the air. As the war progressed, increasing use was made of aeroplanes; reconnaissance, bombing and, inevitably, air fighting. Only gradually were means and methods for the latter developed, and not until the latter half of 1915 did the first successful German fighter-pilots begin to emerge.

In those days, flying was rightly regarded as inherently dangerous. Air combat was even more so; it was so unlike any previous form of warfare that it was positively exotic. Even better, most early combats were one versus one. Fighter-pilots became the single combat champions of the time; the spiritual heirs of the Teutonic Knights of old. They performed their deeds in the lists of the sky, in full view of vast audiences on the ground. And their successes were measurable by the number of their victories; of fallen opponents. For them a measure of chivalry was possible; something virtually unattainable in ground fighting. Desperate for good news to boost national morale, the German press, actively assisted by the high command, swung into action, providing the public with authentic heroes.*

It was against this background that the Richthofen legend began. As his score mounted, he was fêted by the highest in the land and awarded a chestful of medals and decorations. Nor were these only from Prussia and other German states, but from German allies as diverse as Bulgaria and Turkey. Photographs of him were widely on sale, and articles about him appeared in newspapers and magazines. His decision to paint his personal aircraft bright red all over was generally interpreted as a challenge to his opponents, which added to his glamorous image. Then late in his career, while recovering from a serious wound, he wrote a biography called *Der Rote Kampfflieger (The Red War Flyer)*, which spread his fame far beyond his homeland. He was dubbed 'The Red Baron' by his opponents, a unique distinction, and his score of eighty victories was never equalled in the First World War. He has since become the most famous fighter-pilot of all time,† even though his tally was exceeded by no less than 153 German pilots in the Second World War. As a call to arms and an inspiration to his Jagdwaffe successors, he had no equal.

Such is the legend. Without wishing to denigrate his achievements, what is the truth behind it? First, his eighty victories. In the main, these can be confirmed from the records. Just a handful are a bit 'iffy'. Nor was it done without cost. Many times his fighter was hit by return fire, but he

---

* The French had pioneered the ace system for five victories. Later in the war, the German equivalent became the *Oberkanone*, for which ten victories were required.
† US studies of air combat over Vietnam in the 1960s and 1970s were codenamed 'Red Baron'.

escaped unscathed. Then on 9 March 1917, an antiquated FE 8 holed his fuel tank. He force-landed, fortunate that he did not catch fire on the way down. On 6 July he was shot down again, this time by an obsolete FE 2d two-seater. Having suffered a severe head wound, he was extremely lucky to get down in one piece. The final act came on 21 April 1918, when he found the glorious death in action that he had so often visited on others. This was the crucial part of the legend. A dead hero can be immortalised in a way that the living cannot. He becomes idealised; his human failings can be glossed over. So let it be with Caesar!

Of course, Richthofen has had his detractors. A few have accused him of seeking easy victories, citing his tally of two-seaters, which his own fighter outclassed, as evidence. How justified was this? Pull up a sandbag, and we'll take a look.

Of his eighty victories, more than a third were single-seat fighters. Of these, four were inferior DH 2s; two were agile but underpowered Sopwith Pups; a DH 5 and a Sopwith Dolphin. The remainder were three SE 5as, eight Sopwith Camels, four Nieuport 17s, one Sopwith Triplane, and four SPAD 7s, which were all demonstrably at least equal to whichever fighter type he was flying at the time.

The others were a mixed bag. Two bombers, a single-seater Martinsyde Elephant and a two-seater DH 4. Of the other two-seaters, nineteen were obsolescent FE 2 pushers. Three Sopwith Strutters and an FK 8 were the most advanced two-seaters to fall to his guns, but the remainder, BE 2s and RE 8s, mainly engaged on photo-reconnaissance and artillery-spotting missions, were rightly regarded as turkeys in air combat.

The latter were the easiest victims. Slow and unwieldy, often flying alone, with their crews concentrating on their primary task, they were relatively easy to take by surprise. Even when they were escorted, a dive from a high perch, preferably out of the sun, was usually enough to elude the escorts. While it is probably true to say that they were sitting ducks, the fact remains that they could bite back. Neither of the two aircraft which came within inches of killing the Red Baron could be described as first-line fighters.

There is another consideration. Albeit indirectly, photo-reconnaissance aircraft and artillery-spotters contributed more to the effectiveness of the ground war than any other air asset. They were therefore high value targets. Their destruction was arguably Richthofen's greatest material contribution to the war as a whole.

Although an accomplished marksman, the Red Baron was not the greatest aircraft handler around. As he admitted, his first twenty victories were scored before he had fully mastered his machine. His usual technique was to manoeuvre for a position above and astern before plunging down to attack. If his opponent tried to evade, he would try and turn inside him to retain a position of advantage. As a pilot, he was competent enough to gain good shooting positions, close in and with no deflection.

Richthofen was dismissive of what he called stunting, by which he mainly meant looping. He commented, 'One could be quite a splendid stunt flyer and still not be able to shoot down a single plane. In my opinion, stunting is all a waste of time.' He might have recalled his eleventh victory, over the RFC ace Lanoe Hawker. Flying the inferior performing but more agile DH 2, Hawker had fought him to a near draw by superior flying, in a protracted combat which only a lucky shot had ended.

However, he had a point. It must be admitted that superior performance provided the majority of good shooting opportunities. Extravagant manoeuvres were of more use defensively than when on the attack. In the whirl of a dogfight, shooting chances were fleeting, and usually from high deflection angles. The result was much shooting but few hits. It is therefore strange that in the final months of his career, he favoured the superbly manoeuvrable Fokker Triplane over the significantly faster Albatros D V.

Richthofen had been fortunate in his introduction to combat flying. He had been personally selected by the Maestro, Oswald Boelcke, later dubbed 'The Father of Air Fighting', and had been well versed by him in air combat tactics. As a leader, the Baron seems to have added little or nothing to Boelcke's teachings.

Tactically he was naïve. He stated that the decisive factor in victory was personal courage, yet referred to the bravery of his English opponents as often being akin to stupidity. Prussian arrogance? He also stated:

The fighter-pilots should have an allotted area to cruise around in as it suits them, but when they see an opponent they must attack and shoot him down. Anything else is absurd. Nothing else matters to us but the aerial victory.

This was to disregard totally the needs of the mission and the overall strategic situation. In the Luftwaffe of the Second World War, it was to have unimaginable consequences.

What sort of man was Manfred von Richthofen? Ernst Udet, the ranking surviving German ace of the Great War, described him as 'cold-eyed'. He habitually took a nap at lunchtime, to be fresh for the after-noon's operations. His brother Lothar recorded that under his command, life on the ground consisted of eating, sleeping and absolutely no alcohol. Obviously he had little sympathy for the need of his men to unwind. Never a man to court popularity, he led by example, and woe betide a new pilot who failed to live up to his exacting standards.

Ambition was a less attractive side to his character.Following his sixteenth victory he recorded that he was the leading, i.e. top-scoring, fighter-pilot in the Luftstreitkräfte and that this had been the goal he wanted to achieve.

This was stretching the truth. His great tutor and mentor, Oswald Boelcke, had been credited with forty victories, against which Richthofen's score of sixteen was small beer. Boelcke, undefeated in combat, had been killed in a mid-air collision with one of his own men barely three months earlier. Nor was it only Boelcke. Kurt Wintgens had amassed eighteen vic-tories before falling in September 1916. All Manfred von Richthofen could honestly claim was that he was the leading surviving German fighter-pilot.

Also following his sixteenth victory, Richthofen showed signs of pique that he had not yet been awarded the *Pour le Mérite*, the highest Prussian decoration for valour.* Boelcke and Immelmann had both been awarded it after eight victories, but times had changed. Days passed with no sign of the award, and Richthofen felt that he had been overlooked. Ten days later, he was posted to command the so far unsuccessful Jagdstaffel (Jasta) 11. Petulantly, he wrote that he would rather have had the *Pour le Mérite*. Then on 16 January 1917, twelve days after his sixteenth victory, the coveted award was announced. Overnight he became a national hero.

The Trophy Hunter

Richthofen was an avid collector of trophies, a trait that probably stemmed from his passion for hunting. On gaining his first victory, he had ordered a small silver cup on which was engraved the date and the type of his victim. Uniquely he kept up this vainglorious practice with successive victories, each tenth cup being slightly larger than the others. This con-tinued until after his sixtieth victory, when a national shortage of silver forced him to desist.

More understandably, whenever possible he obtained a trophy from

---

* Better known to the British as the Blue Max.

each of his victims – a machine gun, a strip of fabric bearing the number of the victim, etc. As a Jasta commander, he had even more licence. After each victory, he sent one of his officers out, ostensibly to gather details for his remarkably well-documented combat reports, but also to gather souvenirs for his collection.

In addition, he compiled scrapbooks. While this was in some ways understandable, they contained many photographs, some rather ghoulish, of his fallen victims. Over time, his office, and later a room at his home in Schweidnitz, became a gallery of the dead. Cups, mementos and scrapbooks; was this really a chivalrous way of honouring vanquished foes?

In his early days as a Jasta commander, he painted his machine bright red all over; a move which led his RFC opponents to dub him first *'le petit rouge'*, then the name by which he went down to posterity, 'the Red Baron'. In *Der Rote Kampfflieger*, he states that he did it for no particular reason, although he gloated that from then on, '…absolutely everyone knew my red bird. In fact, even my opponents were not completely unaware of it'. One can almost hear him say 'Fee, Fi, Fo, Fum, I smell the blood of an Englishman!'

To digress briefly, Richthofen was not the first pilot to fly an all-red aeroplane in the war. A year earlier, French ace Jean Navarre had gained a fearsome reputation over the Verdun sector. His red Nieuport 11 made him instantly recognisable to his opponents, giving him a psychological advantage even before combat was joined. Could something similar have entered the mind of Manfred von Richthofen?

In a later edition of *Der Rote Kampfflieger*, his brother Lothar gives a far more prosaic explanation. The red colour was adopted to make him instantly recognisable in the air as the leader. It is known that after taking over Jasta 11, Richthofen experimented with colour schemes to make his fighter less visible in the air. When this proved impossible, he went to the other extreme. But not, as *Der Rote Kampfflieger* suggests, instantly; but in easy stages. He started with red wheels and tail, added an all-red fuselage, then progressed to all-over red.

After a mêlée, the Jasta needed to reform, but picking out on whom to reform was difficult.* Red wheels and tail was a start, but possibly not enough at any distance or at certain angles. The red fuselage was almost certainly adequate. The use of all-red was probably for dramatic effect.

There were other benefits. Witnesses to a Red Baron victory could be

---

* The problem was universal. The RFC used streamers to denote leaders.

in no doubt as to who had scored it, while if he was in trouble his men would hasten to his aid. Richthofen certainly revelled in being known to his opponents. He also recounted with relish a myth current at that time, that the Royal Flying Corps had formed a special squadron to hunt him down, with extravagant rewards for the victor. While it is clear that he did not believe the story, it all added to the legend. A whole squadron needed to counter the German champion!

Not that the Red Baron was ever recorded as flying alone, although there were several 'lone wolf' aces current at this time. Invariably he flew at the head of a flight of five, if not the entire Jasta, while later in his career, after Jagdgeschwader 1 had been formed, he often led thirty or more fighters at once.

One thing was certain; his all-red fighter made him a magnet for the British. Reluctantly he allowed the other members of his *Staffel* to paint their aircraft red, but with distinguishing colours on certain areas, such as the tail or control surfaces. In the confusion of the dogfight, this at least made for instant identification between friend and foe, although it worked equally well for both sides.

The practice of personalising aircraft markings spread to other units, and some truly exotic paint schemes appeared. These gave rise to the final part of the legend. The always irreverent British dubbed these large and brightly coloured formations 'Richthofen's Flying Circus'.

Although Richthofen is sometimes depicted as jealously guarding his position, especially against his brother Lothar, he was never seriously challenged for the top spot in the Luftstreitkräfte. He passed Boelcke's tally just under thirty-two weeks after joining Jasta 2. Then on 30 May 1917 his score reached fifty-two, and he was sent on leave. He recorded, 'Strictly speaking, I had been allowed only forty-one; why forty-one is anybody's guess, but I tried to ignore it. I am no record-keeper.'* Given his collection of silver cups and other memorabilia, this seems rather disingenuous.

From this point until his death in April 1918, no other German pilot remotely approached the Red Baron's score, leaving him as the undisputed German champion. His nearest rival was Ernst Udet, who despite having opened his account six months earlier than Richthofen and fighting almost until the end of the war, could only muster sixty-two victories, thirty-nine of them after the Baron's demise.

This then is the Richthofen legend inherited by the Jagdwaffe.

---

* Richthofen was being coy; forty-one was one more than Boelcke.

CHAPTER 2

THE COMMANDERS

Notwithstanding the enduring myth of Teutonic efficiency, the failings of the Luftwaffe in the Second World War stemmed from its command structure. This was deeply flawed. Following the Treaty of Versailles in 1919, the German army was reduced to a rump, with for all practical purposes, no air arm.

Its de facto commander, Generaloberst Hans von Seeckt, was a caricature Prussian: stiff-necked, monocled and moustachio'd, arrogant, conservative to the point where he insisted that Uhlans retained lances, and so inscrutable that he was widely known as 'The Sphinx'. Perhaps surprisingly, he favoured air power, albeit as an adjunct of the *Heer* (army).

In all fairness, he set out to provide the future air arm with high-quality leaders, starting in mid-1920 with a cadre of 180 officers drawn from the former Luftstreitkräfte. It was an interesting selection; all were former staff officers, or were experienced in commanding multi-unit formations. But not one inspirational battle-proven leader.

This was surprising, given that tradition plays a large part in any fighting service, and it was these men on whom tradition in such a new service would be based. The top-scoring surviving German *Oberkanone* of the war, Ernst Udet, with sixty-two victories, was passed over – unsurprisingly, perhaps, as he was a Reserve officer. But so were two former Jagdgeschwader commanders: Bruno Lörzer of JG 3 with forty-one victories and Eduard Ritter von Schleich of JG 4 with thirty-five; both regulars. But long-term, with no aircraft available, Seeckt wanted staff men – organisers, not heroes.

Be that as it may, he laid a firm foundation for the future. The training base at Lipetsk in Russia, which produced the first generation of Luftwaffe flyers, was his initiative. He also actively connived at forming a covert military side of Lufthansa, before a public relations fiasco in 1926 forced his resignation. By this time, the man who was to become one of the prime movers in the new Luftwaffe was on his way up – Erhard Milch.

Erhard Milch

Born in 1892, Erhard Milch became an artillery officer in 1909, and at first served in this role on the Eastern Front. In 1915, he transferred to the Luftstreitkräfte as an observer, rising to command a reconnaissance *Staffel* on the Western Front. For whatever reason, he seems to have been an Anglophile. In May 1918, a British pilot force-landed his badly shot-up aircraft on a German airfield. Taken before the unit commander, Milch, the Englishman astonishingly requested that he be allowed to fly the aircraft that had brought him down.* Even more astonishingly, Milch agreed, with the words, 'Don't try any tricks – you have only ten minutes' fuel.' He later commented:

> Chivalry is only possible between our two peoples. They are close to each other... I was born in the real old Saxon country where some of our words are the same as in English!

Milch's ambition to become a fighter-pilot was never to be realised, but his flair for administration and organisation drew attention from on high. A candidate for staff-officer training, in the late summer of 1918, he became commander of Jagdgruppe 6. For an observer to command a single-seater multi-*Staffel* fighter unit seems strange, but the reason was protocol. At a time when many successful fighter-pilots were Reserve officers, Milch was a regular with flying experience and sufficient seniority.

After the war, Milch worked for the aircraft manufacturer Junkers before joining the state airline Deutsche Lufthansa as a Director. His superb organisational skills quickly made it the world's most efficient airline, drawing comments from future foes that it rarely cancelled flights owing to adverse weather, even when local air-force units were grounded.

He was not allowed to stay there. In January 1933, he joined the still covert Luftwaffe as Göring's deputy. In the following month, he was named State Secretary of Aviation, and given equal rank within the Reichs Air Ministry. His promotion was rapid. *Generalmajor* in March 1934, *Generalleutnant* a year later, following the formal announcement of the formation of the Luftwaffe, *General der Flieger* in April 1936 and

---

* Douglas Bader made a similar request of Adolf Galland in 1941. It was denied.

Generaloberst in November 1938.

Blessed with an enquiring mind, Milch had been instrumental in adopting the blind landing aids used by Lufthansa. He now visited other countries to keep abreast of developments. In October 1938 he visited No. 65 Squadron RAF at Hornchurch. This unit had recently received the reflector gunsight. Peering into the cockpit, Milch enquired, perhaps tongue-in-cheek, how it worked. The pilot, future ace Bob Tuck, dutifully replied that it was so new that he had not yet been instructed in its use. Then to Tuck's horror, an Air Vice Marshal explained it in detail. In fact it was no secret. With British industry unable to produce sufficient quantities, reflector sights for the RAF were being imported from Austria!

Milch was a short man with ruddy cheeks and bright blue eyes. Ambitious, he tended to be sensitive in his relations with colleagues and others. Born to a Jewish father and a Christian mother, in Nazi Germany he had every reason to be touchy. He survived due to some very fancy footwork with official records, probably with Göring's connivance.

Milch had never undergone staff training, and his undoubted organisational and administrative skills were no substitute for those vital middle years when command experience at different levels would have been gained. The second in command of the mighty Luftwaffe was therefore not only an amateur, but was regarded as such by the higher command echelons. But so too was his commander-in-chief!

Hermann Wilhelm Göring

The son of a colonial administrator, Hermann Göring was born in 1893, and served as an infantry officer in the first months of the First World War. In October 1914 he transferred to the air service, at first as an artillery observer. This did not suit his aggressive nature, and in 1915 he trained as a pilot. His first victories were gained on two-seaters, but he then converted to single-seaters. Flying with Jasta 27, which he later commanded, in May 1918 his eighteenth victory brought him the *Pour le Mérite*.

On Manfred von Richthofen's death, command of Jagdgeschwader 1 had passed to Wilhelm Reinhard. Then on 3 July Reinhard and Göring visited Adlershof to test a new fighter. Göring's flight went well, but with Reinhard at the controls, the aircraft broke up and he was killed. Five days later, he was replaced by Oberleutnant Göring, soon to be promoted Hauptmann.

Apart from taking some extended leave, Göring led JG 1 through to the Armistice in November, when he led them home to the Fatherland. On arrival, they wrecked their aircraft rather than surrender them.

It had not been a particularly glorious time for Göring; in the six months between the award of the *Pour le Mérite* and the end of the war, he added only four victories to his previous eighteen. By contrast, Ernst Udet had scored thirty-nine over the same period, more than half of them while Göring commanded the *Geschwader*.

Göring became associated with Hitler and the Nazi Party at an early stage, where he became leader of the *Sturm Abteilung* (Brownshirts), but badly wounded at the time of the abortive Munich *Putsch*, was forced to flee the country. During his lengthy recovery, he became addicted to pain-killing drugs. While this was a propaganda gift to his opponents, too much importance has since been attached to it, as evidenced by the next few years.

Göring returned to Germany in 1927. As a fairly successful business-man, he re-entered politics. His greatest value to Hitler was his entrée into the highest social circles. Men reluctant to meet the vulgar Austrian ex-corporal found it far more difficult to refuse the cultured war hero and former Richthofen *Geschwader* commander. In this way, many industrialists and high-ranking officers were won over to the Nazi cause. Elected in 1927 to the Reichstag as a Deputy, he became its President in February 1932. When in 1933 Hitler came to power, Göring's rise was meteoric. He became *Generalfeldmarschall* in February 1938, having received six promotions in barely five years.

Nor was it just military advancement. In government, Hermann Göring became almost a one-man cabinet: President of Prussia and the Ministries of Aviation, Economics, Forestry and Hunting all came his way. More sinisterly, he became Minister of the Interior for Prussia, which gave him control of the Prussian Political Police, from which he founded the infamous *Geheime Staats Polizei* (Gestapo). The function of this organisation was to impose the will of the Führer on his political opponents. Later, it became part of the SS under Heinrich Himmler.

Abroad, Göring was portrayed as a self-important buffoon, a figurehead for all his various ministries, a dilettante taking the credit for work done by underlings. His reputation as a drug addict, his vanity and love of fancy uniforms and his spectacular girth which fuelled accusations of gluttony all reinforced the myth. But what sort of man was he in reality?

Hermann Wilhelm Göring was a man born out of his time. He would have been far more at home as a Renaissance prince. With a flair for wheeling and dealing, and the exercise of power, he could be benevolent and charming, or an arrogant bully. Or at need, a charming bully. He was cultured. Like Richthofen, Göring enjoyed hunting. But whereas the Red Baron had been a totally dedicated warrior, Göring's interests were far wider, taking in antiques and objets d'art, while a sojourn in Rome in the 1920s fired him with enthusiasm for classical times.

Although the workload of his various ministries was far too much for one man to handle, he was, especially in the years from 1933, extremely energetic and capable. To him in large measure must go the credit for building the nascent Luftwaffe into the formidable fighting force which it became, smoothing the way and making finance available when needed. Albert Kesselring, a pre-war chief of staff, said admiringly of him at this time, 'He was always at his best under pressure, when the rest of us were completely exhausted, and was still able to go on.'*

This was hardly a portrait of a figurehead, a drug addict, or a dilettante. It is more a description of a dominant man who could enthuse and drive his subordinates to achieve a common goal.

Göring carried an aura of authority, even of superiority, that made men instinctively obey. Again, like a Renaissance prince, he could be totally ruthless. Addressing police in 1934 about the need to suppress communists, he stated categorically:

Responsibility must be placed squarely where it belongs. It does not lie with the junior official in the street. I want to hammer it home into your heads that the responsibility lies with me alone. You must be quite clear about that. When you shoot, I shoot. When a man lies dead, it is I who have shot him, even if I happen to be sitting up there in my office in the Ministry. For it is my responsibility alone.†

Ruthless or not, he inspired affection in the populace at large. An accomplished orator, with the common touch to a remarkable degree, he was not averse to jokes about himself. Providing of course that he made them!

---

* Faber (ed.) *Luftwaffe: an Analysis by former Luftwaffe Generals*, New York, 1977.
† Crankshaw, *Gestapo,* London, 1956.

Although in the mid-1930s Göring seemed the embodiment of Teutonic efficiency, this was a façade. Consider the facts. His early interest in and growing collection of art. His intense courtship of his adored first wife Karin, then the wife of another man. After her death, the sumptuous mansion north of Berlin called Karinhall; her mausoleum and her shrine. His close identification with German mythology, the most public sign of which was his exhortation at the funerals of fallen comrades, 'Arise to Valhalla!' Always emotional, he was easily moved to fury or tears. His frequent interventions on behalf of Jewish friends of his second wife Emmy, a former actress, and others, or his love of jewels and fancy uniforms. The fact was that under the Iron Man exterior, Göring was an unabashed romantic.

Nor did he ever let slip an opportunity to associate himself with the glories of the past such as the Order of Teutonic Knights, and the Richthofen legend. The keynote was struck by the foreword to the second edition of *Der Rote Kampfflieger* that he composed in 1933, from which the following extracts are taken:

> ...no weapon of that wondrous and impressive age in which we lived was as striking to the imagination as that of the knightly battle we had to endure, the battle of the flyers who rose up from their fields to engage in the deadly combat of man against man. No one knew if he would come back as the victor or not at all. We Germans must be inspired and imbued with an indestructible pride that of all the champions to soar above the earth, the highest success, the highest honour, the highest renown was won by a German. Manfred Freiherr von Richthofen became not only the greatest battle flyer of Germany, but of the world.

> We will hold Manfred von Richthofen as a great symbol. His memory will help us to use all means in our power to reach our national goal of again giving Germany an air weapon equal to those of other nations, but superior to them in spirit and courageous sacrifice, as was the Jagdgeschwader Richthofen in the World War. It was the highest honour for me as its last commander to be entrusted with the confidence of the leadership of the Jagdgeschwader Richthofen. That mission binds me to the future – I will carry this responsibility – in the spirit of Richthofen.

The message was clear. One day in the future, the new Luftwaffe would be revealed fully formed, to lead Germany into a bright new future. Richthofen would be its knightly hero and symbol; Göring its paladin and torchbearer.

Göring's intensive, almost superhuman, efforts of the early days could not be sustained. With the Luftwaffe out in the open, he increasingly relaxed his grasp, leaving the day-to-day running of the new service in the capable, if ambitious hands of his deputy, Erhard Milch. While this should have been a perfectly practical solution, it soon became a source of friction. Göring was unhealthily proprietorial; it was 'his' Luftwaffe, and no one could be allowed to diminish his standing as commander-in-chief.

His obvious course of action should have been to relinquish at least some of his ministries, and concentrate his undoubted talents on heading the new service. Instead, self-indulgence won. His extravagant tastes and interests demanded a high income, which could only be provided by his portfolio of ministries. He wanted to have his cake, and eat it too.

His next move beggared description. He sought to undermine Milch by reducing his authority, bringing in cronies who bypassed Milch and reported direct to the commander-in-chief. As a case of divide and rule, it was classic. As a way to run an air force, it was a disaster in the making.

Nor did Göring's bombast help. On 9 August 1939, he toured the Ruhr as Economics Minister. In his speech, he stated:

> If an enemy bomber ever succeeds in reaching the Ruhr, my name is not Hermann Göring. You can call me Meier!

At the time it made his audience laugh, but over the years these words came back to haunt him, and by 1943 the joke had worn thin! But by then, all too much of his boasting had proved hollow.

Walther Wever

Wever had spent most of the Great War as a staff officer, in its latter stages working with such luminaries as Hindenburg and Ludendorff, to whom he became adjutant. Then, and in the post-war period, he had shown enough promise as to be touted as a future commander-in-chief.

Wever had two rare gifts. First, he was acutely conscious of what he did not know, and was willing to learn, even to change his mind. Second, he had a flair for getting on with people at all levels, from the megalomaniac Göring to the humblest NCO pilot. Allied to a keen, analytical mind, he was capable of getting things done with a minimum of friction, able to work harmoniously with both Milch and Göring. After a year as head of Training, he became the head of operations, the de facto chief of staff of the covert Luftwaffe, with the rank of Oberst.

Innately conservative, he at first regarded the air arm as an adjunct of the army, but soon became convinced of the merit of strategic bombing. With communism as the perceived threat, his next step was to authorise the construction of prototype bombers, which were unofficially dubbed 'Uralbombers'. Actually, to bomb targets in the Ural mountains from bases in Germany was well beyond the current state of the art, but he took the long view, that advances in technology would one day make it possible.

Like many relatively elderly (mid-forties) officers seconded to the Luftwaffe, he learned to fly, and enthusiastically piloted himself around his command in a fast Heinkel He 70 Blitz. A strong believer in informal discussion, he often carried boxes of cake to help break the ice with junior officers.

Alas, inexperience was his downfall. In May 1936, by now a *Generalmajor*, he took off with his ailerons locked, and was killed in the inevitable crash. With him died not only the possibility of a German strategic bomber force in 1940, but the only man able to hold the balance between Göring and Milch.

While Wever had been the de facto chief of staff, there was never a Luftwaffe general staff as such. In part, this was due to objections from Wever himself, who feared the introduction of an intellectual elite in a small and immature officer corps, as a cause of dissension. Surprisingly, he was backed by both Göring and Milch, who were aware that the officer caste regarded them as meddlesome amateurs. However, this view changed within a year and a general staff was formed.

Ernst Udet

'Udlinger', as he was affectionately known, never rose higher than command of a *Staffel* in the First World War, despite being runner-up to Richthofen with sixty-two victories. Having learned to fly at his own expense, he had started the war as an non-commissioned pilot. When eventually he was commissioned, it was as a Reserve officer, which was sufficient to debar him from higher command. Whereas Richthofen was a 'good enough' flyer but a superb marksman, Udet was an incomparable aircraft handler, who on one occasion fought the French ace Georges Guynemer to a draw. In fact, Udet was by temperament not very German, and certainly not militaristic. A bon viveur, gifted cartoonist and playboy, he was in the British tradition of the talented amateur, unwilling to take anything too seriously.

Failed business ventures post-war saw him barnstorming, flying in three continents, then a stunt pilot in Hollywood. And despite his flair for aircraft handling, he had not the technical skills and aerodynamic knowledge to make even an adequate test pilot. Neither was he a political animal, although on his return to Germany in 1933, he joined the Nazi party, probably at the behest of his old wartime commander Göring. Then in June 1935 he entered the Luftwaffe with the rank of Oberst, and within a year had been appointed Inspector of Fighter and Divebomber Forces.

For this role, which involved little more than flying and reporting, Udet was well suited. But only four months later, he became Head of the Technical Office, responsible for supply and procurement. This involved far more than flying; it was equally a desk job, in which aircraft design and production were even more important than the selection of types for service. Although in the light of later events Udlinger was justified in promoting the Junkers Ju 87 Stuka dive-bomber and the Messerschmitt Bf 109 fighter (Willi Messerschmitt was a friend) as mainstays of the new Luftwaffe, he was unsuited to the task by reason of his lack of administrative experience. In a classic example of the Peter Principle,* Udet had been promoted far beyond his level of competence.

At first, Udet worked harmoniously with Milch, who he taught to fly. But when Göring reorganised the Luftwaffe to curtail Milch's powers, allowing Udet to report directly to his commander-in-chief, friction arose. Both men were of a suspicious nature, and they quickly became estranged. Meanwhile Udet's promotion was rapid; *Generalmajor* on 1 April 1937, *Generalleutnant* on 1 November 1938, and *Generaloberst* in the following year.

As Göring had planned, Udet had undermined Milch, but had paid a heavy price. In November 1941, his health failing, watched by the Gestapo, who were suspicious of his foreign connections, having failed to

---

* The Peter Principle, postulated by Professor Laurence J. Peter, University of Illinois. This states that in any hierarchy, any person who proves competent at one level is automatically eligible for promotion. Provided only that the hierarchy is big enough, a person inevitably arrives at a level in which he is incompetent. Thus it was with Udet.

match production to losses, and increasingly aware that he was incompetent for the job which he held, Udet shot himself.

Albert Kesselring

Born in 1895, Kesselring was commissioned in the artillery, but served on the staff throughout the First World War. He stayed in what remained of the army after the Armistice. An extremely capable administrator, he transferred to the Luftwaffe in late 1933 to head the Administrative Office, but took his allegiance to his new service sufficiently seriously to become a pilot. In 1936 he succeeded Walther Wever to become the first official Luftwaffe chief of staff.

On the face of it he was a good choice; a trained staff officer with a first class mind. A perennial optimist, his benevolent nature concealed an iron will. To his subordinates, he was known as 'Smiling Albert'. Whereas Wever had used cake when visiting a unit, Kesselring mugged up on a technical point. He would then ask questions about it. This quirk soon became known, and units due for a visit would place bets on what it would be. But the fact that he took such pains to impress his junior officers was much appreciated. To them he was 'one of us'.

Unfortunately for Kesselring, the empire-building Milch tried hard to bring the newly-formed Luftwaffe General Staff under his control. Kesselring, the professional officer, was too strong-minded to allow this, and clashes were frequent. Unable, or perhaps unwilling to play political games, he resigned as chief of staff on 30 May 1937. In the following year he headed Luftflotte 1, then in 1940 Luftflotte 2. An outstanding fighting commander, he was promoted to *Generalfeldmarschall* after the successful French campaign.

Hans-Jürgen Stumpf

Kesselring was succeeded as chief of staff by Hans-Jürgen Stumpff, at first *Generalmajor*, then *Generalleutnant*. Five years older than his predecessor, Stumpff was a regular infantry officer during the First World War, and, like him, had remained in the army after it. Transferred to the Luftwaffe in 1933 he became head of personnel, and was probably the oldest of the generals to learn to fly. As chief of staff, he inherited the conflict with Milch, and for the good of the still infant service, decided to capitulate rather than have dissensions tear it apart. The wisdom of this was debatable. He remained chief of staff until January 1939. Promoted to *Generaloberst* in May 1940, his wartime career was unexceptional.

Hans Jeschonnek

The youngest of all Luftwaffe chiefs of staff, Jeschonnek transferred from the infantry to the Luftstreitkräfte in 1917, scoring two victories. After the war he flew briefly with the Freikorps before rejoining the army. Top of his staff training course, he was seconded to tactics and training desk from 1931 in the rank of *Hauptmann*. At one point he became adjutant to Milch, under whom he had served in the First World War, but the two clashed, and he was transferred to KG 152 as *Kommandeur*. Here he attracted the notice of Wever, who saw in him a future successor. This was surprising, as Jeschonnek had an abrasive, very Prussian personality; most unlike the tactful Wever.

Promoted to Major, Jeschonnek became the first *Kommodore* of the *Lehrgeschwader*.* Here he became a proponent of dive-bombing, in which he was supported by Udet. At about this time, Milch severely reprimanded him after a series of fatal accidents caused by low flying over the sea. Relations between the two men never recovered.

In October 1937, by now an *Oberstleutnant*, Jeschonnek became head of operations, the de facto deputy chief of staff, and as a *Generalmajor*, succeeded Stumpff in February 1939. From then on it was all downhill. Being young and fairly malleable, he had won Göring's favour initially. But his abrasive personality had alienated not only Milch, but the senior front-line generals, with the result that he was unable to impose his will on them. With the war going badly, he was buffeted between Hitler, Göring and Milch. Unable to cope with being duty scapegoat, he took his own life in 1943.

Hugo Sperrle

Born in 1885, Hugo Sperrle was truly one of the Old Guard. A pre-war infantry officer, he served with the Luftstreitkräfte during the First World War as an artillery observer. Having recovered from injuries sustained in a crash, he rose to command the air units of the 7th Army. After the war he flew with the Freikorps.

---

* Operational evaluation unit.

Described by Hitler as 'the most brutal-looking of my generals', he wore a monocle. The son of a brewer, he was no aristocrat, but capable rather than outstanding. In 1936, by now a *Generalmajor*, he was selected to command the Condor Legion in Spain. It was not his finest hour, and the infamous bombing of Guernica was a distinct low spot. On his return in 1938, Sperrle was given command of Luftflotte 3, which he retained for much of the war, although following the invasion of the Soviet Union his command became very much a backwater. As a *Generalfeldmarschall* he was retired to the reserve in August 1944.

Wolfram Freiherr von Richthofen

Bearer of the most illustrious name in German military aviation, Wolfram von Richthofen was a cousin of Manfred, and like him, was totally dedicated to the profession of arms. Commissioned as a Hussar in 1913, he fought in the east. Having transferred to the Luftstreitkräfte in October 1917, he flew with Jasta 11 and was credited with nine air victories. Most unusually for a German officer, he studied engineering after the war and achieved a doctorate, before rejoining the *Heer*.

Transferred to the Luftwaffe in 1933, he became head of development in the technical office; a position which, even as a lowly Hauptmann, his engineering background made him well suited. Few Luftwaffe officers of the era were as well qualified to discuss technical matters with aircraft manufacturers.

Progress now was rapid. Two years as Sperrle's chief of staff in Spain was followed by a few months in Germany. Then in December 1938, he returned to Germany to command the Condor Legion as a *Generalmajor*. Back in Germany again, he commanded Fliegerkorps VIII. This was an ironic appointment. In 1934 he had recommended, on perfectly logical grounds, that the Ju 87 dive-bomber should not be put into service, only to be overruled by Udet. His new command, which he would lead successfully through the early years of the Second World War, contained the bulk of the dive-bomber units.

Richthofen was tough-minded and ruthless. Perhaps unjustly, he was often accused of acting the prima donna to get his own way. What is certain was that Jeschonnek, the youthful Luftwaffe chief of staff, was unable to curb him effectively.

Summary

These were the main Luftwaffe commanders at the start of the Second World War. Wever was the de facto chief of staff of the covert Luftwaffe. His greatest attribute was the ability to hold the balance between the commander-in-chief and his deputy. His untimely death was a tragedy for the Luftwaffe. Of the others, commander-in-chief Hermann Göring probably did more than any other man, with the possible exception of the Führer himself, to lose the war. A political appointee, he was a crony of Hitler. His head full of romantic notions, he had no real clue how an air force should be run.

Erhard Milch, his deputy, was an ambitious empire-builder, hell-bent on consolidating his position by manipulating all other departmental heads, chiefs of staff included. In political terms he ran into traffic. As well as some very senior generals, he upset Göring, who was quick to clip his wings. He forced Albert Kesselring to retire from chief of staff. This was a major error; 'Smiling Albert' went on to become not only one of the most distinguished fighting generals, but possibly the best German strategist of the war.

Stumpff and Sperrle can perhaps be categorised as 'good enough'; competent but uninspired.

The most disastrous of Göring's cronies was 'Udlinger' Udet. He was good at playing to the gallery, but little else. Although a first rate aerobatic pilot, he lacked the knowledge to become the head of a technical department. Had he remained General of the Fighter and Dive-bomber Pilots, all might have been well. But as head of the technical department...!

Finally, Jeschonnek. Talented, but young, it is believed that his devotion to the National Socialist cause was a major factor in his appointment to chief of staff. Thrown into the bear pit between Hitler and Göring and the fighting generals, he was never able to cope.

Intelligence

The final major failing of the wartime Luftwaffe was in the field of intelligence. This probably stemmed from Hermann Göring himself. As commander-in-chief, he had several blind spots. For example, he was openly contemptuous of transport pilots. They neither shot down enemy aircraft, nor dropped bombs on enemy targets. And after all, what did intelligence do?

Josef 'Beppo' Schmid

That Josef 'Beppo' Schmid, chief of Abteilung 5, Luftwaffe Intelligence Section, was not held in high regard, can be deduced from his derogatory nickname. He was hardly an ideal choice, especially for a war against England. Not only was he not a pilot; he spoke no English, and had never been out of Germany. Moreover, in 1938 he was a mere major. The importance of this can be gauged by the fact that his English counterpart was an air commodore; the equivalent of a German *Generalmajor*.

Schmid was widely regarded as an unqualified man in a key position. One unflattering description was 'one of the most disastrous men in the Luftwaffe general staff... a boxer's face, without wit or culture. An alcoholic, he started his career with factually false, optimistically exaggerated opinions...'

As Milch said of him, 'The information he provided – it was dreadful. He made a report on Sylt and I thought, "Never have I read such rot". But Göring said, "You know nothing about it". Göring always had the last word.'

Schmid's faulty intelligence assessments would have an ever-increasing influence on the battles to come.

CHAPTER 3

THE FLEDGLINGS

Ever the showman, Hitler had announced the existence of the Luftwaffe like a conjuror pulling a rabbit out of a hat. The fact was that the rabbit had grown too big to be concealed any longer; by 1935 its ears were showing over the brim. To the citizens of the resurgent Third Reich, the impact was nothing less than sensational. Germany now had a modern air force, and the Fatherland could once more hold up its head in the world. To Germany's neighbours, victims in the previous conflict, the Luftwaffe was a source of worry. Military intelligence in Britain and France had of course been aware of the build-up, but the size, composition, and potential of the new German air arm was not known with any accuracy. Thus far, the secrecy surrounding the Luftwaffe had been effective in concealing its weaknesses.

Small Beginnings

A covert organisation, the beginning was necessarily small. At first, the core was centred on Lipetsk. As the Russian winter prevented flying for half the year, this was far from ideal, but it was enough to form a cadre. And at least it was far from the eyes of the main signatories of the Treaty of Versailles, who might well have objected.

In 1925 Werner Junck (five victories in the Great War with Jasta 8), was appointed chief flying instructor at Lipetsk. He was given just two staff instructors, one of whom, Carl-August Freiherr von Schoenebeck (formerly of Jasta 33) had been sent there in the previous year to evaluate the Fokker D XIII fighter.

The first course was a refresher for about thirty *Alte Adler* (Old Eagles), many of them highly decorated. Having to go back to school was not well received by battle-hardened veterans who, in many cases, and possibly with a degree of justification, felt they knew it all. Forced to seek more malleable material, Junck then requested young pilots. At the end of that flying season, he returned with Schoenebeck to Germany on a recruiting drive. Having visited various flying clubs and the DVS (Deutsche Verkehrsfliegerschule – commercial pilot's school) at Stettin, later Schleissheim, they selected a dozen young pilots for the next course.

These first twelve became instructors. Over the seven years between 1927 to 1933, ninety fighter-pilots were trained at Lipetsk, two-thirds of them officer cadets. This was not many; less than the pilot establishment of a single *Geschwader*, but it was a useful start. Of course, Lipetsk was not confined to training fighter-pilots alone; in all about 600 pilots and observers passed through it, but the ratio of fighter-pilots to others was necessarily small, mainly due to the difficulty of keeping them current but covert afterwards.

For example, Johannes Janke arrived at Lipetsk in May 1929 where he flew the Heinkel He 38 and Fokker D XIII. On completing his course he was posted to the *Reklame Staffel*, towing advertising banners with Albatros F 86s. By now, Junck had left to become a test pilot for Heinkel, and was replaced by Schoenebeck. The latter joined Arado as chief test pilot in 1930.

Hans-Heinrich Brustellin, who in 1940 was to lead I/JG 51 against England, was less fortunate. After his course at Lipetsk he returned to the cavalry, with only an annual four-week flying course to keep him up to speed. Hannes Trautloft, who was on the final course at Lipetsk in 1932, also returned to the *Heer*, but not for long. He became an NCO instructor at the DVS, which was then militarised to become the Schleissheim Fighter School. He and Max Ibel appear to have been the only Lipetsk fighter-pilot graduates to be awarded the *Ritterkreuz*.

Lipetsk was never a cheap operation, and its veil of secrecy had become almost impossible to maintain, while its seasonal flying restrictions made it of limited value. With the Nazi accession to power in 1933, it was closed down. An attempt to mount a similar covert operation at Grottaglie in Italy in 1933 foundered because the German pilots, one of whom was future ace and fighter general Adolf Galland, were already better than their Italian instructors. Advanced military flying training was then transferred to Schleissheim. Then when the Luftwaffe became official, secrecy was no longer needed. Recruitment and training could start in earnest.

Recruitment

Recruitment proved no problem. The future Luftwaffe pilots had been children when the previous conflict had ended. They learned at their father's knees (those that still had fathers) the enduring myth that the German army had not been beaten in the field in 1918 but they had been stabbed in the back by defeatist politicians and industrialists at home. The fact that Germany had not been occupied by the victorious Allies was a persuasive argument for this.

They were also told of the iniquities of the Treaty of Versailles, imposed by their vengeful enemies and intended to emasculate Germany militarily. Abroad their country had been ignominiously stripped of its colonies. With the rest of the nation, German youth laboured under a huge perceived weight of injustice. At home, they witnessed civil disorder; fighting in the streets between such diverse groups as Communists, the Stahlhelm (an ex-serviceman's organisation), Hitler's Sturm Abteilung, the SA or Brown-shirts and others, which the police often appeared powerless to control.

Matters quickly went from bad to worse; rampant inflation followed, the worst the world had ever seen, with paper money of huge denomin-ations needed to buy a loaf of bread. This was followed by the world slump, which resulted in six million Germans unemployed.

Conditions were ripe for radical changes. The politicians of the day had failed. Strong leadership was obviously needed to restore Germany to its rightful place in the world. When Adolf Hitler came to power, and not only formally repudiated the Treaty of Versailles but restored the German economy, it seemed to many that such a leader had been found.

Backed by the full resources of the Nazi Party, Hitler became a new Pied Piper, who lured away not only the children of Hamelin, but those of the entire country. In opposition to established movements such as the Scouts (imported from Britain), the Party set up new politically oriented organisations. The more enjoyable outdoor activities, such as cross-country hikes, camping and sing-songs around the campfire, were retained. Added attractions were more glamorous uniforms: riding breeches, jackboots and, most importantly, ceremonial daggers. Nor were rallies and marches neglected; one rally even featured naked maidens riding horses bare-back. The Party really knew how to stage a spectacle. A boy started with the Jungvolk, colloquially known as the *Pimpfe* (squirts), then graduated to the Hitler Jugend; the infamous Hitler Youth. There they were exposed to propaganda films extolling the virtues of the

Teutonic race, and the great Aryan myth of the *Obermensch* (Master Race).

Physical fitness was encouraged, with all forms of sport, particularly in athletics and gymnastics, available. Nor were the girls neglected; the female equivalents were the Jungmädel and the Bund Deutscher Mädel.

Membership of these Nazi youth organisations was not compulsory, any more than Party Membership was compulsory for adults. In fact, non-membership was useful to the party, in that it could indicate political unreliability. But to many youngsters, peer pressure made membership seem desirable. This apart, belonging was fun. Boys are always in a hurry to grow up and become men, and marching, wearing uniform, and carrying a personal weapon, even if it was just a cheapo dagger, was a step in the progress towards manhood.

Even at the time, it was obvious that they were being prepared for military service. Equally, one can argue that Germans have proved more amenable to military discipline than most nations, and patriotism was a strong factor. For German youth at this time, life was good. While the cause for which they later fought was irredeemably tainted, for the most part their original motives were pure enough.

As Germany had become the most air-minded nation on earth, there was no shortage of aircrew volunteers for the Luftwaffe. Moreover, Göring provided inducements to attract the cream of German youth. If on completion of their term of service they failed to find work immediately, they were paid for several months. Or a government loan could be made to set them up in civilian life. And if these benefits, added to the adventure of flying, and duty to the Fatherland were not enough, Göring, always aware of the effect of glamour, introduced a new and smart uniform, with collar and tie replacing the original high-collared tunic.

Even before the Luftwaffe was officially revealed, there were far more aviation candidates than there were vacancies. In 1932, a total of 4,000 applications was received for just twenty DVS places. Among the lucky few was Adolf Galland. As time passed, things got a bit easier, but not a lot. Officer candidates needed the *Abitur* (matriculation), for acceptance. There was however a problem here. More than nine out of every ten young Germans to reach this level had received a classical rather than a technical education. They knew more about ancient Greece and Rome than about the workings of the internal combustion engine. To them, warrior spirit was more important than engineering competence. In what was essentially a technical service, this was a potential source of weakness.

On passing a series of demanding mental and physical tests, the aspiring pilot then spent six months or more at a recruit depot, learning military discipline: square-bashing and exercise. Aviation-related subjects were confined to lectures. The next stage was the A/B Schule, for elementary flying training. This consisted of up to 150 hours flying in biplane trainers. If successful, the aspiring aviator was awarded his pilot's certificate and badge and was assessed as suitable for fighters, bombers, reconnaissance, etc. Those lucky few assessed as suitable then went to Fighter School. This course lasted about three months with about 50 hours flying, culminating with operational types, the Bf 109 or Bf 110.

At this stage the aspirant became truly aware of the dangers of his chosen profession; the accident rate during training, notably on the Bf 109, was on the high side. On graduating, he was posted to an operational unit with about 200 hours in his log book. His rank at this time depended on many things, but often, despite the pilot's badge worn proudly on his left breast pocket, he was a lowly *Gefreiter*, while those destined for eventual commissions were *Fähnenjunker*, or officer cadets.*

The Planes in Spain…

In 1936, the Spanish Civil War broke out. General Franco, the Nationalist (Fascist), leader, requested German aid. Hitler's response was at first limited, but it quickly snowballed to become the Condor Legion; a mini air force entirely consisting of German aircraft and personnel, flying in Spanish Nationalist colours and uniforms. The opposing Republicans (thinly disguised communists) were at least equally aided by Soviet aircraft and personnel.

While the military assistance afforded by the Condor Legion to the Nationalist cause was real enough, the opportunity to use the war as a proving ground for equipment and tactics was too good to pass up. For the Luftwaffe, it proved an enormous slice of luck. In peacetime training, realism is lacking. Rarely does anyone get killed, and then only by accident. Consequently it is impossible to predict how a person will actually perform in war, regardless of how well they have done in training.† Now

---

* A *Gefreiter* was an AC 1, or private soldier; the nearest British equivalent to a *Fähnenjunker* is a navy midshipman.
† Different conflict, same principle. When the 333rd TFS of the USAF were ordered to South East Asia in 1966, young captain Thomas C. Lesan commented, 'We eyed each other surreptitiously, each wondering how we would perform. It was surprising. Some that I thought would be tigers acted like mice, but more often the mice became tigers!'

43

they had a real conflict, the low intensity of which ensured that it could not become too expensive.

In theory, the Italians, also fighting for the Nationalist cause, and the Soviet Union, on the other side, should have been able to benefit equally. In practice this did not happen. The performance of the Italian fighters was inferior to that of the Russian-built and flown Polikarpovs, forcing them to seek both survival and success in manoeuvrability. This was the wrong lesson. The Russians certainly learned many of the right tactics, but these were lost when the majority of their Spanish war veterans were swept away pre-war by Stalin's insane purges.

For the Jagdwaffe, the benefits were threefold. First, by rotating personnel through at frequent intervals, they built up a pool of experienced and battle-hardened pilots. Second, they proved the efficacy of their new and radical monoplane fighter, the Messerschmitt Bf 109. Third, they developed a tactical system superior to that of any other air force in the world.

They had started out with Heinkel He 51 biplanes using the basic *Kette* of three aircraft flying in a V-formation. While a few successes were scored, so inferior was the He 51 to the opposing Russian I-15s and I-16s that it became a matter of urgency to bring in the new and untried Bf 109B. At first there were too few, and as is invariably the case when a new type is brought into action, serviceability left much to be desired.

The two *Staffel* commanders at that time, Gunther Lützow and Joachim Schlichting, attempted to minimise the shortage of aircraft by flying in pairs, or *Rotten*. This was found to have certain advantages. By flying nearly abreast, but with much wider spacings than the *Kette*, the two could cover each other's tails, guarding against the surprise bounce. Altogether it was a far more flexible system. Still later, Werner Mölders formalised a tactical system based on the *Schwarm* of two pairs. To allow radical changes of direction without compromising formation integrity, he rediscovered the cross-turn, which allowed all aircraft to turn at maximum rate without having to adjust their speed.

The cross-turn is not, as has often been said, Mölders' invention; it was certainly in use in 1918. But it was far more useful to fast but widely spaced fighters than to aircraft in close formation. But to him must go the credit for formalising the system. From the outbreak of the Second World War, it proved lethal to many an opponent, and not only was it copied by every other combatant nation; it lasted well into the jet age.

The value of the Spanish experience is shown by the following table, which gives the Second World War records of those who scored four or more victories in Spain.

Name	Spain	WW2	Comments
Werner Mölders	14	101	Rk, El, Sch, B. KIFA 1941
Wolfgang Schellmann	12	14	Rk. KIA Russia 1941
Harro Harder	11	6	KIA England 1940
Peter Boddem	10	nil	KIFA pre-war
Reinhard Seiler	9	100	Rk, El. WIA 1943
Walter Oesau	8	115	Rk, El, Sch. KIA West 1944
Hans-Karl Mayer	8	30+	Rk. MIA North Sea 1940
Otto Bertram	8	13	Rk. Withdrawn 1940 (surviving son)
Herbert Ihlefeld	7	123	Rk, El, Sch. First to last
Wilhelm Balthasar	7	40	Rk, El. KIA France 1941
Horst Tietzen	7	20	Rk. KIA England 1940
Walter Grabmann	6	6	Rk. Zerstörer
Herbert Schob	6	22	Rk. Mainly Zerstörer
Günther Lützow	5	103	Rk, El, Sch. MIA 1945
Joachim Schlichting	5	3	Rk. PoW England 1940
Hubertus von Bonin	4	73	Rk. KIA Russia 1943
Rolf Pingel	4	22	Rk. PoW England 1941
Wolfgang Lippert	4	25	Rk. KIA North Africa 1941
Hannes Trautloft	4	53	Rk.

Rk=*Ritterkreuz*, El=*Eichenlaub*, Sch=*Schwerter*, B=*Brillante*.
KIA=Killed in Action, KIFA=Killed in Flying Accident, WIA Wounded in Action and withdrawn from active service, PoW=Prisoner of War.

At least seventeen others made their combat debuts in the civil war and went on to distinguish themselves as fighter-pilots. They included Adolf Galland, who flew ground-attack sorties, Gustav Rödel, who ended the war with ninety-eight victories and the *Eichenlaub*, and Günther Radusch. After gaining the only victory with the He 112 in Spain, Radusch claimed sixty-four night victories. He also was awarded the *Eichenlaub*.

The final legacy of the Spanish Civil War was its impact on Jagdwaffe training. Whereas in other countries, air-combat practice was normally one versus one, usually between members of the same squadron, the Jagdwaffe practised *Schwarm* versus *Schwarm*, or even *Staffel* versus *Staffel*. While this carried appreciable risks of mid-air collisions, it was judged acceptable in the interests of combat efficiency and heightened realism. It also enabled *Schwarm* tactics and teamwork to be carefully honed, while giving the pilots experience of coincidental support in a confused many versus many scenario. By 1939, the Jagdwaffe had not only the world's best system of fighter tactics; it was the most realistically and professionally trained.

The Pilots

And what of the pilots? They were young and eager, with the high opinion of themselves that is the hallmark of the fighter-pilot. They were totally convinced of their own immortality, despite having seen comrades die during training accidents. This they mentally swept under the carpet; accidents were due to pilot error, and error showed that the fallen had been unworthy to become fighter-pilots. Only the best deserved to survive, and they, the fully-fledged fighter-pilots, were the best!

Should war come, they expected to demonstrate their prowess with a good tally of victories. As their commander-in-chief emphasised, they were the spiritual heirs of the great Manfred von Richthofen, top scorer of the entire war and of all nations. And who should know better than *Oberkanone, Pour le Mérite* holder, and final commander of the Richthofen Geschwader Hermann Göring? War was glorious, he told them. And if any stopped to reflect that the Red Baron had not survived the war, they were told that he died a glorious death in the service of his country. Like soldiers since time began, they were seduced by the siren song of glory.

The pilots themselves were a mixed bag, drawn from every conceivable background. Scattered among them, like nuggets of gold in a gravel bed, were the potential aces. It was impossible to pick them out beforehand; they were of no recognisable type. Inevitably some came from military families; others were sons of blacksmiths, teachers, plumbers and civil servants, priests and ministers. A surprisingly high proportion consisted of younger sons. The nobility was well represented; two princes became aces, as did a *Graf* (count) or two, and several *Freiherren*.

Physically they varied considerably. The cockpit of a Bf 109 was not very roomy, and so single-seater pilots tended to be of moderate height. There were of course exceptions; the towering Hannes Trautloft successfully shoe-horned himself into the Messerschmitt fighter, while at the other end of the scale, at just five feet four inches (163 cm) tall, Josef Priller had to keep his seat raised in order to see out. Some were stocky; others were slightly built but wiry. A few, such as Adolf Galland, exuded glamour; others resembled thinly disguised theological students.

Uniforms and Medals

Appearances meant much to them, and they wore their smart new uniforms proudly. For this reason they often flew in riding breeches and jackboots rather than more practical gear. Rank was indicated not only by epaulettes, but by lapel tabs, the yellow backing of which denoted aircrew. If the unit in which they served had an honorific title, this was worn on a band on the right sleeve. The eagle and swastika common to the German armed forces was worn above the right breast pocket. The pilot's badge was worn on the left breast pocket.

They desired glory and success; not least the outward trappings, the visible signs. The medals! It was the German tradition to wear their badges and medals festooned on their tunics and around their necks, like, as one unkind enemy commented, an overdecorated Tannenbaum.

First came the *Eisernes Kreuz*, awarded for conspicuous bravery or outstanding leadership. This came at two levels; *2 Klasse* was generally awarded for a handful of flights over enemy territory, and the ribbon only was worn in the top buttonhole.

This was followed by the *EK 1 Klasse*, which to fighter-pilots was often awarded for three or four victories. It was worn on the left breast pocket generally, but not always, above the pilot's badge.

Established in 1813, the *Eisernes Kreuz* had, like the *Pour le Mérite*, been a specifically Prussian award. In September 1939, it was established as an all-German decoration, with a new grade, the *Ritterkreuz*, or Knight's Cross of the Iron Cross, to replace the Blue Max. Like its predecessor, it was worn around the neck on a black, white and red ribbon. But whereas the Blue Max had been an officers-only decoration, the *Ritterkreuz* was open to all ranks. For the Jagdwaffe, it was in all but a few cases awarded for a certain number of victories, varying with the perceived difficulty of the various fronts.

In the British and American services, the same award could be won more than once, and was marked with a rosette or cluster on the medal ribbon. This was not the case with the German forces who wore the medals rather than ribbons. As the war progressed, further grades of the *Ritterkreuz* were introduced. The first of these was the *Eichenlaub*, or Oak Leaves, introduced on 3 June 1940, and consisting of three silver oak leaves on the ribbon clasp. September 1941 saw the establishment of the

Eichenlaub mit Schwerter (Oak Leaves with Swords) and the *Eichenlaub mit Schwerter und Brillanten* (Oak Leaves with Swords and Diamonds). In the first of these, two crossed swords featured beneath the oak leaves; in the second, the oak leaves and the hilts of the swords were studded with diamonds. Only one higher award existed; the Golden Oak Leaves; only one was ever made, and that not to a fighter-pilot.

Towards the end of 1941, a new award was instituted, rated above the *EK1* but below the *Ritterkreuz*, possibly because it was feared that the *Ritterkreuz* was becoming devalued. This was the *Deutsches Kreuz in Gold*. Worn on the right breast pocket, it was actually a star rather than a cross, with a swastika in the centre. Other decorations were campaign bars, awarded for specific operations or campaigns, and generally worn above the left breast pocket. If an ace hugged a girl, all this metal could have been quite uncomfortable for her.

Not that the Jagdwaffe ever used the term 'ace'. In the First World War, ten victories made a pilot an *Oberkanone* (Top Gun). In the Second World War, the widely used expression was *Experte*. Unlike *Oberkanone* or ace, this involved no specific number of victories, but was loosely used to describe those who had demonstrated a certain level of expertise in air combat.

Ritterkreutzträger

In all, about 7,500 *Ritterkreuze* were awarded in all services; of whom less than a quarter (about 1,730) were Luftwaffe. Of these, less than one third earned the award exclusively as fighter-pilots. This works out at about one in every hundred Jagdwaffe pilots, which gave it a certain rarity value. This in turn made it the most coveted award of all, and many pilots were so keen to win it that their comrades slightingly described them as having 'throat-ache!'

This was perhaps natural; by their very nature, fighter-pilots are a competitive bunch, and wearing the *Ritterkreuz* marked them as the elite of the elite. As we saw earlier, Manfred von Richthofen himself spent some time fretting that he had been passed over for the *Pour Le Mérite*, even though he had achieved the required victory score.

The practice of awarding the *Ritterkreuz* on the basis of the number of victories was basically flawed. It encouraged a 'pot-hunting' mentality, in which a victory was regarded as more important than protecting bombers or delivering air-to-ground ordnance. On an air-superiority mission, the leader would naturally hog all the best chances. Furthermore, it encouraged unnecessary aggression. Many a young pilot, on nearing the required score, threw caution to the winds, only to pay the ultimate penalty. All these factors were potentially detrimental to the demands of the mission, or in extreme cases, the campaign.

Qualities

The qualities needed by a fighter-pilot are easily stated. He should be a good, confident aircraft handler, with excellent distance vision and quick reactions. Training should have given him a feel for tactics and three-dimensional manoeuvring in space and time. Courage is a much misused term. In the context of air combat, being shot at while sitting on a tank of highly flammable petrol called for self-control above all else; fear was natural, but it had to be mastered. For this, determination was essential. Aggression was potentially a two-edged sword. Unless tempered with caution it could quickly turn into target fixation which leads a pilot into an irrecoverable situation. The 'fangs out, hair on fire' pilot rarely lasted long. Finally he should be an accurate shot, lacking which he might just as well stay at home.

Before appointing a new Marshal of France, Napoleon Bonaparte always asked, 'Is he lucky?' He had a point. There can be no doubt that luck, chance, call it what you will, plays a part in war. What has not been generally recognised is that the most important factor in building a high score is survival. No survival; no score! The easiest way to survive is to avoid being shot down.

Situational Awareness*

It is a matter of record that at least eighty per cent of victims in fighter versus fighter combat were not outfought and shot down. They were taken by surprise, unaware of being under attack until they were either fatally hit, or it was too late. Research shows that high scorers have an extra quality of alertness, an ability to keep track of events in a highly dynamic situation. Called situational awareness, it is unquantifiable but real.

In some pilots it is innate; others learn it the hard way through bitter experience, provided only that they live long enough. It is not an absolute.

---

* For a full discussion of situational awareness, see Mike Spick *The Ace Factor*, Airlife, Shrewsbury, 1988.

Chance still plays a part. Most of the really high scorers in the Jagdwaffe were shot down several times, surviving on every occasion until possibly the last. This was the element of luck.

Overclaiming

The ambition of every young German fighter-pilot was to run up enough kills to gain the *Ritterkreuz*. But what constituted a kill? In a one versus one encounter, when one combatant is seen to go down and crash in friendly territory, where the wreck is available for inspection, there are no problems. But in a multi-bogey fight three or four miles up, the confusion factor is high, and doubts exist. Overclaiming has bedevilled the subject of fighter-pilot scores since air combat began. As a rule of thumb, overclaiming increases in direct proportion to the number of fighters involved. But as most claims were made in good faith, and checked as rigorously as circumstances allowed, it is reasonable to call them victories rather than kills. This terminology has been adopted here.

CHAPTER 4

THE FIGHTER FORCE

Defining the Need

As noted previously, the First World War had seen the emergence of two different air combat philosophies: the manoeuvre fighter, and the performance fighter. Stated simply, the former relied on its outstanding agility to gain a firing position. Once combat was joined, it tried to out-turn its opponent in classic dogfight mode. The ability to turn tightly was of equal value defensively, as it enabled the fighter to keep out of its opponent's gunsight. The latter used its superior performance to gain a favourable position, usually a high perch up-sun, from which to launch an attack, while its ability to close rapidly on an opponent increased the possibility of gaining the advantage of surprise. Defensively, combat could be refused if circumstances were unfavourable, or if joined, it could be broken off more or less at will.

Of course, the difference between the two was not clear cut; the performance and manoeuvrability margins between the two were not all that great. What it basically did was to determine the tactics to be used. For example, the pilot of a manoeuvre fighter could more readily plunge into a whirling multi-bogey dogfight, whereas a performance fighter was at its best when nibbling at the fringes in an attack, disengage, re-attack pattern. Which type was preferred was largely a matter of individual temperament. The Red Baron tended to prefer the superbly agile Fokker Triplane, as did many of the top-scoring German pilots. By contrast, most British and French aces of the late war period scored the majority of their victories with performance fighters.

During the 1920s, strategic bombing was increasingly seen as a potentially war-winning weapon. At first this was no big deal; contemporary biplane fighters were thought to be able to handle the threat. But then came tremendous advances in engine technology, with greater power for less weight; supercharging, which allowed maximum power to

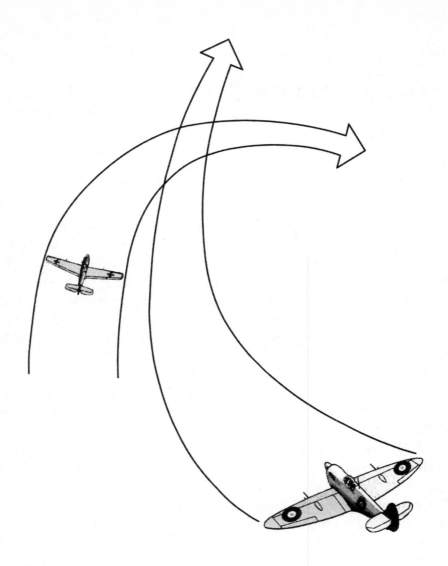

The Break

Standard procedure was to turn hard into the attack, increasing the deflection angle to give the assailant the most difficult possible shot. But if the attacker had already opened fire, and tracers were passing over the wing, flying through them was not always a good idea.

be developed at altitude rather than sea level; and improved fuel efficiency. These promised far greater performance, but other improvements were needed to take full advantage of the increase in power.

The first step was to reduce air resistance, or drag. Now drag increases in direct proportion to the square of the speed. Put simply, doubling the speed quadruples the drag. Therefore to double the speed for a particular aeroplane, four times the power would be needed to overcome the increased drag, assuming that propeller efficiency could be maintained at the same level.

There were many ways of reducing drag. The inefficient biplane configuration, with its two wings, interplane struts and bracing wires, could be replaced by a single cantilevered wing. The landing gear could be made retractable, and the cockpit could be fully enclosed. As many bumps and excrescences as possible could be eliminated; and the shape generally smoothed out, with a light alloy skin to replace the former doped fabric.

There was no free lunch. Span for span, a monoplane wing has less area than the two wings of a biplane, and its construction is heavier. The result was increased wing loading, and with it, greater take-off and landing speeds. Wing flaps were fitted to keep these within acceptable limits, again with a weight penalty. Hydraulically retractable main wheels were obviously heavier and more complex than a fixed undercarriage. However, the increases in weight were more than offset by the reduction in drag, and performance; speed, ceiling, range, and load-carrying capacity, increased accordingly.

The new technology was first applied to bombers, which did not need to be particularly manoeuvrable. By the early 1930s, it had become obvious that the ability of current biplane fighters to intercept the next generation of bombers would be at best marginal. The Germans knew this as well as anybody; developed as a fast mailplane with bomber potential, the Dornier Do 17 first flew in 1934.

The advent of fast bombers sounded the death knell of the biplane fighter. The next generation of fighters needed a fast rate of climb in order to reach the altitude of the bombers quickly. Once there, they needed a significant speed margin in order to catch them in what might prove to be a prolonged chase. The technical advances which had given the bombers a head start were now applied to fighters. There was now no doubt; performance had to take priority over manoeuvrability.

In some ways, the emergence of the new Luftwaffe was very fortunately timed. When it was revealed, it was still numerically small; its

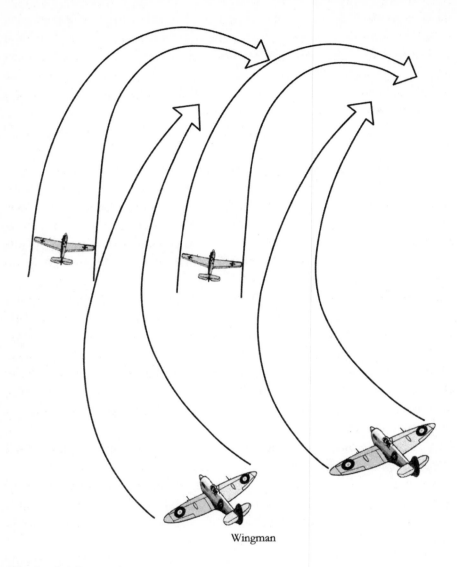

Wingman

The Sandwich

The fighter being attacked turns into the attacker. If the attacker follows, the Kacmarek *can drop in behind to sweep it off his leader's tail. Problems arise when the attacker also has a wingman who can engage the* Kacmarek.

fighter component consisting of Heinkel He 51 and Arado Ar 68 biplane fighters. Consequently, the accelerated growth of the Jagdwaffe coincided with the next generation of fighters, forming a brand new arm from the ground up. By September 1939, few of the obsolete biplane fighters remained in service. Many Heinkels had been lost in Spain; others were turned over to the Nationalists at the end of hostilities. Most of the remainder ended up as advanced trainers.

The Messerschmitt Bf 109

The Reichsluftministerium (RLM) issued a specification for a fast mono-plane fighter in the summer of 1934. Four companies competed, and after flying trials in October 1935, the Bayerische Flugzeugwerke fighter was declared the winner and ordered into production. Ironically, it was powered by a Rolls-Royce Kestrel engine, as the intended Junkers Jumo was still under development.

In what was his first foray into fighter design, the tall and angular Professor Willi Messerschmitt produced the Bf 109, a small but equally angular fighter, which was destined to become famous. Maximum performance was attained by the simple expedient of wrapping the smallest possible airframe around the most powerful available engine. It had all the latest innovations; a cantilever monoplane wing, retractable main wheels, a monocoque metal fuselage, and an enclosed cockpit. It was however, not the first. In the allegedly backward Soviet Union, the Polikarpov I-16, with all these features, had first flown on the final day of 1933, some twenty-one months earlier than the Bf 109.

Even on the prototype, wing loading was more than half as much again as that of the biplane fighters it was to replace. To keep short-field performance within acceptable limits, high-lift devices were fitted: automatic leading edge slats, large slotted flaps and slotted ailerons. This was far-sighted; every fighter suffers from creeping weight-growth during its operational life, and the Bf 109 would be no exception. By 1940, wing loading had increased by a third as much again, while by the end of the war, it had increased by a full two-thirds.

The leading edge slats, which featured on all Messerschmitt fighters, were a mixed blessing. During hard turns, they had a tendency to open asymmetrically, causing the ailerons to 'snatch' and one wing or the other to dip. In combat this could be embarrassing.

The Bf 109 had other faults. Its narrow track main gear was from the

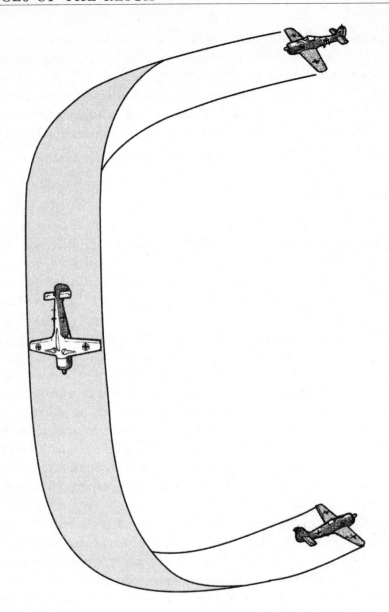

The Abschwung

The most widely used method of disengaging was the Abschwung. It consisted of a half roll to inverted (or a bunt); followed by a vertical dive during which aileron-turning could be used to give a pull-out in any desired direction. Not recommended against a better-diving opponent such as the P-47 Thunderbolt.

outset a source of weakness, and would remain so throughout its service life, while low-speed handling started as poor and in the much heavier late models became truly vicious. It tended to swing on take-off, and if lifted off too soon, could easily roll onto its back. On the landing approach, as it neared the stall, the port wing could drop without warning. A horrendous 1,500 Bf 109s were lost in take-off and landing accidents in the first two years of the war, often with fatal results. It was not a beginner's aircraft.

Publicity and propaganda were the lifeblood of the Third Reich. In July 1937, an International Military Aircraft Meeting took place at Dubendorf in Switzerland. To capitalise on this, the RLM sent a Dornier Do 17 bomber and a team of Bf 109s. It was an outstanding success. The Dornier showed that it could handily outpace the fighters of competing nations, while the German fighters swept the board, winning the dive and climb and speed events, and the team event was won by three Bf 109Bs. One of these was flown by future *Experte* Hannes Trautloft. Nor was that all. In November of that year, the Bf 109V-13, fitted with a DB 601 specially boosted to give 1,650 horsepower for short periods, set a world speed record for landplanes of 379.39 mph (610.48 kph).

Even before these momentous events, the Bf 109 had received its baptism of fire. Three pre-production aircraft arrived in Spain in December 1936, followed by sixteen Bf 109Bs in March 1937, and a further twenty-nine in July. Here it was discovered that the armament of three 7.9-mm MG 17 machine-guns was inadequate, although Harro Harder claimed eleven victories with it. The Berta was followed into action in spring 1938 by the Bf 109C with four MG 17s, the greatest exponent of which was Werner Mölders, with fourteen victories.

Next off the production line was the Bf 109D. Powered by a DB 600A rated at 960 horsepower, the Dora was armed with two MG 17s and an engine-mounted 20-mm MG FF cannon. Few of these were built, although a handful saw action in the early months of the Second World War. With cockpit canopies removed, a handful were used as makeshift night fighters.

The first major production variant was the Bf 109E. The Emil was powered by the DB 601A, rated at 1,100 horsepower and fitted with fuel injection instead of conventional carburation. In combat, this was a tremendous advantage, as it allowed the nose to be stuffed straight down without the engine cutting through fuel starvation during negative-g manoeuvres. Conventionally aspirated fighters were left floundering in its

57

wake. As the *Abschwung*, this became a standard evasion manoeuvre throughout the war. It hurt the pilot, but was much better than being shot down.

The propeller was of variable pitch, with the angle of the blades controlled electrically by the pilot. While this optimised performance, particularly when climbing, in combat it was just one more call on the pilot's attention, making the Emil a rather 'busy' aircraft to fly to its limits.

Armament on the various Emil subtypes varied. Some carried an engine-mounted cannon, but this had a tendency to jam, and was little used. Most carried two 20 mm Oerlikon cannon in the wings, supplemented by two cowling-mounted MG 17 machine-guns. The greatest advantage of the MG FF was its light weight. Compared with the French 20 mm Hispano-Suiza, its muzzle velocity was little more than two-thirds, while its rate of fire was exactly half. Consequently, weight of fire was lacking.

The lower the muzzle velocity, the greater the bullet drop, the less the effective range, and the greater the difficulty of aiming. The lower the rate of fire, the less effective it is at scoring hits on a fleeting target. Be that as it may, the best shooting is done at close range and non-manoeuvring targets, and for that the Revi reflector gunsight was the equal of any.

At combat speeds, handling was good, apart from the tendency for the leading edge slats to open asymmetrically under g-loading. The Emil could out-dive any of its contemporaries, but a prolonged steep dive at full throttle carried its own problems. As speed increased, control forces mounted alarmingly. The ailerons became heavy, reducing rate of roll, affecting the ability to change direction.

Rather worse was the effect on the rudder. Engine torque, combined with the rotating effect of the propeller slipstream, tried to screw the whole aircraft round its longitudinal axis. While this could be countered with a bootful of opposite rudder, at very high speeds it was an enormous strain on the pilot's leg. Even worse, rolling against the torque became nearly impossible. Elevator forces in a high velocity dive were also excessive, and an awful lot of sheer muscle was needed to pull out, making it a rather sedate process. At low level, with the ground coming up fast, this was not a good idea. On later variants, cockpit-operated trim tabs were introduced to overcome these problems.

Keeping the airframe small made the cockpit very cramped. This had two knock-on effects. The pilot's heel-line was high, making his legs almost horizontal. In a high-g turn or pull-out, his blood could not drain down very far, giving him an inbuilt resistance to grey-out. Nor could the Revi reflector gunsight be placed centrally, as in most other fighters. Instead it was offset to line up with his 'shooting eye'.

In air warfare, nothing ever stands still. A fighter that at one point has a distinct edge over its opponents, may well find itself outclassed just weeks later. The battle for air superiority was waged just as fiercely on the drawing boards of the opposing designers as in the sky.

The Emil was replaced on the production lines by the Bf 109F, or Friedrich, which had been designed around the more powerful DB 601E engine. Housed in a new symmetrical cowling, driving a smaller-diameter propeller but with a larger spinner, this was rated at 1,300 horsepower. A redesigned wing had rounded tips and a slightly greater span, but less area. Frise-type ailerons and plain flaps replaced the former slotted surfaces, although the leading edge slats were retained. Other drag-reducing measures were a retractable tailwheel, a cantilever tailplane in lieu of the braced original and shallower underwing radiators with boundary layer by-passes.

With the Friedrich, attempts to mount a reliable cannon in the nose finally came to fruition. It was a new weapon; the 15 mm Mauser MG 151 cannon, mounted between the cylinder banks to fire through the propeller hub. Apart from accessibility, this was the ideal location. Wing-mounted weapons were subject to vibration and torsion, which caused bullet scatter. The solid engine mounting was aligned with the longitudinal axis of the aircraft, and did not need to be harmonised at a point ahead. The two cowling-mounted MG 17s were retained.

Although many pilots regarded the smaller-calibre cannon as a retrograde step, the MG 151 offered many advantages. Its muzzle velocity was much greater than that of the MG FF, its flatter trajectory giving improved accuracy, while its rate of fire was approximately double that of the older weapon.

Marksmen such as Werner Mölders favoured this arrangement, although many other *Experten*, including Adolf Galland, felt that the average pilot, who was no marksman, would benefit from the scatter effect. Few however went to the lengths of Walter Oesau, who refused to fly a Friedrich until his Emil was grounded by lack of spares.

The Friedrich entered service from January 1941. In many ways, the early models were the peak of Bf 109 development; in both handling and appearance it was superb. Later of course it was found to lack hitting power. On the F-4 the 15 mm cannon was replaced by the 20 mm

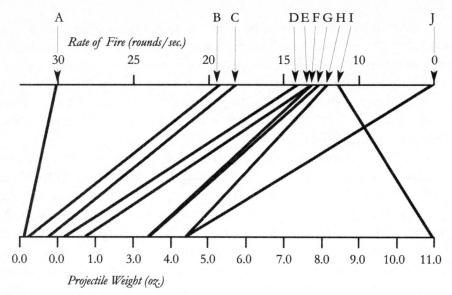

Rate of Fire (rounds/sec.)

A   B C   D E F G H I   J

30   25   20   15   10   0

Projectile Weight (oz.)

0.0   0.0   1.0   3.0   4.0   5.0   6.0   7.0   8.0   9.0   10.0   11.0

Key
A   Russia: 7.62 ShKAS
B   Britain: .303 Browning/Germany: 7.9 MG 17
C   Germany: 13 mm MG 131
D   USA/Britain: Browning .50
E   Russia: 12.7 UBS
F   Russia: 20 mm ShVAK
G   Germany: Mauser 151/20
H   Britain: 20 Hispano-Suiza
I   Germany: 30 mm MK 108
J   Germany: Oerlikon 20 mm MG FF

Aircraft Guns: projectile weight (oz)/rate of fire (rounds/sec)

With one exception, German aircraft guns were not outstanding. The 7.9mm MG 17 performed almost identically to the .303 Browning used by the RAF, but both were vastly inferior in rate of fire to the Soviet 7.62mm ShKAS. The MG 17 was replaced by the 13mm MG 131, which had a higher rate of fire but a lighter projectile than the American 50 calibre Browning and the Soviet UBS. The Oerlikon 20mm MGFF cannon was the worst-performing weapon of its type, with a pathetic rate of fire, and was superseded by the Mauser MG 151/20 which gave a rate of fire slightly less than the Soviet 20mm ShVAK for the same projectile weight, and slightly more than the British 20mm Hispano, the projectile weight of which was some 25% greater. But much greater destructive powers were needed against US heavy bombers, for which the 30mm Rheinmetal Borsig MK 108, with a projectile weight more than three times greater, was adopted.

MG151, which had a muzzle velocity of 2,500 ft (762 m)/sec, and a rate of fire of 750 rounds per minute. Still later two MG151/20s were fitted underwing in gondolas. This did nothing for manoeuvrability, and the remorseless cycle of creeping weight growth was under way.

The most widely produced variant was the Gustav, which entered service from the summer of 1942. With virtually the same airframe as the Friedrich, it was powered by the DB 605A engine, rated at 1,475 horsepower, boosted for short intervals by GM-1 nitrous oxide injection. While this restored the power/weight ratio, the added torque aggravated the low-speed handling problems, which became downright capricious. In fact, with wheels and flaps down, the Gustav had to be flown on to the ground at full throttle.

Nor was this all. Against opponents fitted with armour and self-sealing fuel tanks, the MG17s were relatively ineffective, and were replaced by two 13mm Rheinmetall Borsig MG131 heavy machine-guns. To house them, large bulges (*Beulen*) were fitted over the breech blocks. These did nothing for drag or handling.

For the bomber destroyer role, still heavier armament was needed. This emerged as the extremely destructive 30mm MK108; just three or four hits of this were generally enough to bring down a heavy bomber. The rate of fire for such a big weapon was excellent; 660 rounds per minute, but muzzle velocity was on the low side, at 1,750ft (533m)/sec. On the Bf 109G-6, the engine-mounted 20mm MG151 was replaced by the MK108, while the G-6/U4 carried these huge weapons in underwing gondolas in lieu of the MG 151/20s.

Thus laden, the Gustav was a turkey against enemy fighters. Rate of roll was significantly reduced and acceleration was poor. Wing loading had nearly doubled from the original prototypes. By 1944, fighters equipped to destroy bombers themselves needed protection from enemy escort fighters, although the introduction of the Erla Hood (later known as the Galland Hood) on the G-6 improved the view 'out of the window' considerably.

More Bf 109s, about 31,000, were produced than any other fighter in history. But by the end of the war, overweight, underpowered and tricky to handle, it was well past its prime. Had it been just a bit larger, its development potential might have been enough to handle ever-increased power, while its wing loading and handling would not have suffered so badly.

During the war, Messerschmitt made several attempts to design a replacement for the Bf 109, notably the Me 309 and Me 209A, but without success.

The Focke-Wulf FW 190

Never as famous nor as glamorous as the Bf 109, the Focke Wulf FW 190 was in many ways a far better fighter. Of course, it should have been; chronologically it was designed and flown almost three years later, at a time when aviation technology was moving fast.

Whereas the Bf 109 had been a rather delicate thoroughbred, Focke-Wulf designer Kurt Tank set out to produce a 'squaddy-proof' fighter, tough enough to withstand a great deal of operational mistreatment. First flown in June 1939, development problems, the most serious of which concerned engine overheating, delayed its combat debut until September 1941. The engine in question was the BMW 801 radial, with 14 cylinders arranged in two banks, and cooling the lower cylinders in the rearmost bank for a long while caused problems.

The use of a radial engine in a fighter was a departure for the Jagdwaffe, which hitherto had preferred the liquid-cooled V-12 as used in the Bf 109. Once again, it was a trade-off. The liquid-cooled engine was sleek, and had a relatively small frontal area, giving reduced drag compared to the radial, with its heavily finned cylinders spread out like the petals on a flower. On the other hand, lacking the plumbing and radiators of a liquid-cooled engine, power for power, the radial was lighter and less complex. It was also less vulnerable to battle damage, as many a Bf 109 pilot, forced down by a minor hit on his coolant system, could testify.

The first major production variant was the FW 190A-3. It was powered by the BMW 801D, rated at 1,700 horsepower at sea level. With the aid of two-stage supercharging, it could put out 1,440 horsepower at 18,700 feet (5,700 metres). Close-cowled, it was fronted by a twelve-bladed cooling fan. On the ground, forward view was restricted due to the diameter of the engine, but in the air, a slight downward tilt of the thrust line, which gave the FW 190 an odd nose-down attitude in level flight, provided an adequate view forwards.

Dimensionally larger than the Bf 109, but still smaller although rather heavier than its main opponent, the Spitfire V, the FW 190 had pleasingly simple lines. This was in part due to the importance laid on ease of production. The low-set cantilever wing was evenly tapered, and only slightly rounded at the tips. Aileron trim tabs were fixed, adjusted on the ground with a tool akin to a tuning fork. This unlikely system worked remarkably well. Unlike the Bf 109, the main gears were tough, wide track, well suited to operations from semi-prepared strips, and retracted inwards.

Another difference from the Messerschmitt fighter was the cockpit canopy. Whereas that of the latter was side hinged and heavily framed, the single-piece canopy of the FW 190 slid rearwards, giving excellent vision all round, marred astern only by 14 mm-thick armour for head protection. The seat was semi-reclining (shades of the F-16 some four decades later), and with its high heel line, gave the pilot good g-resistance.

The FW 190A was a superb dogfighter, even though its wing loading was some 20 per cent above that of contemporary Spitfires. While it could not turn as tightly as the British fighter, its beautifully harmonised ailerons gave it a far superior rate of roll, allowing it to change direction much faster. As in a multi-bogey combat it was rare to follow an opponent through more than about 135° before becoming vulnerable in one's turn: transient manoeuvrability, i.e. the ability to change direction rapidly, was far more valuable than sustained manoeuvrability. For the Spitfire V, the ability to turn in very small-diameter circles at a high rate of degrees per second was a purely defensive attribute.

Against the agile British fighters, Bf 109 pilots had been forced to use slashing attacks; diving from a high perch before zooming up to reposition for a second attempt. Rarely did they stay and fight. Given the manoeuvring constraints on even the Bf 109F, this was tactically correct. But now, with the FW 190A, the Jagdwaffe could stay and mix it with the best.

The FW 190A out-accelerated, outclimbed, and outdived the Spitfire VB with ease, and had a higher maximum speed, although it was largely matched by the Spitfire IX. The main failing of the German fighter was that power fell away at altitudes above 22,000 feet (6,700 metres). It was mainly for this reason that the Bf 109, with its good high-altitude performance, was kept in production. Everything possible was done to reduce pilot workload on the FW 190A, including *Kommandgerät*, an early example of automation. This automatically controlled engine revs, boost, fuel mixture and propeller pitch, leaving the pilot free to fly and fight the aeroplane. An electrically operated tail trimmer was yet another unusual feature, intended to tighten the turn still more. In hard turns, sufficient lift was provided by increasing the angle of attack (alpha) of the wings. While increased alpha involved higher induced drag, a high power-to-weight ratio was able to push the FW 190 'round the corner' quite effectively.

Although a superb day-fighter, instrument flying was not easy, while

Weight of Fire (lb/sec)

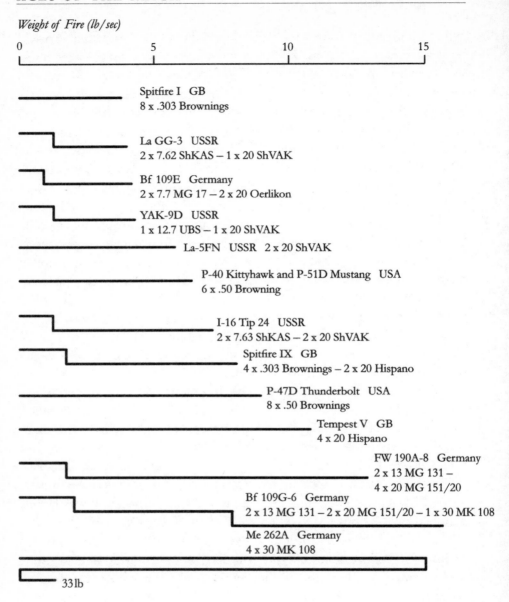

Second World War Fighters: comparative weights of fire (lb/sec)

When in the early years the rifle-calibre machine-gun was found to be inadequate, the move towards bigger but fewer guns tended to increase the weight of fire. But not always. The weight of fire of Soviet fighters actually declined, and the high point of the pre-war Polikarpov I-16 tip 24 was never equalled. Similarly, the Americans stayed with the 50-calibre Browning, which proved adequate, while the British, committed from an early stage stall characteristics were totally unforgiving. The stall was sudden; it came with no prior warning, marked by a violent drop of the port wing. A high-g stall, i.e. a stall during hard manoeuvring, which occurs at much higher speeds than a stall in straight and level flight,* was potentially lethal at low level, where there was little room for recovery. The wing drop was sufficiently violent to snap-roll the aircraft through 180° into the opposite bank, after which it would enter a spin. Knowing this, many FW 190A pilots were reluctant to manoeuvre hard at low level.

With just four MG 17 machine-guns, the FW 190A-1 was inadequately armed. This was quickly corrected; on the A-2 the two wing-root mounted MG 17s were replaced by 20 mm MG FF cannon. The A-3 retained the two cowling-mounted MG 17s; the MG FFs were moved outboard and replaced in the wing roots by the superior 20 mm MG 151. But as these fired through the propeller arc, the rate of fire was slowed by the need for synchronisation gear. That aside, four cannon and two machine-guns was quite exceptional for the time; one of the first British pilots to encounter the FW 190A-3 described it as 'streaming tracer like a fire engine!' Not a good simile, but descriptive!

Development continued. The A-4 featured MW 50 water-methanol injection, which boosted engine output to 2,100 horsepower for short periods. The A-5 had the engine moved forward by 5.9 inches (150 millimetres). A later variant was a dedicated bomber destroyer, with the MG FF cannon outboard replaced by 30 mm MG 103 cannon. From the A-7, the cowling-mounted MG 17s were replaced by 13 mm MG 131 heavy machine- guns, while the ultimate bomber destroyer, the FW 190A-8/R8 Sturmbock, carried two MG 151 cannon in the wing roots and two 30 mm MK 108 cannon outboard in underwing gondolas.

An airborne tank, the Sturmbock was heavily armoured, and carried bullet-proof glass panels scabbed onto the canopy sides and quarterlights.

---

* Normal stalling speed at sea level was 127 mph (204 kph). In a moderate 4g turn, this doubled to 254 mph (409 kph). Above about 6g, a high speed stall was nearly inevitable. In the stress of combat, the line was easily crossed.

to the superb 20 mm Hispano-Suiza cannon, increasingly relied on this weapon. But whereas the Allies only needed to counter single- and twin-engine aircraft, the Germans were faced with the formidable American heavy bombers, against which they needed a tremendous weight of fire, culminating in the Me 262 which could deliver 33 lb/sec; nearly three times that of the most heavily armed Allied fighter, the Tempest V.

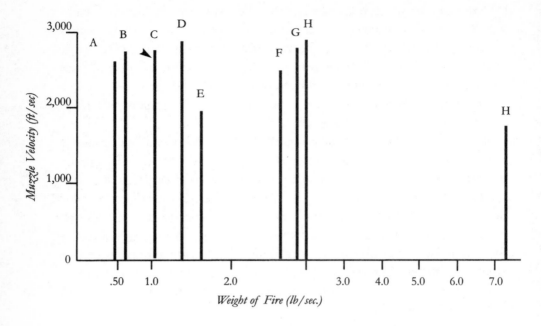

Key

A	Britain/Germany: .303 Browning/7.9 MG 17
B	Russia: 7.62 ShKAS
C	USA/Germany/Britain: Browning .50; the arrow marks 13 mm MG 131
D	Russia: 12.7 UBS
E	Germany: 20 mm MG FF
F	Germany: Mauser 151/20
G	Russia: 20 mm ShVAK
H	Britain: 20 Hispano-Suiza
I	Germany: 30 mm MK 108

Aircraft Guns: weight of fire (lb/sec)/muzzle velocity (ft/sec)

High muzzle velocity not only increases effective range; the imparted energy makes the projectiles more destructive. Against small and medium aircraft, 20 mm cannon were adequately lethal. The MK 108 was a heavy bomber-killer in which muzzle velocity was sacrificed in favour of a huge high-explosive round. The penalty was a low muzzle velocity resulting in a short effective range.

Thus protected, they could brave the storm of fire from the massed guns of American bomber formations like the Teutonic Knights shrugging off arrows as they charged to contact. But weighed down with armour and weaponry they lacked performance and manoeuvrability, and were sitting ducks for Allied escort fighters. Like the Bf 110 before them, they needed fighter protection.

The FW 190A was extremely versatile. Quite apart from its being an air superiority fighter and bomber destroyer, it was widely used for ground attack, anti-shipping and reconnaissance. Demands on production for these missions meant that it never entirely supplanted the Bf 109 as the premier fighter of the Jagdwaffe, even though in most ways it was better suited to the air superiority task.

There was however a final and very superior fighter variant. This was the FW 190D-9, commonly known as the Dora, or long-nose. Powered by the Junkers Jumo 213A water-methanol injected liquid-cooled engine rated at 1,776 horsepower, it had an annular radiator which gave the impression of being a radial. The fuselage was stretched and the fin and rudder were enlarged.

The Dora had a better climb and dive performance than the FW 190A and it accelerated faster. Transient performance suffered slightly; roll and pitch rates were a bit slower. In a sustained turn it was slightly better; it did not bleed off speed as quickly as its predecessor. Entering service in autumn 1944, the Dora proved itself a formidable opponent even against the most modern British and American fighters. But by then it was the same old story; too little, far too late.

The Zerstörer

During the 1930s, several nations began to develop long-range heavy fighters. Their purpose was threefold; bomber escort, deep penetration air superiority and extended pursuit of enemy intruders.

The key to long range was of course fuel capacity combined with fuel economy. Fuel capacity demands a large tank capacity, while economy is best achieved at modest speeds and in the thin air at high altitudes.

Even the best engines of the era could only put out about 1,000 horsepower, and to shackle one of these to a fighter with adequate fuel could only result in a large, unmanoeuvrable low-performance turkey. Modest economic cruising speeds were also a non-starter (although the Japanese used them successfully in the Pacific), because over Europe, they would

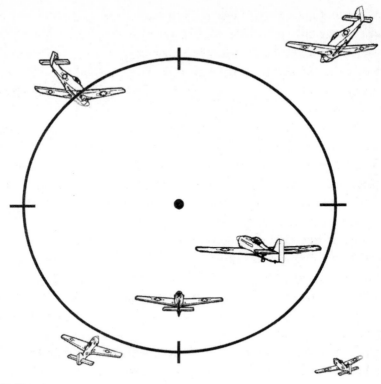

Angle-off Shooting

Some idea of the difficulty of angle-off shooting is shown here. In each case, the aim-point is accurate.

make the long-range fighter a sitting duck. What was needed was therefore a long-range fighter able to hold its own against the defenders.

In a valiant attempt to meet these conflicting requirements, Willi Messerschmitt fell between two stools. Given the state of the art at that time, it was an impossible task.

The result was the Messerschmitt Bf 110, which first flew in May 1936. To meet the power requirements it was twin-engined. Unavoidably, it had a wingspan of 53 feet 5 inches (16.28 metres), two-thirds greater than that of the Bf 109, which was guaranteed not to give a sparkling rate of roll. Wing area was 137 per cent larger; not quite enough to give parity in wing loading with the Bf 109E, but a worthy attempt. Like its stablemate, it had leading edge slats and trailing edge flaps. In its main fighter incarnation, the Bf 110C, it could turn quite well, but hampered by poor rate of roll, it was slow in establishing the turn.

Aware that agile single-engined fighters would have little difficulty in getting on the tail of the Bf 110, Messerschmitt built in some discouragement in the form of a rear gunner. Not that a single 7.9 mm swivelling machine-gun could offer much protection, but every little helped. To give the gunner a clear field of fire, he used endplate twin fins and rudders. Willi Messerschmitt may or may not have been aware that the only really successful two-seater in the First World War had been the Bristol F2B. But that had been an immensely powerful single-engined fighter; not a twin! Nor had it possessed anything exceptional in the way of range or endurance.

So far, so good! But...! The RLM requirement had not been entirely clear, perhaps because while a long-range fighter sounded like a good idea, no one had firm ideas as to its actual employment. Bombers carried observers for navigation; perhaps the new fighter ought also. So Willi Messerschmitt made provision for a third crew member, all three housed under a long glazed canopy. As the Jagdwaffe quickly discovered, for daylight operations this was a waste of space. But as we shall see in a later chapter, for night-fighting it was a godsend!

Powered by two DB 600s, prototype Bf 110s were even faster than the Bf 109B, although lacking acceleration. This was a good omen for the future. The Bf 110C Cäsar was fitted with two DB 601As, giving a total of 2,200 horsepower and a maximum speed of 349 mph (562 kph) at altitude. This was pretty fast by any standards. Fixed forward-firing armament was heavy; two 20 mm MG FF cannon and four MG 17 machine-guns in the nose.

The Bf 110 was generally popular with its pilots, due to its viceless handling. A captured example flown by an experienced RAF pilot was described as 'a twin-engined Tiger Moth!' While this looks like a compliment, a certain Fleet Air Arm pilot described a Tiger Moth as 'an airborne brown paper bag!' So we don't know!

So, what was the Bf 110 worth? Although fast, it lacked manoeuvrability and acceleration. Even worse, it lacked range. It could not escort bombers on deep penetration raids. Willi Messerschmitt had attempted to design a long-range escort fighter, but had failed on both counts. True, it could go a bit further than its single-engined counterpart, but the difference was not really significant.

Even before the war, the Bf 110 was recognised as a non-starter, and it was scheduled for replacement by the Bf 210. That this never came about was due to simply appalling instability and handling problems experienced

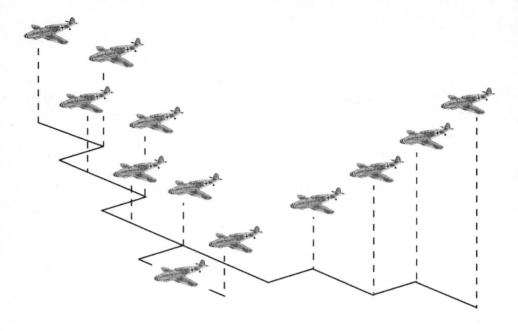

Variations on a Staffel *Formation*

The Staffel was a very flexible formation, with the Kapitän and his Schwärm low and in front, and the other two Schwärme stepped upon either side. The latter show two different formation combinations.

by the latter. But when war broke out, it was in service, it was available, and it was used.

For the Jagdwaffe, the question became, how best to use the heavy fighter. The question was answered in typically bombastic fashion by Luftwaffe Commander-in-Chief Hermann Göring. He named the heavy fighter units *Zerstörer* (Destroyers), and declared them to be elite units; his Ironsides. Promising young pilots were posted to the *Zerstörer* units, to the detriment of the single-seater force. At the same time it was found that the third crewman, the observer, was not really necessary; a pilot and a radio operator/gunner were quite adequate. This was just as well; observers were in short supply, due to the rapid expansion of the bomber force.

Jagdwaffe Unit Composition

The composition of Jagdwaffe fighter units was nearer that of l'Armée de l'Air than any other. As there are no exact English or American equivalents, we must stay with that of the Luftwaffe. The basic fighting and administrative unit was the *Gruppe*, which was led by a *Kommandeur*. His actual rank was a *Hauptmann*, a Major, or in extreme cases, an *Oberstleutnant*. At the outbreak of war, the *Gruppe* typically consisted of thirty-four to forty fighters, made up of three *Staffeln* of ten to twelve aircraft, plus a *Stab*, or staff flight, of about four aircraft.

The *Staffel*, which was roughly equivalent to an overgrown RAF flight, was commanded by a *Staffelkapitän*: a *Leutnant*, an *Oberleutnant* or a *Hauptmann*. The largest tactical formation was the *Geschwader*, consisting of three *Gruppen* and a four-ship *Stab*, for a total complement of 106 to 124 fighters. It was commanded by a *Kommodore*. He was often a *Major*, sometimes an *Oberstleutnant* or, in extreme cases, even an *Oberst*.

This description was not set in stone; as the war progressed it was not unusual for an extra *Staffel* or two to be added to a *Gruppe*, or an extra *Gruppe* to be added to a *Geschwader*. Neither was it unusual for a *Staffel* or *Gruppe* to be completely detached from its parent *Geschwader* for extended periods, during which time it operated autonomously.

Day-fighter units were *Jagdgeschwader*; heavy fighter units were *Zerstörergeschwader*, while night-fighter units were *Nachtjagdgeschwader*. For normal usage these were abbreviated to JG, ZG, and NJG. There were also two *Lehrgeschwader* (LG), responsible for operational and tactical evaluation.

Within the *Geschwader*, *Gruppen* were designated with Roman numerals, e.g. II/JG 11, III/ZG 76, etc. *Staffeln* were also designated within the *Geschwader* rather than the *Gruppe*, using Arabic numerals. Thus 2/JG 26 would be part of I/JG 26, while 7/ZG 2 would be a component of III/ZG 2. But later, with increased unit sizes, things were not so clear cut. Also, with the Second World War raging, it was rare for any unit to be at full strength.

From mid-1940, Jagdwaffe leaders were selected on merit rather than seniority, with success in combat as the main, but not absolute criterion. If for example, replacement officers in a *Staffel* were inexperienced, it would then be led in the air by an experienced NCO with the honorific title of *Staffelführer*.

Nor was it a given that all aircraft in a *Geschwader* or *Gruppe* were of the same type. This was particularly the case with the *Lehrgeschwader*, which included both fighter and bomber *Gruppen*. In these cases a designator was used, e.g. 3(Jagd)/LG 2 indicated that this unit flew the Bf 109, whereas II(Z)/LG 1 indicated a *Zerstörer* unit. Then later in the war, a small unit might be set up to evaluate a new fighter type. These were generally designated *Kommando* (Kdo) followed by the name of the commander, e.g. Kdo Nowotny.

CHAPTER 5

VICTORY BY DAY

The Road to Götterdammerung

Having achieved union with Austria, and the bloodless annexation of Czechoslovakia, the Führer became overconfident. His next target was Poland. Although Britain and France had earlier guaranteed Polish sovereignty, he felt that these were just empty words. In any case they were badly placed to intervene quickly, and even if they tried, a rapid victory would present them with a fait accompli, after which he could negotiate a settlement.

The one real threat to his plans was the Soviet Union. This was finessed by a non-aggression pact with Joseph Stalin, which virtually assured him of a clear run. There was of course a price to be paid; the Russians had to be allowed to occupy eastern Poland. Not that this mattered in the long-term; in his dreams of European domination, the Soviet Union was next.

Initially it all seemed to be going according to plan. On 1 September 1939, German forces crossed the Polish border, and after a whirlwind campaign, overran Poland in just five weeks. Towards the end, the Soviet Army moved in and occupied the eastern part of the country, creating a buffer zone between Nazi-dominated western Poland and the Russian border. As half-expected, Britain and France, in that order, declared war on Germany. Nor, over the coming months, could they be persuaded to enter a negotiated peace. It was Hitler's first major, and possibly his greatest, miscalculation.

Both on the ground and in the air, the Polish campaign was a numerical and technical mismatch. The best Polish fighter was the PZL 11c of 1933 vintage. It had a high-set braced gull wing, fixed undercarriage and an open cockpit. Its armament of two KM Wz.33 7.7 mm machine-guns was far too light, although when the war started, this was in the process of being doubled. Powered by a Bristol Mercury radial engine, its maximum speed was about 242 mph (390 kph) less than even the Bf 109C. Rate of

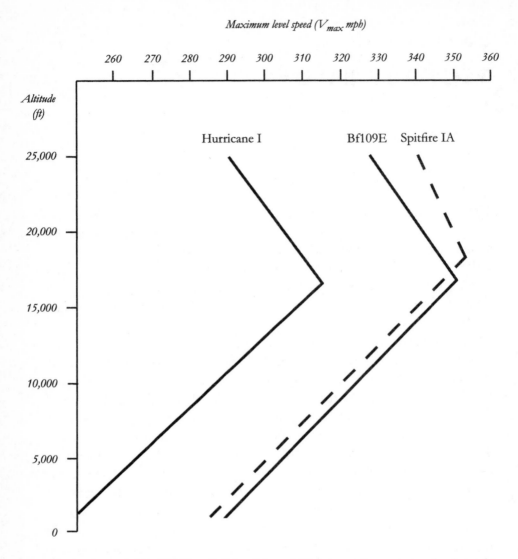

Maximum level speed (V_{max}. mph)

Altitude (ft)

Hurricane I   Bf109E   Spitfire IA

Comparison of Bf 109E vs Spitfire IA and Hurricane I: maximum level speed/ altitude

The Bf 109E is a bit faster than the Spitfire IA below 17,500 ft where it reaches its maximum, but beyond this it is inferior, the difference increasing rapidly up to 25,000 ft. While the Hurricane I is inferior overall, it remained a formidable opponent. This diagram is based on data from physical trials carried out by Rolls-Royce at Hucknall in December 1940.

climb was inferior to that of the Bf 109, but slightly better than that of the Bf 110. Only in one area was it superior to the invaders: lightly wing loaded, it could out-turn them. The other Polish fighter type was the even more elderly P 7, from which the P 11c had been developed.

For effective air defence, the two essentials are an early warning and control system to get the fighters to where they are needed in time, and security of base. The first consisted of a network of observers on the ground, which relied heavily on landlines. With an invading army storming across the country, this was not a good idea, and it collapsed within a week. Security of base was rather better; the period of international tension prior to the attack had allowed the Polskie Lotnictwo Wojskowe (PLW) to disperse its assets. When on the first day the Luftwaffe sought to destroy it on the ground, the blow fell largely on empty airfields. Not until 14 September did the Luftwaffe manage to mount a really effective airfield strike.

Outnumbered and outclassed, the Polish fighters fought back hard. But whereas the dispersion of the Polish air arm had saved it from destruction on the ground, it made concentration of force against massed German bomber raids doubly difficult.

While on paper the air battle looked a walkover, the largely inexperienced Jagdwaffe pilots took it seriously. Bf 110 pilot Helmut Lent of 1/ZG 76, the son of a Protestant minister, recalled his thoughts on the eve of battle.

How will the enemy react? Will he accept our challenge? Will our long-held wish to defeat the enemy in a chivalrous man to man duel be fulfilled? Or will there be a clash in massed squadrons?*

He need not have worried about the answer to the first question. The proud traditions of the Polish Lancers lived on strongly in the PLW, which would certainly rise to the defence of its homeland. But some seem unrealistic; even immature. Chivalry? One-on-one duels? These were the myths of the Richthofen era, and were no more true in 1939 than they had been two decades earlier.

Ironically, the first German air victory of the campaign was not scored by a fighter-pilot. On the first morning, a P 11c of 122 Squadron fell to the guns of Stuka pilot Frank Neubert of I/StG 2. This was not an

---

* Helmut Lent in *The Lent Papers*, Peter Hinchliffe, Bristol, 2003.

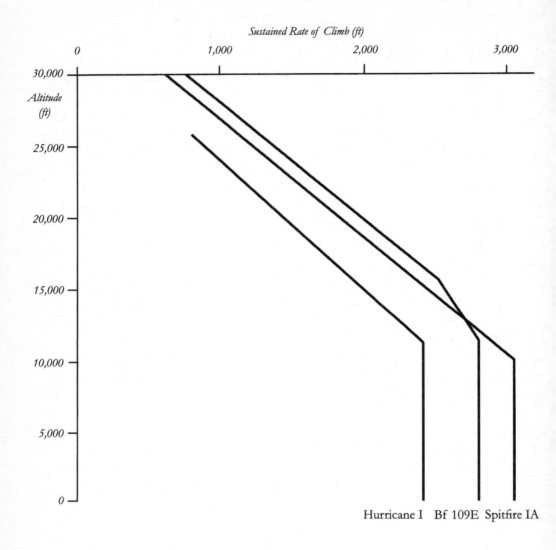

Comparison of Bf 109E vs Spitfire IA and Hurricane I: sustained rate of climb/ altitude

The Bf 109E is inferior to the Spitfire IA (Rotol constant speed propeller) up to 13,500 ft, but thereafter is slightly superior. The Hurricane I not only lags overall but reaches its operational ceiling at 26,000 ft. This diagram is based on data from physical trials carried out by Rolls-Royce at Hucknall in December 1940.

isolated case; several Dornier 17 pilots adopted an aggressive stance when confronted by Polish fighters. On the first morning, the Bf 110 received its baptism of fire. The *Zerstörern* of I(Z)/LG 1, escorting Heinkel 111 bombers, tangled with Polish fighters. In a short, sharp action, two P 7s were shot down, but the Kommandeur, Spanish veteran Walter Grabmann, was wounded. This was not a good start.

That afternoon, I(Z)/LG 1 was out again, led by Hauptmann Schlief, one of the winning Bf 109 team at Dubendorf in 1937. High over Warsaw, Schlief spotted a formation of P 11cs climbing towards him. His first diving attack was easily foiled by the agile Poles. After a brief skirmish, one of his Bf 110s became isolated and apparently vulnerable. As a Polish fighter lunged towards the *Zerstörer's* tail, Schlief dropped in astern and shot it down from close range.

This 'decoy duck' was a trick from the First World War, but was none the less effective for that. A solitary enemy aircraft at a lower level was a great temptation. The clever bit was to get in the attack before its friends, lurking above, could intervene. On this occasion, the tremendous performance advantage of the Bf 110 proved decisive. The hot-headed Polish pilots were slow to learn, and four more fell for the same ruse in this action.

Combats were not always to the advantage of the Jagdwaffe. On 2 September, I/ZG 76 lost three aircraft while claiming only two victories, one of which was a P 11c shot down by future *Experte* Helmut Lent. Then on 12 September, Lent became a victim in his turn. Preoccupied with strafing aircraft on the ground, he was attacked from behind by a Polish fighter. With an engine knocked out, he force-landed; luckily behind friendly lines.

In all, the Luftwaffe lost sixty-seven Bf 109s and a dozen Bf 110s, plus 109 level- and dive-bombers. In all, about ninety fell to ground fire, leaving ninety-eight as air-combat victims. Fighting fiercely in defence of their homeland, the Polish fighter-pilots claimed 126 victories, a relatively modest overclaim. Polish losses in air combat amounted to about seventy, with the remaining 190 either destroyed on the ground, shot down by flak, or, and this was a considerable cause, friendly ground fire.

Unlike victory claims, figures for air-combat losses are generally fairly accurate. Given that this is the case here, the badly outnumbered Polish fighter arm, technically and tactically overmatched and inexperienced in combat, seems to have had slightly the best of things. How could this be?

First, the Bf 109s had been withdrawn from the front after the first

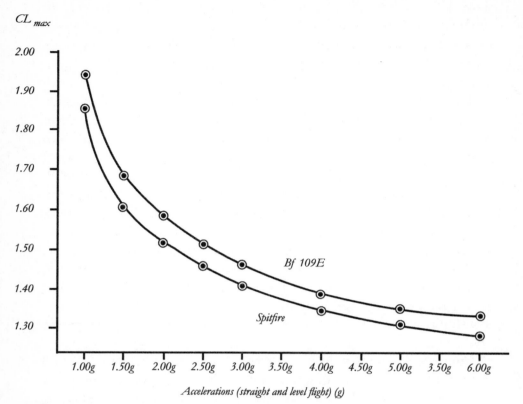

CL_{max}

Accelerations (straight and level flight) (g)

Wing loadings:
Bf 109E 32 lb/ft^2
Spitfire IA 24.8 lb/ft^2
— approximately 30% advantage

Comparison of Bf 109E vs Spitfire IA: acceleration/CL_{max}

As shown here, CL_{max} varies with acceleration (g forces). Although the German fighter has the advantage, partly provided by leading edge slats, this is more than offset by the much lower (thirty per cent) wing loading of the Spitfire. This diagram is based on data from physical trials carried out by Rolls-Royce at Hucknall in December 1940.

week of hostilities, leaving the less potent but longer-ranged Bf 110 to hold the ring. Second, a high proportion of Polish pilots had been flying their fighters for eight years or more, and were totally familiar with them. Not so the Jagdwaffe, the rapid expansion of which meant that it was a relatively young force. Notwithstanding the leavening of Spanish Civil War veterans, few had flown their respective fighters for more than a year or so. And as previously noted, the Bf 109 was not a beginner's machine.

As for the new tactical system, they certainly used the *Schwarm* and the *Rotte*, but the need to use the vertical plane against better-turning opponents, so convincingly demonstrated in Spain against the agile Polikarpovs, seems to have been largely ignored. Why was this?

Deflection shooting was officially discouraged as a waste of ammunition; victories were most surely obtained with a no-deflection shot from astern. But unless they could manoeuvre into a favourable position at the start of the engagement, this could only be obtained by using a curve of pursuit. This in turn caused two problems. First, very precise judgement was needed for the distance-speed-altitude-time-angles involved. A very few gifted pilots did this instinctively. For the rest, it came only with long practice. Second, a curve of pursuit approach increased the possibility of being spotted. Once this happened, all chance of surprise was lost, and the enemy could take counter-action.

The outcome was usually that manoeuvre combat was joined; the old-fashioned dogfight. This was of course in full accord with the Red Baron legend and the myth of chivalry, reinforced by the teachings of the several *Alte Adler* who held command positions at this time, to the detriment of the Spanish experience. It would take another year and many losses before this trend was reversed.

One thing is certain. In theory, the Jagdwaffe operated like a well-drilled machine, but in practice, this was not the case. Under the stress of what Carl von Clausewitz* called 'frictions', things often come unglued. The Jagdwaffe wanted individual combat and glory, but this was largely denied them. One versus one combat varied between rare and non-existent, and a free for all was the rule. The final factor was the fanaticism with which the patriotic Poles defended their homeland.

---

* Carl von Clausewitz, *Vom Krieg (On War)*, 1832.

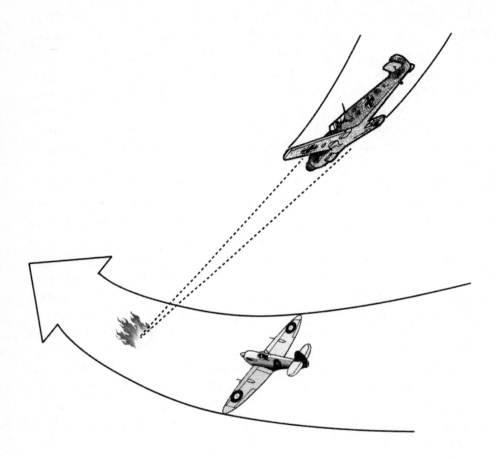

Deflection Shooting

In anything other than a straight shot from astern (or head-on), the aim had to be slightly ahead, so that the target and the shells arrived at the same time at the same place. At extreme deflection angles, the target would have vanished below the nose of the attacking fighter before the correct angle had been achieved. This called for judgement beyond the ability of the average fighter pilot.

Birth of the Experten

The top-scoring Jagdwaffe unit was the *Zerstörer*-equipped I(Z)/LG 1, which claimed thirty victories during the war, with Werner Methfessel leading the pack with four. In second place was JGr 102 with twenty-eight victories. JGr 102 was nominally a *Zerstörer* unit (I/ZG 2), flying Bf 109Cs and Ds pending delivery of the Bf 110, which was in short supply. It was led by Hannes Gentzen, who with seven victories, was the top Jagdwaffe scorer of the campaign. As this unit was employed mainly for air defence, only five of the twenty-eight were fighters. Gentzen's own tally included five bombers.

In third place, following Gentzen and Methfessel, was Wolfgang Falck, *Staffelkapitän* of 2/ZG 76, with three victories. A surprisingly high number of pilots who made their combat debut over Poland were destined to become high-scoring *Experten*. A few of them opened their account in the Polish campaign, but many did not. This was not lack of ability; in the main it was lack of opportunity and lack of combat experience.

The following table shows the *Ritterkreutzträger* who began in Poland:

Name	Unit	WW2	Comments
Gordon Gollob	I/ZG 76	150	Rk, El, Sch, B. 1st to reach 150.
Helmut Lent	I/ZG 76	110	Rk, El, Sch, B. 102 at night. RO Walter Kubisch Rk. Both KIFA 5.10.44.
Hans Philipp	I/JG 76	206	Rk, El, Sch. 2nd to reach 200. KIA 8.10.43.
Karl-Gottfried Nordmann	I/JG 77	93	Rk, El. KIA 11.2.44.
Friedrich Geißhardt	I(J)/LG 2	102	Rk, El. KIA 5.4.43.
Erwin Clausen	3(J)/LG 2	132	Rk, El. MIA 4.10.43.
Gustav Rödel	I/JG 21	98	Rk, El. Veteran of Spain
Dietrich Hrabak	II/JG 54	125	Rk,El.
Walter Ehle	3/ZG 1	36	Rk. 33 as night-fighter. 2 in Poland. KIFA 17.11.43.
Wolfgang Falck	2/ZG 76	7	Rk. 3 in Poland. Father of night-fighting.
Ludwig Franzisket	I/JG 1	43	Rk.
Walter Grabmann	I(Z)/LG 1	6	Rk. Plus 6 in Spain
Erich Groth	2/ZG 2	c12	Rk. KAS 11.8.41.
Herbert Kaiser	III/JG 77	68	Rk. Ended with JV 44 *contd*

Name	Unit	WW2	Comments
Johannes Lutter	II/ZG 76	12	Rk. Mainly an attack pilot.
Klaus Quaet-Faslem	I(J)/LG 2	49	Rk.KIFA 30.1.44.
Wolfgang Schellmann	I/JG 77	14	Rk. Plus 12 in Spain. MIA 22.6.41.
Hannes Trautloft	2/JG 77	53	Rk. Plus 4 in Spain.

Rk = *Ritterkreuz*, El = *Eichenlaub*, Sch = *Schwerter*, B = *Brillante*.
KIA = Killed in Action, MIA = Missing in Action, KAS = Killed on Active Service,
KIFA = Killed in a Flying Accident.

It is perhaps surprising that Wolfgang Schellmann, the second highest scorer in Spain, achieved so little in later campaigns. Yet others who had not flown fighters in Poland later did well when transferred to the Jagdwaffe. Reconnaissance pilots Franz Dörr claimed 128 victories; 122 of them in the East with JG 5; while Herbert Friebel, flying with IV/JG 51 in the East, claimed 58 victories before he was killed over Poland on 15 May 1944. Two army observation pilots also did well. Friedrich Rupp flew with 7/JG 54, mainly in the East, but was shot down into the North Sea on 15 May 1943 while attacking US heavy bombers. His score was 52, including two 'heavies'. Helmuth Schulte retrained as a night-fighter in 1943. Assigned to NJG 5, he ended the war with a score of twenty-five. Former Lufthansa pilot Fritz Lau flew transport missions in Poland. He also retrained as a night-fighter. With NJG 1, he achieved twenty-eight night victories in just seventy-eight sorties. All the above were awarded the *Ritterkreuz* as fighter-pilots. Finally, there is Adolf Galland, who flew Henschel Hs 123 biplanes in Poland as a *Schlacht* pilot. A winner of Germany's highest award, he ended the war as a *Generalleutnant* with 104 victories; all in the West.

War in the West

In the West, the period known variously as the *Sitzkrieg*, Phoney War, or *Drôle de Guerre*, had begun. Careful not to escalate the conflict by causing civilian casualties, Britain and Germany restricted themselves to attacks on naval targets. The Franco-German border saw intensive frontier patrols and reconnaissance missions.

The first Jagdwaffe victories in the West occurred on 4 September 1939, when Alfred Held and Hans Troitsch of II/JG 77 each shot down a British bomber over the North Sea. Over the next few months, an increasing toll was taken of British bombers, which, seeking naval targets, flew in unescorted formations.

The greatest Jagdwaffe victory of the *Sitzkrieg* period came on 18 December. A formation of 22 Wellingtons was detected off Wilhelmshaven, and thirty-two Bf 109s and sixteen Bf 110s were scrambled to intercept. First into action were six Bf 109Cs of the specialist night-fighter *Staffel* 10(N)/JG 26. Their *Staffelkapitän*, Johannes Steinhoff, claimed the first of his eventual 176 victories. Other units followed, including I/ZG 76, which had arrived from the East only the day before. Adding to their Polish tallies, Helmut Lent claimed three, Gordon Gollob two, and Wolfgang Falck one, although Lent and Gollob each had one claim disallowed.

Jagdwaffe losses were two Bf 109s and their pilots; another with engine damage which was wrecked in a forced landing, and several Bf 110s badly damaged. One of the latter was flown by Wolfgang Falck, who with both engines hit and stopped, managed to stretch his glide to the nearest airfield; and another whose pilot and gunner were both wounded.

British losses were appalling; twelve (fifty-five per cent of them) were shot down, and three more badly damaged. Faced with such unsustainable losses, the British all but ceased daylight raids by unescorted bombers. In all it was a famous victory, marred only by one thing.

A total of thirty-four claims were made. Not only was this in error by almost three to one; it was more than half as many again as the entire bomber force involved. With many victims falling in the sea, a physical check on wrecks was not possible. In the event, only the two claims mentioned were disallowed.

Meanwhile, down on the Franco-German border, things were boiling up. With both sides flying patrols between the Maginot and Siegfried lines, clashes were inevitable. The first occurred on 8 September 1939, when a *Schwarm* of Bf 109Es of I/JG 53 fought five Hawk 75s of GC *(Groupe de Chasse)* II/4. Experience and reputation counted for little; one of the two Bf 109s downed was flown by Werner Mölders, who force-landed with engine damage. It was thirteen days before he redressed the balance by claiming a Hawk 75; the first of his 101 victories in the Second World War.

The Hawk 75 was a much underrated fighter. Although inferior in performance and armament to the Bf 109E, in all other respects it was a far better fighting machine. Finely harmonised controls and a wing loading barely three-quarters that of the German fighter made it far more manoeuvrable, while a constant-speed propeller enabled the engine to run at maximum efficiency at all speeds and altitudes.

On 6 November, Hawk 75s taught the Jagdwaffe a harsh lesson. Hannes Gentzen, still the top scorer of the Jagdwaffe, spotted a Potez 637 reconnaissance aircraft far below, escorted by nine Hawk 75s of GC II/5. Seeking to add to his laurels in Poland, he led his 27 Messerschmitts down. He failed to attain surprise, and in the ensuing dogfight, the agile Hawks outfought his Bf 109s, shooting down four, and damaging a further four which force landed. The only French casualty was a single crash-landed Hawk.

Luftwaffe Commander-in-Chief Hermann Göring was not best pleased. Sending for the unhappy Gentzen, he gave him a truly monumental dressing down. Gentzen continued to fly, adding ten to his score, but was shot down and killed on 26 May 1940. He had outlived Bf 110 pilot Werner Methfessel, his nearest rival in Poland, by just nine days. Methfessel had added just four more to his score before he fell in combat on 17 May.

From early 1940, the Luftwaffe made increasingly deep penetrations of French territory, and combats became ever more frequent. Then on 10 May the storm broke. On the ground, the *Heer* outflanked the Maginot Line by violating Belgian and Dutch neutrality. Spearheaded by the Luftwaffe, German forces swept into and across France and the Low Countries, overwhelming the small and ill-equipped Belgian and Dutch air forces in just days.

On the offensive, the Jagdwaffe not only had the initiative; operating mainly in *Gruppe* strength they usually had a numerical advantage over the smaller French and British formations. But this was not always the case. Surprise was always the dominant factor in air combat, and often the few could remain unobserved where the many would have been spotted.

This was demonstrated on 12 May. By subterfuge, Adolf Galland had finally got his transfer to fighters, to *Stab*/JG 27. But war involves paperwork, and when the *Blitzkrieg* started, he was tied to his desk. It was two days before he managed to sneak away to freelance with veteran of both Spain and Poland, Gustav Rödel. Near Liège, they encountered eight Hurricanes of No. 73 Squadron RAF, which Galland misidentified as Belgian.* In a classic bounce from above and astern, Galland and Rödel took them by surprise and shot down three.

---

* By this date all Belgian Hurricanes had been destroyed on the ground. Almost certainly these were RAF Hurricanes of No. 73 Squadron. As Galland was over Belgium at the time, his error is understandable.

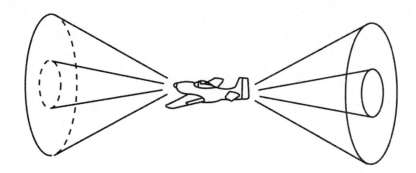

Gun Attack Angles

The most successful attack angles were made from within a 15° angle from astern, or at a pinch, from head-on. A 45° angle was better than nothing, but few victories were scored from angles greater than this.

As the Panzers swept through France, Allied fighter units, falling back as their airfields were overrun, and with their organisation breaking down, became increasingly unable able to mount an organised defence. By now a few high-scoring *Experten* were emerging. A few, like Galland, had a hunter's nose, but in the main they were unit leaders who got the first crack in an attack. Many others had few opportunities.

Mölders had claimed ten victims during the *Sitzkrieg*, all except one fighters. In the seventeen days following the opening of the ground campaign in France, he claimed ten more. Then on 29 May, with his score at twenty, he was awarded the *Ritterkreuz*, the first Jagdwaffe pilot to be so honoured. Five more victories followed, but on 5 June he fell victim to a Dewoitine D 520 of GC II/7. Baling out of his stricken fighter, he became a prisoner of war. But not for long; he was freed when France capitulated three weeks later.

Like Mölders, the second fighter-pilot to be awarded the *Ritterkreuz* was also a high-scoring Spanish veteran; Wilhelm Balthasar. *Staffelkapitän* of 1/JG 1 at the outbreak of war, he did not open his account until 11 May 1940. But then he quickly outstripped Mölders, with twenty-three victories in just thirty-four days, to become the leading scorer in the French campaign.

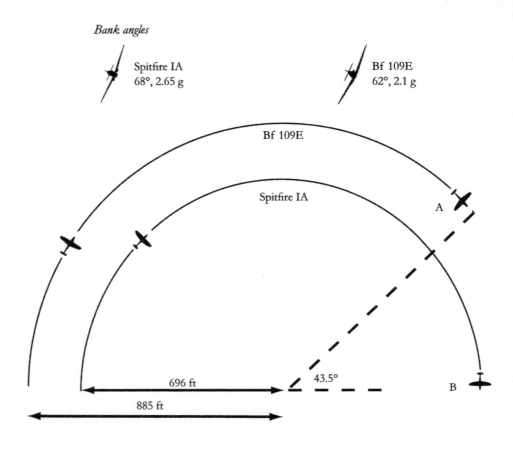

Bank angles

Spitfire IA
68°, 2.65 g

Bf 109E
62°, 2.1 g

Bf 109E

Spitfire IA

A

696 ft

43.5°

B

885 ft

A = Bf 109E: position after 9.5 seconds; true air speed 152 mph
B = Spitfire IA: position after 9.5 seconds; true air speed 157 mph

Comparison of Bf 109E vs Spitfire IA: minimum radius sustained turn at 12,000 ft

In a sustained turn, in which neither speed nor altitude is lost, the Bf 109E lags the Spitfire by nearly 5°/sec; the German fighter only able to sustain an acceleration of 2.1 g compared to the 2.65 g of the British fighter. In combat, speeds would rarely be this slow, and both fighters would be trading altitude for speed in instantaneous manoeuvre. Be that as it may, the Bf 109E was generally disadvantaged in a turning fight. This diagram is based on data from physical trials carried out by Rolls-Royce at Hucknall in December 1940.

The Battle of England

With France subjugated, the Führer confidently expected the British to sue for peace, but it was several weeks before he accepted that this was not going to happen. For the Luftwaffe as a whole, this was a sorely needed breathing space. Most units were withdrawn to Germany to re-equip and train replacement pilots. For weeks, the only *Jagdgeschwader* on the Channel coast was JG 51, led by its *Kommodore*, forty-eight-year-old *'Onkel'* (Uncle) Theo Osterkamp.

Osterkamp, a *Pour le Mérite* holder from the First World War with thirty-two victories with Marinejagdstaffel 2, had for some considerable time commanded the *Jagdfliegerschule* at Schliessheim. Then in late 1939 he had formed JG 51, which he led in action against France and Britain, adding another six victories to his tally.

Rested and reinforced, other fighter units returned to the Channel coast. But the campaign to come was unlike anything previously experienced. The Jagdwaffe now faced a well-trained and equipped foe, backed by radar early warning and a well-rehearsed fighter-control system, with 20 miles (32 kilometres) of sea protecting its bases from the advancing Panzers. The defending Hurricanes and Spitfires were more manoeuvrable than the Bf 109E, while the latter was their equal in performance.

A major failing of the Bf 109 was its short endurance. Thus the bombers, which depended on it for protection in daylight, had their radius of action restricted to a small area of southern England.

The result was a hard-fought aerial campaign. As well as a superior tactical system the Jagdwaffe usually had the advantages of height and position. But these were often squandered, as once battle was joined, the German pilots stayed to mix it with their more manoeuvrable opponents. Many survived only by sheer luck, among them future high-scoring *Experten* Heinz Bär of 7/JG 51, and Hans-Joachim Marseille of 4/JG 52. Bär returned badly shot on six occasions and ended in the Channel on a seventh; Marseille expended four fighters.

The shortcomings of the Bf 110 long range fighters had been cruelly exposed over Poland and France, but given their build-up as Göring's 'Ironsides', they had to be used against England. Casualties were heavy; it soon became clear that the long-range fighter itself needed fighter protection. On 15 August, no less than twenty-six *Zerstörern* were lost. I/ZG 76, flying long-range escort over the North Sea, lost seven of twenty-one, including Kommandeur Werner Restemeyer, who had been the third

87

member of the winning Bf 109 team at Dubendorf. In a separate action over southern England, II/ZG 76 lost seven, with an eighth damaged beyond repair, and III/ZG 76 four, the latter including its Kommandeur Hauptmann Dickore. A singleton was lost from II/ZG 2, while the fighter-bomber unit Erprobungsgruppe 210 lost six, including its *Kommandeur*, Swiss-born Walter Rübensdörffer.

Leadership Changes

By mid-August, the defeat of RAF Fighter Command seemed as far away as ever. Göring, dissatisfied with results, decided that the fault lay in the *Geschwader* leadership. He had a point. Theo Osterkamp had added six to his First World War score, which was no mean achievement for a relatively elderly gentleman, but he was the exception. The other *Kommodoren* had achieved virtually nothing. To Göring, the solution was simple. They should be replaced by high achievers, who would lead their *Geschwadern* in the air.

Some accounts make this appear an almost overnight process, with success in combat and youth the only criteria for promotion. This was not the case. In practice it was fairly gradual, and the replacements were mature, tried, and proven *Kommandeure*.

Changes commenced in late July, when Osterkamp was booted upstairs to become *Jafü* (fighter leader) 2. But Mölders, his replacement, was shot down and wounded on the following day, and Onkel Theo returned to lead JG 51 for three weeks until he recovered. Almost a month later, the twenty-eight-year- old Galland replaced the thirty-two-year-old Gotthard Handrick at the head of JG 26.

At about this time, Galland and Mölders, both exercised to reduce mounting losses, discussed tactics. Though friends, in many ways they were opposites. Galland was a hunter; Mölders's approach was more cerebral. Naturally they disagreed, and after an acrimonious exchange, Mölders stated that while Galland could become the Luftwaffe's Richthofen, he preferred to be its Boelcke. Their main point of agreement was that dogfighting with the agile British fighters was not a good idea. Instead, the Jagdwaffe should adopt the dive and zoom tactics which had been so successful in Spain. But this could not be done overnight.

At the end of August, three more *Kommodoren* were replaced. Günther Lützow took over JG 3 from Carl Vieck; Günther Freiherr von Maltzahn replaced Hans-Jürgen von Cramon-Taubadel at JG 53, while Hannes

Trautloft supplanted Martin Mettig at JG 54. Then on 3 September, First World War veteran Harry von Bülow-Bothkamp was replaced as *Kommodore* of JG 2 by Spanish veteran Wolfgang Schellmann.

Like Mölders; Lützow, von Maltzahn and Trautloft were all noted teachers as well as leaders. Galland was a hunter/leader, with thirteen scalps in the six weeks of the French campaign. Appointed *Kommandeur* of III/JG 26, his score had risen rapidly. Schellmann, *Kommandeur* of II/JG 2 had scored more slowly, but his outstanding record in Spain spoke for him.

One star was rising rapidly. Helmut Wick of 1/JG 53, recorded his first victory on 22 November 1939. His tally had risen to fourteen when France fell. In July 1940 he became *Staffelkapitän* of 3/JG 2. Awarded the *Ritterkreuz* for twenty victories on 27 August, the seventh Jagdwaffe pilot so honoured, he was appointed *Kommandeur* of I/JG 2 on 7 September. His fortieth victory came on 4 October, followed by the *Eichenlaub* two days later. He was the third fighter-pilot (after Mölders and Galland) so decorated. His virtuosity could not be denied. He became *Kommodore* of JG 2 on 19 October, supplanting Schellman, who moved sideways to take over JG 27 from Lipetsk veteran Max Ibel. At 25, Wick was by far the youngest of the new *Kommodoren*.

Also promoted was Wilhelm Balthasar. His 1/JG 1 had been redesignated 7/JG 27 on 9 July, and shortly after he was appointed *Kommandeur* of III/JG 53, But despite his Spanish and French record, he found victories hard to come by over England. Having added just one to his score, he was seriously wounded by Spitfires over Canterbury on 4 September and barely managed to regain France.

A total of thirty-eight *Ritterkreuze* were awarded for success in air combat during 1940. On 1 August Adolf Galland became the third Jagdwaffe recipient following his seventeenth victory. On 20 August, Spanish veterans and Staffelkapitäne Horst Tietzen and Walter Oesau of 5 and 7/JG 51 respectively, followed with twenty victories apiece, although Tietzen's award was posthumous.

Fourteen were Spanish Civil War veterans. Two were killed in action in 1940, Tietzen and Hans-Karl Mayer. Heinz Ebeling of 9/JG 26 (18 victories) became a prisoner of war. Otto Bertram of III/JG 2 (thirteen victories plus eight in Spain) was withdrawn from the front line as a last surviving son, his two brothers having fallen over England.

Of the *Ritterkreuzträger* who survived 1940, eighteen (half) gained higher awards; the same number failed to survive the war, and three became prisoners. On 5 September Oberfeldwebel Werner Machold of

7/JG 2 was awarded the *Ritterkreuz* for twenty-one victories; the first NCO so honoured. At the opposite end of the rank and age scale, Generalmajor Osterkamp received his on 22 August, partly for leadership and partly for six victories over men young enough to be his sons. At forty-eight, *'Onkel'* Theo was the oldest recipient. The youngest was another rising star, twenty-two-year-old Joachim Müncheberg of 7/JG 26.

Even though *Zerstörer* pilots were originally hand-picked as an elite, the twenty-victory standard was not applied to them. Given the inferiority of the Bf 110, it was remarkable that four of them reached double figures. Leading the pack was Hans-Joachim Jabs of II/ZG 76, with nineteen victories. He was followed by Erich Groth, *Kommandeur* of II/ZG 76 and Heinz Nacke of 6/ZG 76 with twelve apiece, and Rolf *'Schlitzohr'* (Slitear) Kaldrack, *Kommandeur* of III/ZG 76 with eleven.

The table shows the first twenty *Ritterkreuzträger of* 1940:

Name	Unit	Rk Date	Score	Remarks
Werner Mölders	III/JG 53	29.5.40	20	Plus 14 in Spain. KIFA 22.11.41. Total 115.
Wilhelm Balthasar	7/JG 27	14.6.40	23	Plus 7 in Spain. KIA 3.7.41. Total 47.
Adolf Galland	Stab/JG 27 III/JG 26	1.8.40	17	Total 104
Walter Oesau	7/JG 51 III/JG 51	20.8.40	20	Plus 8 in Spain KIA 11.5.44. Total 123
Horst Tietzen	5/JG 51	20.8.40 *Posthumous*	20	Plus 7 in Spain. Total 27
Helmut Wick	1/JG 53 3/JG 2	27.8.40	20	KIA 28.11.40. Total 56
Hans-Karl Mayer	1/JG 53	3.9.40	20	Plus 8 in Spain. MIA 17.10.40. Total c 38
Werner Machold	7/JG 2	5.9.40	21	PoW 6.6.41. Total 32
Gerhard Schöpfel	9/JG 26 III/JG 26	11.9.40	20	Total 40
Herbert Ihlefeld	I/LG 2 (I/JG 77)	13.9.40	21	Plus 7 in Spain Total 130
Joachim Müncheberg	7/JG 26	14.9.40	20	KIA 23.3.43. Total 135
Rolf Pingel	2/JG 53 I/JG 26	14.9.40	15	Plus 4 in Spain. PoW 10.7.41. Total 26

Name	Unit	Rk Date	Score	Remarks
Hermann-Friedrich				
Joppien	I/JG 51	16.9.40	21	KIA 25.8.41. Total 70
Günther Lützow	I/JG 3	18.9.40	15	Plus 5 in Spain. MIA 24.4.45.
	Kdre JG 3			Total 108
Wolfgang Schellmann	I/JG 77	18.9.40	10	Plus 12 in Spain. MIA 22.6.41.
	II/JG 2			Total 26
	Kdre JG 2			
Hans (Assi) Hahn	II/JG 2	24.9.40	20	PoW 21.2.43. Total 108
Wolfgang Lippert	3/JG 53	24.9.40	12	Plus 4 in Spain. KIA 23.11.41.
	II/JG 27			Total 29
Gustav Sprick	8/JG 26	1.10.40	20	KIA 28.6.41. Total 31
Hans-Joachim Jabs	II/ZG 76	1.10.40	19	Total 50; 22 day, 28 night.
Erich Groth	2/ZG 2	1.10.40.	12	KAS 11.8.41. Total 12?
	II/ZG 76			

Rk = *Ritterkreuz*, KIA = Killed in Action, MIA = Missing in Action, KAS = Killed on Active Service, KIFA = Killed in a Flying Accident.

Pot Hunting

More than two decades earlier, Manfred von Richthofen had made it clear that the prize that he most valued was to be the top-scoring German fighter-pilot. While the Richthofen myth was hard to resist, it set an unfortunate precedent. An unseemly race for top spot developed, often to the detriment of teamwork and the needs of individual missions. Mölders, wounded at the end of July and out of action for three weeks, was soon overtaken by Balthasar. Only after the latter was wounded on 4 September did Mölders recover his lead, hotly pursued by Galland and Wick.

Mölders scored his fortieth victory on 20 September, for which he was awarded the *Eichenlaub*, another Jagdwaffe first. Galland was just five days behind; also with forty. Wick was in hot pursuit; his *Eichenlaub* came on 6 October with his forty-second victory. By now, Wick was suffering from the 'fangs out, hair on fire' syndrome, taking increasing risks to achieve his aim. 'I want to fight and die fighting', he was reported as saying. He got his wish. Having briefly taken the lead on 28 November, he was shot down into the Channel shortly after, his score at fifty-six.

The final day of the year saw Galland in the lead with fifty-eight victories, followed by Mölders with fifty-five. It was a two-horse race. Of the competition, Wick and Hans-Karl Mayer were dead; Balthasar was still out of action. The rest of the field was nearly out of sight. In third place was Oesau with 39; fourth was Joppien with 31; and fifth was Müncheberg with 23. The latter was quite remarkable. Although Müncheberg frequently flew as Galland's *Kacmarek*, he had a flair for picking out his own victims while continuing to protect his leader.

In the battle for England, the Luftwaffe had met its first serious reverse. While it was true that the Jagdwaffe had shot down rather more British fighters than they had lost, this was hardly surprising. The RAF fighters usually tried to slip past the escorts and 'have at' the bombers. By doing so, they inevitably became vulnerable to counterattack. The fact was that not only had the Jagdwaffe signally failed in their primary duty to give effective protection to the bombers; their own losses had been painful.

Jagdwaffe Malaise

Many Jagdwaffe pilots suffered from 'throat-ache'; a condition arising from an unfulfilled ambition that could only be cured by a *Ritterkreuz* hung around the neck. In 1940, the *Ritterkreuz* demanded twenty victories, but these were hardly likely to be gained while protecting bombers. Consequently bomber escort duty was understandably unpopular.

The German propaganda machine played a large part. High-scoring fighter-pilots were heavily publicised; they featured in popular magazines, on cinema newsreels, and were depicted on glossy postcards sold throughout the Reich. Home on leave, it was impossible not to be recognised. This was enough to turn the head of many a youngster.

Three other conditions assailed the Jagdwaffe in 1940. The first was *Kanalkrank* or Channel sickness. This arose from the fact that on long overwater flights in a single–engined fighter, the engine always sounded rough. It was bad enough over the Dover Straits, but units based in Normandy were faced with an eighty-mile Channel crossing. As Julius Neumann, *Staffelkapitän* of 6/JG 27 commented, 'the Channel or the Spitfires were bad enough, but the two together...'

Another condition can only be described as 'Spitfire snobbery'. Few Jagdwaffe pilots could bear to admit that they had been worsted by the supposedly inferior Hurricane, even though the latter was twice as likely to be encountered. They could only admit to losing to the very best.

Finally, like every other air force in every other war, they overclaimed, often by as much as three to one. The majority of claims were made in good faith, and as far as possible they were carefully checked. Confusion accounts for much, plus the human weakness, often evident in peacetime, of seeing what one expected rather than what actually happened. When overclaiming obscures the knowledge of defeat, it is good for morale. But in this case, it badly misled the naive Luftwaffe intelligence branch, with dire consequences.

In that fateful summer of 1940, the main task of the Jagdwaffe had been to gain air superiority over southern England to allow Operation Seelöwe, the invasion of England, to proceed uninterrupted. In this they failed.

CHAPTER 6

THE CONFLICT WIDENS

Background

The failure to gain air superiority over southern England in 1940 was widely regarded by the Jagdwaffe as a mere setback, rather than the defeat which later events proved it to be. Surely the campaign would be renewed in 1941, and the 'Lords'* defeated?

Hitler thought otherwise. His primary aim had always been to subjugate the Soviet Union, creating a Pan-Germanic empire throughout most of Europe. This would give the Reich control of the industrial and agricultural potential and mineral riches of Russia; not least the southern oil fields, while providing the promised *Lebensraum* for its people.

So far, the non-aggression pact with Stalin had held while the Third Reich was heavily engaged in the West. But could it possibly last through another whole year, while Hitler dealt with Britain? For the Führer, ambition and necessity dovetailed neatly. Planning for the invasion of the Soviet Union began in December 1940. Codenamed Operation Barbarossa, it was scheduled to begin in mid-May, by which time the snow would have melted, the floods subsided and the dirt roads become passable. The USSR was to be overrun by winter in a *Blitzkrieg*-style campaign. Then after a period of rest and re-equipment, German forces would return to the West in the spring of 1942, to settle with perfidious Albion.

Many German commanders were concerned at having to fight a war on two fronts, but the Führer correctly calculated that as the British had little offensive capability at that time, they could be contained by relatively small forces for the time being. During the spring of 1941, strong German forces were deployed to the East, leaving just occupation troops

---

* A First World War expression for the English, popularised in the Jagdwaffe by Theo Osterkamp.

and a small Luftwaffe contingent to hold the ring in the West.

*Der Gröfaz** had reckoned without his Italian ally Mussolini. *Il Duce* had conquered and colonised Abyssinia and Eritrea in 1935, then occupied Albania in 1939. With France on the verge of defeat in June 1940, he cast covetous eyes on Corsica and Tunisia. Greed won; he took Italy into the war on the side of Germany.

While this effectively closed the Mediterranean to British shipping, it brought Italian forces in Libya into direct conflict with the British in Egypt. Even worse, British naval and air forces on Malta were ideally placed to interdict the Italian sea lanes to Libya.

Italian attempts to neutralise Malta from the air failed dismally, while in the Western Desert, the Italian army suffered a series of resounding defeats. To make matters even worse, *Il Duce* had invaded Greece from Albania, only for the British to rush in reinforcements.

Hitler had little choice but to support his ally. In quick succession he despatched Luftwaffe units to Sicily to neutralise Malta, and sent German air and ground forces to North Africa. To clear the southern flank of his invasion of Russia, he launched a *Blitzkrieg* attack on Greece through Yugoslavia, rounding it off with the costly airborne invasion of Crete.

These operations were a drain on scarce resources, but while they impacted on Operation Barbarossa, they did not delay it. Spring came late to Eastern Europe that year, and the muddy roads remained all but impassable to wheeled vehicles until mid-June. The invasion was finally launched on 22 June 1941, a critical six weeks later than planned.

As in Poland, France and the Balkans, the on-rushing Panzers, spearheaded by the Luftwaffe, swept all before them, reaching the outskirts of Moscow before General Winter interposed his veto. The German advance resumed in the spring of 1942, albeit more slowly. The vast distances and poor road and rail communications took their toll. Meanwhile Russian resistance was stiffening. The end of 1942 saw the limit of the German advance in the East.

The Channel Front

Poor weather during the first months of 1941 limited air activity on the Channel coast, and there was little more than desultory skirmishing. By

---

* A contraction of *Größter Feldherr Aller Zeiten* (greatest military commander of all time), a scurrilous name for Hitler.

late spring, many Jagdwaffe units were already redeploying to the East. One of the last to leave was II/JG 52, which departed Ostend on the final day of May.

Back on the Channel coast, only two *Geschwader* remained; JG 2 Richthofen, commanded by the now recovered Wilhelm Balthasar, operated from south of the Seine down into Brittany, while the hard-charging Adolf Galland remained at the helm of JG 26 Schlageter,* two *Gruppen* of which were based north of the Seine and one in Belgium.

By early 1941, the rapidly expanding RAF Fighter Command was experimenting with offensive operations on both small and large scales. At first these were tentative, but from mid-June huge fighter sweeps, with a few bombers thrown in to force the Jagdwaffe to react, became frequent, sometimes even twice a day. The slow build-up had, however, given the Luftwaffe time to cobble together a radar network and fighter control system. As British radar reached deep into France at high altitude, the resultant air battles were the first in which ground control was available to both sides.

Although opportunities were few in the first half of 1941, Mölders had claimed thirteen victories before JG 53 deployed to the East, regaining the lead from Galland with sixty-eight. By 21 June the latter had added a further eleven victories, bringing his tally to sixty-nine, for which he was awarded the *Schwerter*. On the following day, the opening day of Operation Barbarossa, Mölders claimed four Russians. His score at seventy-two, he also was awarded the *Schwerter*.

By contrast, Balthasar's progress was pedestrian. By 2 July he had added another seven to his score, bringing it to forty, and was awarded the *Eichenlaub*. His triumph was short-lived. On the following day he was shot down and killed by Spitfires over Aire-sur-la-Lys. He was replaced by Walter Oesau, who on 6 February 1941 had been the third fighter-pilot to be awarded the *Eichenlaub*; his score was also forty.

From June 1941, the Bf 109F started to replace the Emil, but even with this new machine, dogfighting with the agile Spitfires was not a good idea. Instead, the heavily outnumbered Jagdwaffe tended to peck at the fringes of British formations, using hit and run tactics.

This worked well; the British fighters, often more than two hundred strong, frequently got in each other's way. The confusion factor was high,

---

* A less than inspiring honour title. Albert Leo Schlageter was a saboteur executed by the French in 1923.

Adolf Galland succeeded Mölders as General der Jagdflieger. *On 19 November 1942, aged thirty, he was promoted to become the youngest general in the entire* Wehrmacht. *Uniquely he wears his collar closed at the neck, displaying his* Ritterkreuz mit Eichenlaub, Schwerter und Brillanten *to advantage. He appears to have discarded the row of medal ribbons over his top left pocket, but retains the honorific* Schlageter *armband of his former unit JG 26.*

Former blacksmith's apprentice Hermann Graf is seen here with fighter designer Willi Messerschmitt. The second pilot (after Gollob) to reach 150 victories, and the first to reach 200, the publicity machine hailed him as a people's hero. He flew mainly in the East with JG 52, although he accounted for ten heavy bombers on Home Defence with JG 11.

Cap jauntily askew, Austrian Walter Nowotny is carefully posed to look heroic in this portrait of 19 October 1943, when he was awarded the Brillanten. *255 of his 258 confirmed victories were scored in the East with JG 54. He was killed flying the Me 262 on 8 October 1944.*

The top-scoring night Experten *discuss problems, April 1944. Heinz-Wolfgang Schnaufer (right) survived the war with 121 night victories. After the award of his* Schwerter, *he was presented with a piglet, signifying that he was a 'lucky swine'. Helmut Lent (left) was his closest rival with 102 night and eight day victories. Whereas Schnaufer survived the war, Lent died after a daylight flying accident on 5 October 1944.*

Two Spanish Civil War Experten. *'Franzl' Lützow (left), Kommodore of JG 3 Udet, is seen here in France on 7 October 1940. To his left is Wilhelm Balthasar, then Kommandeur of III/JG 3. In 1941 in the East, Lützow became the second fighter pilot (after Mölders) to reach 100 victories. In staff positions from July 1942, he later became the spokesman for the fighter pilot's 'mutiny', after which he converted to the Me 262. He was killed in combat on 24 April 1945. Balthasar, the tail of whose fighter this is, was shot down and killed over France on 3 July 1941, with a total of forty-seven victories.*

Chunky good looks, with blue eyes and blond hair, made gifted pilot 'Jochen' Müncheberg a pin-up throughout the Reich. Alas it was not enough to win the hand of film star Carola Höhn, seen here with him in Sicily in Spring 1941. She married a bomber pilot! Müncheberg was killed over Tunisia on 23 March 1943 when he collided with his 135th and last victim.

Above: RAF pilot Howard Squire of No. 54 Squadron, stands beside his downed Spitfire on 26 February 1941; the 30th victory of Herbert Ihlefeld, Kommandeur of I(J)/LG 2, seen with him. A Spanish Civil War Experte, *Ihlefeld served with many units, ending the war as* Kommodore *of the He 162-equipped JG 1.*

Left: Otto Schulz was one of the mainstays of II/JG 27. He opened his account over England in August 1940, then in 1941 scored two in the Balkans and three against Russia. He added 42 in the Western Desert, including RAF ace Neville Duke on 30 November 1941. His score at 51, he was posted missing near Sidi Rezegh on 17 June 1942.

Günther Rall (centre) celebrates his 200th victory on 29 August 1943. Over the next three months he brought his score to 250, the second pilot (after Nowotny) to reach this figure. With 275 victories, mainly in the East, he became the third-highest scorer of all time. To his left is Walter 'Graf Punski' Krupinski, who after a slow start, amassed 197 victories, and ended the war flying with Galland's JV 44.

Former flying instructor Wilhelm Batz came late to II/JG 52, but quickly made up lost ground with a tally of 237 victories, all except five in the East. He is seen here in distinguished company: to his right is Gerd Barkhorn, to his left Otto Fönnekold, who claimed 136 victories before being shot down and killed by US fighters on 31 August 1944.

Werner Streib, the 'Father of Night Fighting', thoughtfully examines the rear turret of what appears to be a Wellington bomber, shot down by him in 1941. He was the fourth-highest scoring night Experte. *From March 1944 he became* Inspekteur der Nachtjäger, *his war total 66.*

Erich Hohagen gained ten victories over England in 1940 with 4/JG 51, then another twenty in the East in three months, but his career was constantly interrupted by wounds. A noted aerobatic pilot before the war, he was briefly a fighter instructor in 1942; his most distinguished pupil was Hartmann. He returned to the West first with JG 2, then with JG 27, sustaining a bad head wound with the latter. Undaunted, he converted to the Me 262, and flew with JG 7 and JV 44. His fifty-five victories were amassed in more than 500 sorties.

Johannes 'Macky' Steinhoff had a remarkable career. Pre-war he flew naval aircraft; then Bf 109Ds at night, before reverting to day fighting, when he flew against England in 1940, then Russia. Having replaced Müncheberg at the head of JG 77, he fought over Tunisia, Sicily, then Italy. A leading 'mutineer', he was sacked from JG 7, but flew with Galland's JV 44 until badly burnt in a takeoff accident on 18 April 1945. His final score was 176, 148 in the East, and six with the Me 262.

Horst 'Jakob' Tietzen had the unfortunate distinction of being the first fighter pilot to be awarded the Ritterkreuz posthumously. After seven victories in the Spanish Civil War, he flew with II/JG 51 against France and England, and was soon among the leading scorers. He is seen here in August 1940, with eighteen victory bars painted unusually on the fin rather than the rudder. On 18 August he was shot down and killed off Whitstable by a Hurricane of No. 501 Squadron, having claimed just two more.

Three distinguished Experten *of II/JG 2 in Tunisia. Left is Kurt Bühligen, who started as an* Unteroffizier *and rose to command the Richthofen Geschwader. He scored 112 victories against Western-flown aircraft, including twenty-four four-engined bombers. Second from right (pointing) is Adolf Dickfeld; 136 victories, 115 in the East, and eleven four-engined bombers. Far right, looking startled, is Erich Rudorffer, a master of mass destruction, with one-day scores of seven, eight, and eleven twice. He was himself downed fifteen times.*

Otto Kittel smiles self-consciously for the camera after receiving the Eichenlaub *in April 1944. After a slow start, he became top-scorer of JG 54 with at least 267 victories in the East. He was shot down and killed by Il-2m3s over Courland on 14 February 1945.*

Like Ehrler, Theodor Weißenberger flew in the North and was nominated for the Schwerter. *He gained twenty-three victories as a Bf 110 pilot before coming to JG 5 in September 1942, where he notched up another 152 in the East. Transferred to the West, he claimed another twenty-five, before converting to the Me 262. Having succeeded Steinhoff as* Kommodore *of JG 7, he claimed eight jet victories.*

The 'victory stick', carried here by Dietrich Hrabak, was a tradition from Richthofen's days. Kommodore *of JG 52, then JG 54, he scored 125 victories; 109 in the East. He once enquired why a Schwarm of Bf 109s were unable to shoot down an Il-2, only to receive the classic reply; 'Herr Oberst, you cannot bite a porcupine in the arse!'*

One of the largest men ever to fly the Bf 109 in combat, Hannes Trautloft was, with Mölders, Lützow and Maltzahn, one of the great tutor/leaders. A veteran of Lipetsk and the Spanish Civil War, he was appointed Kommodore *of JG 54 Grünherz on 25 August 1940, leading them until July 1943, after which he joined Galland's staff. His fifty-seven victories included four in Spain, and forty-five in the East. The picture is believed to commemorate his 500th sortie.*

Former Arbeitdienst *leader Helmut Lipfert was a survivor. hot down thirteen times by Soviet flak and twice by fighters, he was never injured. Flying with II/JG 52 from 16 December 1942 in the East, then as* Kommandeur *of I/JG 53 from February 1945 in the West, he claimed a total of 203 victories, including two heavy bombers.*

Walter 'Gulle' Oesau flew 130 sorties in Spain, gaining eight victories. Flying with III/JG 51 against France and England he was soon among the leading scorers, reaching forty on 5 February 1941. As Kommandeur *of III/JG 3 in the East, he claimed forty-four Russians in five weeks, but in July then called back to the West to replace Balthasar. On 26 October 1941 he became the third pilot to reach 100. After a spell as* Jafü Bretagne, *he returned to combat as* Kommodore *of JG 1 in home defence, accounting for ten US heavy bombers. On 11 May 1944 he was shot down and killed by Lightnings over the Eifel; his total was 123.*

which worked to the advantage of the Jagdwaffe, whose victory/loss ratio was also high, 3:1 or sometimes more. This should have been damaging to RAF morale, but fortunately for them, the adverse ratio was masked by overclaiming.

Sufferers from 'throat-ache' had a singularly lean time on the Channel Front during 1941/42. A mere nine *Ritterkreuze* were awarded to single-engine pilots on the Channel Front in 1941: six to members of JG 2 future high scorers such as Erich Rudorffer, Egon Mayer, Kurt Bühligen, Josef 'Sepp' Wurmheller; and two to members of the former '*Wick Schwarm*', Erich Leie and Rudi Pflanz. The sole representative of JG 26 was Austrian Johann Schmid, with twenty-five victories by 21 August. He was lost on 6 November when he dipped a wingtip into the sea while circling a downed Spitfire, his final score being forty-one.

Eichenlaub awards went to Balthasar and Siegfried 'Wumm' Schnell of JG 2, 'Pips' Priller of JG 26, and two *Kommandeure* of JG 51 before they left for the East, Walter Oesau and Hermann-Friedrich Joppien. Shortly after his return to the West, Oesau's score reached eighty, and he was awarded the *Schwerter*, the third fighter-pilot to be so honoured. Then on 26 October, his tally climbed to one hundred; again as the third fighter-pilot to achieve this, after Mölders and Lützow. Like them, a high proportion of his victories had been scored in the East.

The new and potent FW 190 had entered service on the Channel Front in the autumn of 1941, but not until the new year did it really make its presence felt, outclassing even the Spitfire V. Now the Jagdwaffe could stay and mix it like never before.

But despite this, not a single *Ritterkreuz* was awarded to a member of either JG 2 and JG 26 in the whole of 1942. The established *Experten* were still scoring, but relatively slowly; this was almost certainly an indication of how difficult conditions really were. 'Sepp' Wurmheller, after a brief sojourn in the East, transferred to III/JG 2 in July. On 19 August he claimed seven victories over Dieppe, despite a broken leg and concussion. He was awarded the *Eichenlaub* on 13 November with his score at sixty; all but nine in the West.

Galland continued to be the scourge of the Channel Front. After the death of Mölders in November 1941, he was appointed *General der Jagdflieger*, his tally now having risen to ninety-four. Then on 28 January 1942 he became the second soldier of the Reich to be awarded the *Brillanten*.

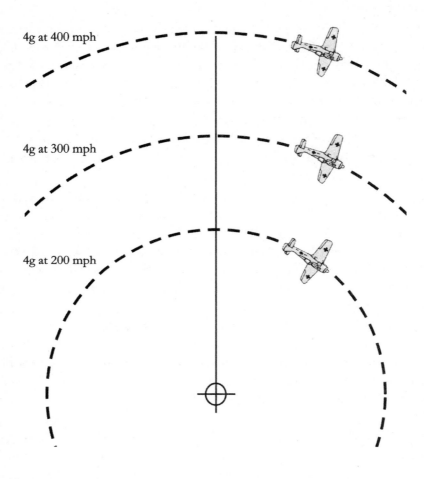

4g at 400 mph

4g at 300 mph

4g at 200 mph

The Effect of Speed on Turn Radius

Shown here to scale are the turn radii of a fighter at the same acceleration(4g), but at three different speeds. Turn radius increases with speed, but rate of turn (deg/sec) diminishes.

Malta and the Western Desert

To support the Regia Aeronautica against Malta, a single *Staffel*, 7/JG 26, arrived in Sicily in February 1941. Led by *Ritterkreuzträger* 'Jochen' Müncheberg, who had drilled his men not to enter a turning fight, but to dive and zoom, they quickly established an ascendancy over the island's Hurricanes. In April they spent three days in Italy, assisting the Balkan operations. They claimed two victories in this short period; both obsolete Avia BH 33E biplanes of the Yugoslavian Air Force, which fell to Müncheberg and future *Ritterkreuzträger* Klaus Mietusch.

Having returned to Sicily, they continued to score. On 7 May, Müncheberg was awarded the Eichenlaub for his 43rd victory. Arriving in Sicily with a score of 23, he had claimed 19 against Malta plus the one Jugoslavian fighter. This was remarkable on two counts; firstly the rest of the Staffel had claimed only 22 between them; secondly, amazingly, not a single Bf 109 was lost.

Only one *Ritterkreuz* was awarded for the Balkan operations, and that was posthumous. Sophus Baagoe of 5/ZG 26 was shot down by ground fire over Crete on 14 May, his score fourteen. A few other *Experten* had interesting experiences. Herbert Ihlefeld, the *Kommandeur* of I/JG 77, by then well on his way to forty victories and the *Eichenlaub* was shot down and taken prisoner, but was soon freed. Max-Hellmuth Ostermann of 7/JG 54 scored his ninth victory; a Jugoslavian Bf 109E, in a confusing combat between opposing aircraft of the same type. Kurt 'Kuddel' Ubben, the *Staffelkapitän* of 8/JG 77, came down behind enemy lines, but was rescued by Storch; while Wolf-Dietrich Huy of III/JG 77, running short of fuel, landed at a British airfield near Corinth, only to find it abandoned. Anxiously, he and his wingman refuelled, before returning to base.

In 1941 the best British fighters were held back for home defence; Malta and the Western Desert had to make shift with what could be spared; Gladiators and elderly Hurricanes, which were adequate against the Regia Aeronautica and Bf 110s of III/ZG 26.

The Bf 109Es of I/JG 27 had arrived in Sicily in March, but achieved little; a single victory over Malta. Then in early April they transferred to the desert. Their *Kommandeur* was Eduard Neumann, who had claimed five victories over England in 1940. Despite achieving only eight more by December 1944, he was widely considered to be one of the great Jagdwaffe leaders.

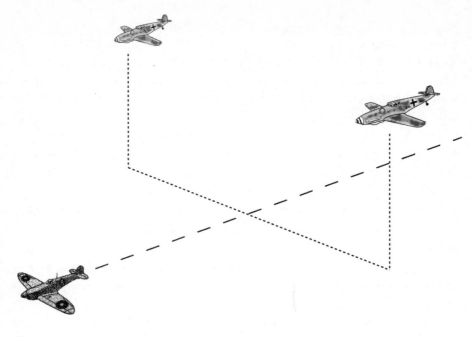

Boxing

If a solo Allied fighter could be caught by a Rotte, *they would take station on each side. If the leader* (Rottenführer) *attacked, and the victim broke into the attack, he was nicely set up for the* Kacmarek *to pull in behind.*

He brought with him a galaxy of future *Experten*: Ludwig Franzisket, Gerhard Homuth, Friedrich Körner, Karl-Heinz Redlich, Werner Schroer, Hans-Arnold Stahlschmidt, Günther Steinhausen, and, greatest of all, Hans-Joachim Marseille.

In the desert, both sides concentrated on providing support for the ground forces. Targets were diffuse, and difficult to spot in the featureless terrain. This being the case, most sorties were carried out at medium to low level, both for ease of spotting and accuracy of attack. In any case, the British drew the short straw. As their tired Hurricanes were unable to match the altitude performance of the Bf 109E, there was little point in even trying for the highest perch. Even when in June 1941 the Curtiss Tomahawk made its first appearance in theatre, the low altitude rating of its Allison engine made little difference.

Although the Jagdwaffe usually had altitude and positional advantages, clear skies and unrestricted visibility made surprise hard to achieve. Consequently most encounters ended in a dogfight at medium to low level. This made the no-deflection shot from astern a very rare occurrence. A hard-turning opponent ahead not only vanished from the bottom of the gunsight; it vanished from view altogether. By the time the correct deflection had been achieved, it was hidden somewhere under the nose!

Matters were not helped by the fact that their opponents, fed up with the fact that the Jagdwaffe were almost invariably in a position of advantage above, often adopted the defensive circle when threatened.* This was a tough nut to crack; the tail of every fighter was covered by the one behind.

The diameter of the circle was necessarily large; it was impractical for its component fighters to turn at their maximum rate. In theory, a Bf 109E could slip inside it, turning more tightly, and attack. In practice, it was extremely dangerous. If the next Allied fighter in the circle reacted quickly, the 109 would present it with a close-range modest deflection shot.

While the *Jagdflieger* could come at the circle from any angle, this demanded a level of skill in deflection shooting that few pilots possessed. It was Marseille who finally solved the problem, using three-dimensional manoeuvring to defeat the two-dimensional defensive circle, combined with the 'you can't miss if you stick your nose in the enemy cockpit' method.

Typically he would approach from above, trade altitude for speed, then from outside the circle, he would come up from the blind spot under his target's wings. He would give a short burst as the target disappeared under his nose, then he'd be up and over to attack another aircraft on the far side of the circle.

Marseille did not develop this method overnight. It called for incredibly precise flying, which he honed by unrelenting practice against his fellows, often to their annoyance. But once he had demonstrated that it could be done, he had many imitators.

Although 'Jochen' Marseille had seven victories on arrival in the desert, he took a while to settle in. Others were swifter. By 14 June the scholarly looking Gerhard Homuth, *Staffelkapitän* of 3/JG 27, added seven to bring his total score to twenty-two, for which he was awarded the *Ritterkreuz*. He left the theatre in July 1943, his score sixty-three. Others so decorated were Karl-Wolfgang Redlich, *Staffelkapitän* of 1/JG 27, who by 9 July had raised his score from nine to twenty-one, and Ludwig Franzisket who by 20 July had increased his tally from fourteen to twenty-two.

---

* The *Lufbery* originated in the First Word War War and was widely used by Bf 110s in the West in 1940. Göring tried to rename it the offensive circle, without success.

Franzisket showed generosity of spirit on 14 June. After shooting down a Hurricane near Gazala flown by South African ace Kenneth Driver, an action during which his own aircraft was badly damaged, he met his victim over breakfast. On learning that Driver's wife was in Cairo, he flew to the Allied side of the lines and dropped a message for her.

From late June 1941, the Mediterranean and North Africa were always overshadowed by events on the Eastern Front, but the Jagdwaffe was often used as a fire brigade, sent hither and thither to douse the latest conflagration. For example, II/JG 27 arrived in the desert in September, fresh from the East. Its *Kommandeur*, Wolfgang Lippert, did not last long. On 23 November he fell victim to a Tomahawk and died in a British hospital ten days later, his score at twenty-nine. II/JG 27 was equipped with Bf 109Fs, and I/JG 27 was also converting to the Friedrich.

The failure to neutralise Malta saw Axis shipping losses rise to unacceptable levels that autumn. Something had to be done, and with flying curtailed by the arrival of the Russian winter in November, units could be spared from the East. In late November, all three *Gruppen* of JG 53, led by Kommodore Günther, Freiherr von Maltzahn, arrived in Sicily, while Karl-Heinz Krahl's II/JG 3 arrived in December. In that same month, III/JG 27 arrived in North Africa, only to lose one of their greatest *Experten* almost immediately. Erbo, Graf von Kageneck, had been awarded the *Eichenlaub* in October. *Staffelkapitän* of 9/JG 27, having added only two to his score of sixty-five, he was shot down by a Kittyhawk near Agedabia on 24 December and died of his wounds.

From early in 1942, the Hurricanes defending Malta were swamped by superior numbers and outfought by better aircraft. Under continual bombardment, the island ceased to be a base for offensive operations, despite the arrival of Spitfires from March onwards. But just when the battle seemed to be won, the demands of other fronts intervened. II/JG 3 and I/JG 53 returned to the East in May, while III/JG 53 crossed to North Africa to reinforce the outnumbered and hard-pressed I/JG 27. Only II/JG 53 was left in Sicily, in company with Italian fighter units. These moves coincided with an accession of British strength on the island; Malta was back in business.

In the early months of 1942, targets were few, the Jagdwaffe many, and victories over Malta were hard to come by. This changed from April, when reinforcements of Spitfires started to reach the island. Even when II/JG 77 returned from the East, the Jagdwaffe on Sicily was increasingly forced on to the defensive.

It was during this year that the top scorer against Malta emerged. Gerhard Michalski of II/JG 53, had flown continually from Sicily since December 1941. Initially a *Staffelkapitän*, he was appointed *Kommandeur* on 1 June 1942. On 4 September he was awarded the *Ritterkreuz* for a total of forty-one victories. He continued to score, reaching a total of twenty-six against Malta-based aircraft.

Meanwhile the Star of Africa was rising. Having honed his technique, Marseille began an orgy of quick-fire destruction. On 8 February 1942 his thirty-third victory made him the leading scorer in the desert, having overtaken Homuth, Redlich and Franzisket along the way. It was a position he never lost.

Ten more victories in the next two weeks took his overall total to fifty and the *Ritterkreuz*. He received the *Eichenlaub* on 6 June for seventy-five victories, and he was appointed *Staffelkapitän* of 3/JG 27 two days later. The *Schwerter* for 101 victories followed on 18 June. On 1 September he set a new record of seventeen victories in one day. This raised his total to 126, and he became the fourth soldier of the Reich to be awarded the *Brillanten*. But on 30 September his Gustav caught fire. Forced to bale out, his parachute failed to open. In those last frenetic few days, he claimed twenty-five more victories, bringing his total to 158; all against Western-flown aircraft, and all but seven in the desert.

Although none could match the man whom Galland called 'the unrivalled virtuoso', he inspired several *Experten* in I/JG 27 to emulate him. Among them were Werner Schroer, whose sixty-one victories (of an eventual 114) was the next highest score in the desert. Schroer was closely followed by Hans-Arnold 'Fifi' Stahlschmidt with fifty-nine. He was lost on 7 September. Günther Steinhausen was killed near El Alamein on 6 September 1942 with his score at forty, while Friedrich Körner claimed thirty-six victories in a year, only to be shot down and taken prisoner on 4 July 1942.

Otto Schulz of II/JG 27 arrived in the desert with six victories in October 1941. Posted missing on 17 June 1942, his forty-two victories included British aces 'Imshi' Mason and Neville Duke, although Duke survived. Gustav Rödel of the same unit registered thirty-two victories from his war total of ninety-eight. All the above were awarded the *Ritterkreuz*. Schroer went on to win the *Eichenlaub* and *Schwerter*, while Stahlschmidt was belatedly awarded the *Eichenlaub* sixteen months after his death.

Towards the end of 1942, defeat at El Alamein combined with Allied landings in Algeria irremediably reversed the tide of war in the Mediterranean. With this, Malta lost its importance. From this point on, the Jagdwaffe would fight on the defensive.

On the Road to Moscow

In the East, the Luftwaffe prepared for its most ambitious task yet. Outnumbered by roughly five to one in fighters alone, they sought to reduce the imbalance by launching a devastating surprise attack. To destroy the Soviet air force was beyond their means; there were more than 200 airfields in the forward area alone, of which only thirty-one were attacked initially, by level bombers supplemented by Bf 109 Jabos. On the first day of Operation Barbarossa, 22 June 1941, 1,489 Soviet aircraft were claimed destroyed on the ground.

With many airfields still untouched, the Soviet air force fought back hard, mounting an estimated 6,000 sorties on the first day alone. Bitter skirmishes erupted when fighters met fighters. The main Soviet fighters of this era were Polikarpov I-15 biplanes and I-16 monoplanes as encountered in the Spanish Civil War. While they lacked the performance of the German Bf 109E/F, they were far more agile. The I-16 was particularly formidable. Attacked from astern, it could break into an attack fast enough to turn it into a head-on 'shoot-out at the O.K. Corrall' type of exchange. Given that the cannon of the I-16 Type 24 not only outranged the Bf 109F-3 but had triple its weight of fire, this was not a healthy place to be. More modern Soviet fighters were the MiG-3, optimised for high altitude interception but less good lower down where most combat took place, and the LaGG-3, widely regarded as a turkey, but lethal if well flown.

In addition to the destruction on the ground, the Luftwaffe claimed another 322 in the air; 172 by the Jagdwaffe; the rest by the *Flakartillerie*, which was a branch of the Luftwaffe. A significant number of these were bombers. Operating from undamaged airfields in the rear, they flew in unescorted gaggles of twenty to thirty aircraft and paid heavily. Based near Costanza in Romania, 8/JG 52, led by Staffelkapitän Günther Rall, accounted for eighteen Soviet bombers in the first few days of Barbarossa.

Elsewhere, victories depended on opportunities. Wolf-Dietrich Wilcke, *Kommandeur* of III/JG 53, claimed five on that first day to bring his tally to eighteen. Elsewhere, Werner Mölders brought his score to seventy-two with four victories, for which he received the *Schwerter*, just one day after

Galland in the West. Lothar Keller, *Kommandeur* of II/JG 3, also claimed four to bring his score to twenty. However, it was not done without cost. Four days later he was killed in a mid-air collision while flying a Storch; an ignominious end for an *Experte*. Other *Ritterkreuzträger* who did not survive the early days in the East included Heinz 'Pietsch' Bretnütz, Spanish Civil War veteran and *Kommandeur* of II/JG 53. Wounded while downing a Soviet bomber, his thirty-seventh victory, he force-landed behind enemy lines. By the time German forces freed him, it was too late. He died in hospital five days later. Wolfgang Schellmann, *Kommodore* of JG 27, baled out after being damaged by debris from an I-16. Taken prisoner, he was reportedly shot by the NKVD* two days later.

Many other *Ritterkreuzträger* failed to survive the year in the East. Spanish Civil War veteran Hans Kolbow, *Staffelkapitän* of 6/JG 51, had downed five Soviet bombers in a single sortie on 25 June. With his tally at twenty-seven, fifteen of them in the East, he was shot down and killed by ground fire on 16 July. His *Ritterkreuz* was posthumous.

Not all fell to enemy action. Hubert 'Hubs' Mütherich, *Staffelkapitän* of 5/JG 54, died when his fighter went over on its back in a forced landing near Leningrad on 9 September; his total was forty-three. Staffelkapitän Kurt Sochatzy of 7/JG 3 was shot down twice behind enemy lines, but managed to return. But on 12 August, he was forced to bale out when he collided with an I-16 over Kiev and was taken prisoner, with his final score at thirty-eight. Erich Schmidt of III/JG 53 went missing after being hit by Soviet anti-aircraft fire near Dubno on 31 August, his score forty-seven. Heinrich Hoffmann of 12/JG 51 fell to an Il-2 on 3 October, his score sixty-three, only one of which was in the West. He was awarded a posthumous *Eichenlaub*. Finally Edmund Wagner of 9/JG 51 was killed on 13 November in action against Pe-2s.

The most distinguished Jadgwaffe pilot to die in 1941 was Werner 'Vati' Mölders. Following the award of the *Schwerter* for his 72nd victory, Mölders quickly eclipsed the eighty of Manfred von Richthofen. By 15 July he had brought his Luftwaffe score to 101 – victories in Spain were Condor Legion, not Luftwaffe. He was then appointed *General der Jagdflieger*, and withdrawn from combat flying, although he still managed to add an occasional sneaky victory while visiting the troops.

Late in 1941, the greatest surviving *Oberkanone* of the First World War, Ernst Udet, shot himself. Recalled to be part of the honour guard at his

---

* Better known in modern times as the KGB.

state funeral, Mölders was killed when his He 111 crashed in bad weather on 22 November. He also was given a state funeral at which Reichs-marschall Göring, always a tauroboliast, exhorted him, 'Arise to Valhalla!' As a devout Roman Catholic, 'Vati' Mölders would have found this singularly inappropriate.

The most successful fighter-pilot in the East during 1941 was Günther 'Franzl' Lützow. *Kommodore* of JG 3 with eighteen victories in the West, he was awarded the *Eichenlaub* on 20 July with forty victories, and on 11 October became the fourth soldier of the Reich to receive the *Schwerter*, for ninety-two victories. On 25 October his score reached 101, not counting five in Spain, so he became the second centurion of the Jagdwaffe. Stab/JG 3 was credited with 106 victories during this period, of which 'Franzl' had claimed eighty-three. Although, like Mölders, he was then barred from combat flying, he remained as *Kommodore* of JG 3 until the following August, adding two unofficial victories in 'accidental' encounters.

Lützow was closely followed by one of his *Kommandeure*, Gordon Mc Gollob, who took over II/JG 3 on 1 July. By 26 October he had accounted for seventy-nine Soviet aircraft to add to his previous six previous victories. Having received the *Ritterkreuz* on 18 September, he was then awarded the *Eichenlaub*. Shortly after, he was assigned to the test centre at Rechlin.

Had he stayed in the East, 'Gulle' Oesau would probably have eclipsed both. *Kommandeur* of III/JG 3, with forty-two victories and the *Eichenlaub* prior to Barbarossa, he claimed forty-four victories in barely five weeks. Awarded the *Schwerter* on 15 July, the third soldier so honoured, he was recalled to the West soon afterwards to replace Balthasar as *Kommodore* of JG 2. Once back in the West, his scoring slowed, but on 21 October, he became the third pilot to achieve 100 victories.

Before Barbarossa, the benchmark for the *Ritterkreuz* was twenty victories and forty for the *Eichenlaub*, give or take a few either way. But the unprecedented slaughter in the East soon made it apparent that victories in the East were far more easily come by than in the West. The value of the *Ritterkreuz* lay in its rarity, but too many awards would degrade it. To avoid this, the figures were revised sharply upwards, typically with 20 more added to each. At the same time, the German Cross in Gold was introduced as a sort of intermediate award.

During 1941, seventy-six *Ritterkreuze* and eighteen *Eichenlaube* were awarded to fighter-pilots, but as few were entirely for operations in the

East, no meaningful conclusions can be drawn.

But if the awards list was high, so were the casualties. Twelve were killed in action, the most notable of whom was Hermann-Friedrich Joppien, *Kommandeur* of I/JG 51. A ruthless character* whose forty-two victories in the West had won him the *Eichenlaub*, by 25 August he had amassed a further twenty-eight in the East. But on that date, near Bryansk, he appeared to lose control during a hard turn and crashed.

Four more simply went missing, including Erich Schmidt of III/JG 53. Hit by flak over Dubno on 31 August, he baled out over enemy territory and was never seen again. He had scored forty-seven victories, eighteen of which were against England.

Three became prisoners; *Experte* Kurt Sochatzy, *Staffelkapitän* of 7/JG 3 with thirty-eight victories, was three times shot down behind enemy lines. Twice he got back, but for him it was third time unlucky.

Four died in flying accidents, of whom Werner Mölders was the most prominent. Winfried Schmidt, Staffelkapitän 8/JG 3, was wounded for the fourth time on 11 July, then assessed as unfit for flying duty, while Josef 'Joschko' Fözö, Kommandeur II/JG 51, was permanently incapacitated after a take-off accident on 11 July.

Early in 1942 the winter-wise Soviet armies counterattacked, gaining ground in the northern and central areas. For the first time, the *Heer* was forced to cede ground, although the siege of Leningrad was maintained. The front in the north and central areas was finally stabilised, and the late spring offensive was launched in the south. It had three objectives; Stalingrad, the Caucasus oil fields and the complete occupation of the Crimea.

The Jagdwaffe prepared for another blood-letting. They were not disappointed. Victories still came easily, although not as easily as they had in 1941. The Soviet air force was growing in numbers, while new and improved Lavochkin and Yakovlev fighters were entering service in ever increasing numbers. The average Soviet pilot was still undertrained, but improving, and in an echo of the Cigognes in the First World War, many promising pilots were being grouped in Guards Fighter Regiments. These élite units would prove formidable opponents.

The race for top spot continued. In May 1942, Gordon Gollob returned to the Eastern Front as *Kommodore* of JG 77. By 24 June, his

---

* During operations over England in 1940, Joppien was castigated by Mölders for strafing a passenger train.

score had risen to 107, and he was awarded the *Schwerter*. Against far easier opposition, he swiftly outstripped Oesau. Then on 21 June, Friedrich Beckh, *Kommodore* of JG 52 for just eighteen days, was posted missing after forced landing behind Russian lines near Kharkov. Gollob replaced him as a temporary measure, scoring his 150th victory on 30 August. He was awarded the *Brillanten* and posted to a staff job.

Gollob did not hold his lead for long. Hermann Graf of 9/JG 52, had opened his score on 3 August 1941. Another forty-one victories brought him the *Ritterkreuz* on 24 January 1942. Appointed *Staffelkapitän* in March, the *Eichenlaub* arrived on 17 May with his score at 104. Perhaps surprisingly, the *Schwerter* came just two days and two victories later. His score continued to mount, and on 4 September he became the second pilot to reach 150, five days after Gollob. On 26 September he was awarded the *Brillanten* for 172 victories. Still scoring at an incredible rate, on 2 October he became the first pilot to pass 200. Wounded shortly afterwards, he did not return to the East until October 1944.

Awards in 1942

In all, 105 *Ritterkreuze* were awarded to day-fighter-pilots in 1942. Of these, eighty-eight went to Bf 109 pilots for operations mainly or exclusively in the East, and eleven for those in the Mediterranean and North Africa. Four were awarded to Bf 110 pilots, two in the East and two in the Mediterranean, with a further two going to pilots who achieved respectable scores as *Zerstörer* before converting to the Bf 109. The most notable was Theodor Weißenberger, with twenty-three Bf 110 victories out of the thirty-eight which earned him the *Ritterkreuz* on 13 November 1942.

The *Eichenlaub* went to thirty-two day-fighter-pilots; twenty-seven of them in the East, the majority of their scores around 100, while the *Schwerter* went to just ten, including such great *Experten* as Heinz Bär and Hans Philipp, the seventh and eighth so honoured, for ninety victories on 16 February and eighty-two victories on 12 March respectively. On 23 June Leopold Steinbatz of 9/JG 52 became the first NCO to receive the *Schwerter*, albeit posthumously. Often flying as Hermann Graf's *Kacmarek*, he was shot down by Russian anti-aircraft fire on 15 June, with a score of ninety-nine.

The unrelenting years of war had not been kind to the Jagdwaffe, and casualties had been high. A high proportion of replacements were NCOs, or even in many cases Gefreiter. In 1942 this was reflected in the fact that forty-five *Ritterkreuze* went to NCOs, six of them lowly Unteroffiziere.

The war in the East was brutal, and rarely did the Russians show mercy to their prisoners. Many German pilots were posted missing in the East, and were never seen again. Others were beaten to death. On 22 May, Hans Strelow of II/JG 51 was the youngest holder of the *Eichenlaub*, awarded just two days before his twentieth birthday. Down behind enemy lines on 25 May, he shot himself rather than be captured. His final score was sixty-eight.

In 1942, thirty-three *Ritterkreuzträger* were killed in action, twenty-six in the East. Of the fifteen posthumous awards, twelve were in the East. Two died in accidents, both in North Africa. The incomparable Marseille was one,, the other was Helmut Belser of 8/JG 53 after a take-off accident. Six became prisoners; four of them in the Mediterranean, while two more suffered wounds severe enough to debar them from combat flying.

By the end of 1942, Germany was everywhere defensive. In the West, the British night-bombing campaign was intensifying, while by day the USAAF was preparing to take the offensive. In North Africa, the Axis armies were caught between East and West, while in Russia German forces were in full retreat from the Caucasus, and at Stalingrad, a whole army was cut off. The tide had turned.

CHAPTER 7

STRATEGIC DEFENCE

As seen in chapter 5, the British plan of raiding in daylight, with massed formations of bombers defending themselves against fighter attack with their multi-gun power-operated turrets, was a failure. Faced with the inevitable, they switched to night raiding, thus bringing about the scenario for which the Jagdwaffe was least well prepared. This was hardly surprising. Defence of the Fatherland against air attack was primarily the responsibility of the *Flakartillerie*, also a branch of the Luftwaffe. At the time, Germany had the best anti-aircraft guns in the world, and plans were afoot to introduce radar-aimed gun laying, of which great things were expected.

While there can be little doubt that radar-laid flak would have been very effective against massed formations of bombers flying predictable courses, this was not the threat that it faced. Instead, British bombers roamed the night skies over the Reich singly, in a haphazard manner. Changing altitude and course frequently in a defended area, they degraded the efficiency of the guns. Not that they inflicted much damage; often the bombers were unsure of their position over a blacked-out Europe, and the bombing was scattered and inaccurate. It was however a constant irritant and, for Göring personally, a loss of prestige.

The Luftwaffe made token experiments with night-fighters, but the problems seemed intractable. If the bombers had difficulty in finding their targets, the *Jagdflieger* had even greater difficulty in finding the bombers! Matters were not helped by the fact that from shortly after take-off, the night fighters had only a vague idea of their own whereabouts.

Searchlights were of less help than anticipated. Cloudy conditions were the norm, and these rendered them almost useless. Even in clear conditions, they illuminated only the underside of a bomber, which remained invisible to fighter-pilots at a higher altitude. And if the fighter was lower, it was forced to give chase while climbing. This reduced the speed of pursuit. Unless the fighter was exceptionally well placed at the moment of visual contact, it stood little chance of catching the bomber before it passed out of range of the searchlight.

Even when the fighter neared its target, it was not only likely to be blinded by the searchlight; it was often shot at by 'friendly' flak. A handful of victories were scored, but these were entirely fortuitous; the fighter just happened to be in the right place at the right time. The Bf 109Ds of the specialist *Nachtjagdstaffel* were quickly recognised to be ineffective; something better was needed.

By chance, this was readily to hand. Even before the war, the shortcomings of the Messerschmitt Bf 110 had been evident, and it was scheduled for replacement by the improved Bf 210. As a day-fighter it was already proving a turkey. By now an aircraft in search of a role, it was available.

At night its lack of manoeuvrability was no handicap. Its benign handling and blind-flying instrumentation were positive advantages. Its performance was adequate against the bombers, and its armament was destructive enough to inflict lethal damage in a single short burst. It could remain on patrol for significantly longer than the Bf 109. Finally, it had a second crewman to help with lookout and navigation.

The problems of finding individual bombers, widely spaced in time and distance, over the vast blacked-out area of western Europe seemed intractable, but while these were being addressed, another method was tried. Bombers could most easily be found in the vicinity of their bases. And while, like the Continent, England was blacked out at night, the bomber airfields had to be illuminated. Night bombers needed a flarepath to take off in darkness, and equally a flarepath for landing.

Intruders

Thus was born in the summer of 1940 the idea of intruder missions. For a start, the navigational problems of the German intruders operating over England were nowhere near as severe as those of British bombers raiding Germany. Distances were much shorter; a landmark could usually be found when crossing the coast, and deep incursions inland were not required.

In even halfway decent visibility, a flarepath could be seen from many miles away. Even though it would be switched off at the first sign of an intruder, its approximate location would have been noted. Night-fighters patrolling in the vicinity of these airfields would not only severely hinder bomber operations; they would have a fair chance of finding some airborne targets.

The *Nachtjagdflieger* even received unexpected help from their opponents. On the morning prior to a raid, British bombers carried out air tests, including their radios. These were monitored by the Luftwaffe listening service, which quickly deduced that a noisy morning followed by a quiet afternoon indicated a raid that night. Not only that; although direction-finding was insufficiently accurate to locate specific airfields, it did indicate areas. Information thus gleaned was passed on to the intruder units, which were thus alerted to the fact that a raid was planned.

The intruder mission not only required a lengthy flight across the North Sea; it also called for an extended time on patrol, awaiting 'trade'. But while the endurance of the Bf 110 was good enough for air defence, it was far too short for the intruder mission. Fortunately for the *Nachtjagdflieger*, there was an alternative ready to hand.

'Short legs' had been one of the failings of the Bf 110 as a *Zerstörer*, and as an interim measure, a few bombers had been modified with a 'solid' nose containing heavy armament. Two that had were the Junkers Ju 88C–2 and the Dornier Do 17Z-10. Both had the endurance of a bomber, plus the added bonus of an internal weapons bay. A few bombs scattered across an airfield, assuming that it could be found once the lights had been swiftly doused, would rarely do significant material damage, but could cause a great deal of disruption.

The bombers had two points of greatest vulnerability. The first was on take-off when they lurched, heavy laden, into the air, barely under control. This had the advantage of catching them before they could deposit their lethal cargo on the Fatherland. But given the inaccurate nature of British bombing, which more often than not was agricultural, this hardly mattered. And in the summer months, this was hardly feasible. At this time of year, bombers often departed at dusk or before, heading into the gathering darkness as they approached the enemy coast. Daylight intruding was not a viable proposition.

The second vulnerable time was on the bombers' return. The crews were tired and off guard. Seeking to avoid a mid-air collision with their fellows, they often burned their navigation lights. And a lit-up bomber was fair game.

Surprisingly, the intruders failed to make much impression on the bombers during 1940. They claimed eighteen victories, but lost eleven, six in crashes, one shot down by an RAF night-fighter and four that simply went missing. The following year was rather better; 123 claims were made. RAF records show just eighty-six aircraft attacked by intruders, although many others went down in unknown circumstances. But less than half the losses were bombers; most of the rest were trainers.

Given that the effect on RAF bomber operations was minimal, the price was high. Some twenty-eight intruders were lost. Of these, seven fell to night-fighters; two are believed to have been shot down by 'friendly' intruders, two collided with the aircraft that they were attacking; one was shot down by a bomber; ten were involved in crashes, while six simply went missing.

In November 1941, Der Gröfaz decreed that intruder missions must cease; he wanted British bombers shot down over the Reich where the populace could see them. It was an idiotic decision. Granted the intruders should have done better than they did, and if continued, they might have had a significant braking effect on RAF bomber operations in the following year.

Successful I/NJG 2 intruder pilots, 1940–41:

Name/Rank	Intruder Victories	Total	Remarks
Wilhelm Beier/Fw	14	36	Rk.
Hans Hahn/Fw*	12	12	Rk. KIA 11.10.41, collision with target.
Alfons Köster/Ofw	11	29	Rk. Killed in landing accident 7.1.45.
Kurt Herrmann/Oblt	9	9	PoW 10.3.41, shot down by anti-aircraft fire.
Paul Semrau/Oblt	9	46	Rk+El. KIA by Spitfires, 8.2.45.
Hermann Sommer/Ofw	9	19	KIA 11.2.44.
Heinz Strüning/Fw	9	56	Rk+El. KIA 24.12.44.
Heinz Völker/Lt	9	9	KIA 22.7.41. Collided with target.

Rk = *Ritterkreuz*, El = *Eichenlaub*; KIA = Killed in Action.
* This Hans Hahn should not be confused with day fighter *Experten* Hans 'Assi' Hahn or Hans von Hahn.

Not until June 1940 was the night defence of the Reich taken seriously, with the formation of NJG 1; the first true night-fighter *Geschwader*. Its *Kommodore* was Wolfgang Falck, a *Zerstörer* pilot with seven victories by day, who from experience was aware of the absolute need for radar in night interception. Just weeks later, Nachtjagddivision 1 was formed. In a classic example of poacher turned gamekeeper, it was commanded by former bomber, Kommodore Josef Kammhuber. It was an inspired combination; Kammhuber the meticulous organiser, vastly experienced in bomber operations, and Falck, the inspirational fighter leader. Together they set out to forge a new defensive system.

Until such time as the system could be made ready, the *Nachtjagdflieger* were forced to continue their unrewarding 'catseye' patrols, with and without the aid of searchlights. The spell was finally broken on 20 July 1940. A Bf 110 flown by Werner Streib, a former *Zerstörer* pilot with one day-victory to his credit, shot down a Whitley bomber.

It was the start of a lucky streak for Streib. On six more occasions in the next ten weeks he was in the right place at the right time, accounting for three Wellingtons in a single sortie on 1 October. He was awarded the *Ritterkreuz* on 6 October, the first *Nachtjagdflieger* decorated for success in the air.*

The turn of radar-assisted ground control came shortly after. After a series of experiments with a Freya radar fitted with a crude height-finding gadget, an operational trial was run, with a Do 17Z flown by Ludwig Becker of 4/NJG 1. Like Falck, he was one of the handful of 'true believers'. On 16 October, his ground controller guided him towards a Wellington bomber, which he shot down for his first victory. But while this was the first German radar-aided night victory, it was atypical, achieved in cloudless skies and bright moonlight.

In average conditions, something far more accurate was needed. Using what was immediately available, Kammhuber cobbled together a system called *Himmelbett*. This consisted of a Freya for early earning, and two short-ranged but more accurate narrow-beam Würzburg gun-laying radars. Freya made the initial contact, then handed it on to a Würzburg, which tracked it accurately. Meanwhile the other Würzburg tracked a defending fighter. The ground controller then steered the fighter towards the last reported position of the bomber.

Himmelbett boxes were set up in an unbroken chain across the British line of approach; every bomber heading for Germany was forced to run the gauntlet. It had however one great weakness. The controller had to steer the fighter to within visual contact, and in average visibility, this meant a distance of 650 ft (200 m) or so. This was not totally impossible, just extremely difficult.

---

* Falck received the *Ritterkreuz* on 1 October, but all his seven victories had been by day.

For the pilots, night fighting could be totally frustrating. To fly night after night, sometimes for weeks on end, and never once set eyes on a bomber, was disheartening, and many asked to be transferred to daylight operations. Helmut Lent, with eight day-victories, was one. At night, he failed to score for several months. Persuaded to keep trying by Falck, Lent finally opened his night account in May 1941. He went on to gain 102 night victories before his death, ironically in a daylight accident.

A clash of cultures did not help. Most *Nachtjagdflieger* had come from the *Zerstörer* units: Göring's élite Ironsides. Proud fighter-pilots, imbued with the Richthofen tradition, they took a dim view of being directed apparently aimlessly around a seemingly empty night sky by some chair-borne warrior.

The final piece in the puzzle was airborne fighter radar. No longer did the ground controller have the near-impossible task of bringing the fighter to within visual distance of a bomber. It was now sufficient to bring it within radar range; typically 2,500 to 4,000 m. Once again the pioneer was Ludwig Becker, who scored the first German airborne radar-aided victory on 9 August 1941. As the Bf 110 had originally been designed as a three-seater, this allowed a radar operator, plus his black boxes, to be squeezed in. The extra weight did nothing for performance and handling; nor did the draggy aerials projecting from the nose.

Although a vast step forward, improved results were far from immediate. Having resented being ordered around the night sky by a ground controller, it was a further affront to the *amour propre* of a formerly élite fighter-pilot to have to take directions from his radar operator, often his inferior in rank. But gradually, inspired by Streib, Becker and others, pilots came to appreciate that night interception was a matter of teamwork.

Compatibility of temperament was a major factor; most night fighter *Experten* scored the majority of their victories with the same 'sparker'.* There were also numerous cases where pilots changed their sparkers until they found one with whom they were compatible. As the majority of night *Experten* were officers, and most sparkers were NCOs, it is unlikely to have been the other way round very often.

Compatibility in this field is difficult to define. Most pilots preferred a running commentary, so that they always knew what was going on. A few seconds of silence made them restive. Others preferred a minimum of chatter, with few but decisive instructions. As familiarity grew, mutual

---

* Radar operator.

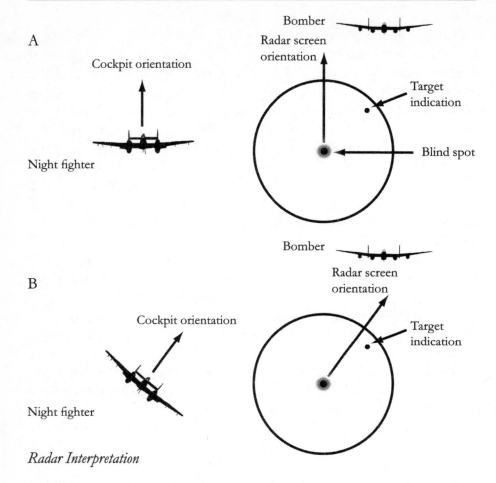

A

Cockpit orientation

Night fighter

Bomber

Radar screen
orientation

Target
indication

Blind spot

B

Cockpit orientation

Night fighter

Bomber

Radar screen
orientation

Target
indication

Radar Interpretation

Whereas a day fighter pilot could see where his target was and what it was doing, at night things were much more difficult. Radar showed the sparker where the target was; he had to work out what it was doing from a succession of contacts, then steer his pilot close enough to within visual distance. Depicted is a very basic problem. In (A) the sparker gains a contact rather higher and off to starboard. He instructs his pilot to begin a gentle turn, but as the fighter banks, (B), the contact appears to be almost dead ahead but much higher. This is due to orientation of the fighter vis-à-vis its target. Only when the fighter levels out on its new course does a true relative position appear, but further contacts will make it appear to be drifting to port. And had the contact initially been on a radically different course, the problems would have been compounded. Only the most gifted sparkers could handle the mental gymnastics involved. The fuzzy spot in the centre of the radar screen indicates minimum radar range. Once this is reached, the sparker's voice goes up an octave, as the fighter is very close to an unseen target, and a midair collision is a distinct possibility. The key to night fighting was teamwork and trust!

trust grew also. With practice, the pilot could deduce much from the tone and pitch of his sparker's voice. When an interception was imminent, it rose gradually, but if it suddenly jumped an octave, they were far too close to the unseen target for comfort.

The *Himmelbett* system had been tailored to the threat, which consisted of a hundred or so bombers wandering through the night sky in an unco-ordinated manner. The result was that only rarely did a defended box have to deal with more than one at a time. With practice, the defenders improved. At the end of 1941, Werner Streib led the field with twenty-two night victories, closely followed by Paul Gildner (the first NCO night *Experte* to be awarded the *Ritterkreuz*) with twenty-one and Helmut Lent with twenty. British losses started to rise, reaching four percent in April 1942.

In war, nothing ever remains constant. British tactics changed on the night of 30 May, when almost a thousand bombers raided Cologne. Tightly spaced in time and distance, they surged through the *Himmelbett* belt on a narrow front. The defending fighters in the few boxes they flew through were swamped, while the rest were left patrolling impotently far from the action.

At a stroke, the effectiveness of the *Himmelbett* system had been re-duced by seventy-five to eighty per cent. While a more flexible free-hunting defence was needed, this would produce a scenario in which twin-engined night-fighters roamed freely amid a bomber stream which was still largely composed of twin-engined Wellingtons. Haunted by the thought of own goals, which on at least two occasions had occurred over England, Kammhuber could not approve this. Instead, he reinforced the *Himmelbett* system, deepening it with more boxes and patrolling each box with two fighters instead of one. This was a waste of scarce resources.

By now, only two-thirds of the *Nachtjagdwaffe* consisted of Bf 110s. More than a quarter were Dornier Do 215s and 217s, while nearly ten per cent were Junkers Ju 88s. As night-fighters, the Dorniers were a makeshift, less potent than the Bf 110G. Ideally there should have been a greater pro-portion of Ju 88s, but this was constrained by the demands of other fronts.

The year saw eight more *Nachtjagdflieger* awarded the *Ritterkreuz*. Among them were former intruders Paul Semrau, Heinz Strüning and Alfons Köster, with fourteen, twenty-three and sixteen victories respectively. On 1 July Ludwig Becker was so decorated for twenty-five victories, as was Reinhold Knacke with thirty. Two aristocrats also featured; the Austrian Egmont Prinz zur Lippe-Weissenfeld on 16 April with twenty-one victories, and on 2 October Heinrich Prinz zu Sayn-Wittgenstein with twenty-two, many of which had been scored against the Soviet Union. Another high scorer in the East was Rudolf Schönert with twenty-one. All except Köster went on to receive the *Eichenlaub*, albeit two were posthumous awards.

While Cologne could only be described as a tactical defeat, by the autumn of 1942, bomber losses had again started to rise. By 31 December, Helmut Lent, who had received the *Eichenlaub* on 6 June, led the field with forty-nine night victories, most shared with sparker Walter Kubisch. Equal second were Reinhold Knacke and Ludwig Becker with forty apiece. Knacke set a record of five victories in one night on 16/17 September with his regular sparker Kurt Bundrock, who shared in thirty-five of his eventual total score of forty-eight (four by day), while Josef Staub, Becker's sparker, had shared in all forty of his. In equal fourth place were Paul Gildner, and the fast-scoring Egmont Prinz zur Lippe-Weissenfeld with thirty-eight each. Of these, only Bundrock survived the war. After Knacke's demise he flew with Werner Streib.

White Stars by Day

At the start of 1943, a new threat was emerging. The second half of the previous year had seen the USAAF build up a strategic bomber force in England, committed to precision daylight raiding. The main bomber was the heavily armed Boeing B-17 Flying Fortress with which, despite British advice to the contrary, the Americans confidently expected to be able to beat off enemy fighters.

The US 8th Air Force commenced its offensive in the final months of 1942, with raids on targets in France, and were met by the resident *Jagdgeschwader*. Making the traditional attack from astern, they were greeted by a lethal storm of fire from the bombers long before they themselves reached effective shooting range. This had all the potential for an adverse kill/loss ratio.

Egon 'Conny' Mayer, the experienced *Kommandeur* of III/JG 2, addressed the problem by introducing an attack from head-on and slightly high. This had two advantages. The high closing speed made the exposure to enemy fire very brief, while the protection of the bombers was weakest in front. The disadvantage was that firing time was equally brief. Few bombers were shot down in a single head-on pass, but hits in the control cabin often knocked them out of formation. And stragglers were vulnerable.

The Americans first ventured over Germany on 27 January 1943. The FW 190As of JG 1 rose to defend Wilhelmshaven, but lacking the experience of their Channel coast colleagues, attacked from astern. While they shot down three B-17s, they lost seven of their own. Mayer's tactics were vindicated.

It was quickly apparent that against the USAAF Viermots,* the German fighters needed a greater punch. The added weight and drag of more and larger guns reduced manoeuvrability, but against unescorted bombers, this was acceptable. Experiments were also made with air-to-air bombing and 21-cm rocket mortars, but these proved far too inaccurate to be effective.

Zerstörer units were used against the US heavies, and even Bf 110 night-fighters were pressed into service. This was sheer folly; the *Nachtjagdflieger* were unused to daylight formation attacks, while both aircraft and crews were too valuable to risk in this way. This was underlined on 26 February 1943, when Ludwig Becker was shot down and killed by US bombers; his tally was forty-six, all at night. For more than a year, night-fighters continued to be used in daylight, although the top night *Experten* were held back.

The bombers were the real threat, and the Jagdwaffe was ordered to concentrate on them, avoiding the Allied escort fighters wherever possible. In the early days, this was easily achieved by delaying attacks until the escorts turned back. Jagdwaffe victories mounted, culminating in the two Schweinfurt raids of August and October, when sixty bombers were lost on each incursion, with many more damaged beyond repair. Both were tactical victories for the defenders; never again would the USAAF mount unescorted deep penetration raids. But already the scenario was changing.

Escorts to Berlin

By the middle of 1943, American escort fighters were barely able to reach the German border. Within months they could reach central Germany, while by March 1944, they could go all the way to Berlin. The one redeeming feature was that with a bomber stream many miles long, the escorts could not be everywhere at once. With luck, they might be avoided.

---

* *Viermot*: a contraction of the German for four-engined; also known as *Mobelwagen* (pantechnicons). Originally coined for American heavy bombers, it was only applied to British bombers if they were encountered by day.

This was at odds with the Richthofen knightly ethos, in which chivalry, skill and valour predominated, and where victory and honour went to the better man. Against the Viermots, victory and survival became a matter of sheer chance, with little scope for individualism and even less for chivalry. The attitude of many was summed up by Hans Philipp.

Against 20 Russians trying to shoot you down, or even 20 Spitfires, it can be exciting; even fun. But curve in towards 40 Fortresses and all your past sins flash before your eyes. And when you yourself have reached this state of mind, it becomes that much more difficult to have to drive every pilot of the *Geschwader*, right down to the youngest and lowliest NCO, to do the same.

At the end of March 1943, 'Fips' Philipp was the very successful *Kommandeur* of I/JG 54 in the East. Holder of the *Schwerter*, his score had reached 203, 177 of them on the Eastern Front. On 1 April he was transferred to JG 1 as *Kommodore*, only to find that the daylight defence of the Reich was a different world. Over the next six months he claimed just two victories, both fighters. On 8 October he claimed his first Viermot, only to be shot down and killed by Thunderbolts shortly after.

The *Ritterkreuz* was the most prized German decoration, and hitherto had been awarded to fighter-pilots on the basis of their victory scores. In an attempt to modify Jagdwaffe attitudes, OKL now offered a carrot. Points would be awarded for success against the bombers. The complete destruction *(Abschuss)* of a Viermot counted as three points plus a victory. Knocking it out of its tight formation *(Herausschiessen)* counted as two points plus a victory, while finishing off a badly damaged bomber was worth one point (but no victory).* Points were added to victories obtained in the usual manner, with forty points the nominal requirement.

With the carrot came a stick. Göring, under pressure to halt the raids, sought scapegoats. Unable to understand this new form of warfare, he began to threaten fighter leaders with courts-martial for cowardice. This totally undermined his leadership.

The only way to gain a respite from the air assault was to inflict unacceptably high losses on the bombers. Throughout 1943, Jagdwaffe units had gone into action in *Gruppe* strength; due to unserviceability this

---

* There is some evidence to show that finishing off a damaged bomber was also counted as a victory later in the war.

was typically about twenty or so fighters. It was not enough; attacks by such small formations were all too easily disrupted by the ever-present escorts. The immediate solution was to operate where possible in *Geschwader* strength.

General der Flieger Adolf Galland pondered the problem. He rightly concluded that the head-on attack gave too little time to inflict lethal damage, whereas the traditional attack from astern gave a much greater chance of success. The next step was how to achieve this without unacceptable casualties.

Experiments were already under way with the *Sturmböcke*, heavily armed and armoured FW 190A-8s, which could drive through the defensive fire like knights of old through an arrow storm. But heavy and unman-oeuvrable, these would be all too vulnerable to the agile escort fighters. Galland's solution was to form a *Gefechtsverband*, consisting of a *Sturmgruppe* of FW 190A-8s, protected by two or three *Begleitgruppen* of Bf 109Gs. The first such unit was JG 3 Udet, formed in early 1944.

Shooting down four-engined bombers was a specialised field, in which some were more successful than others. It took enormous nerve to keep driving in while 50-calibre bullets drummed on one's fighter like hail, while hoping that the *Begleitgruppen* could fend off the angry escort fighters. The nervous strain was enormous; the *Kommandeur* of IV (Sturm) /JG 3 from April 1944 was Wilhelm Moritz, formerly of JG 51. Com-pletely exhausted, he was withdrawn from combat in November 1944, having claimed eleven Viermots.

In all 67 *Jagdflieger* reached double figures against the Viermots, although these were not all necessarily shoot-downs.

Casualties were high, although many fell to the escort fighters rather than return fire from the bombers. Of the top sixty-six, sixteen were killed in action, two in ramming attacks, while four were wounded too severely to continue combat flying. Of the high scorers, Egon Mayer was shot down by Thunderbolts on 2 March 1944, while Hugo Frey fell to return fire from B-17s on 6 March, having earlier shot down four of their number on the same mission.

The following table shows the top Viermot *Experten*:

Name	Viermots	Total	Notes
Walter Dahl	36	128	Rk+El. JG 3, 300
Georg-Peter Eder	36	78	Rk+El. JG 2, 1, 26, 7.
Anton Hackl	32	192	Rk+El+Sch. JG 11, 76, 26, 300.
Konrad Bauer	32	68	Rk, nom. El. JG 3, 300.
Werner Schroer	26	114	Rk+El+Sch. JG 54, 3, 27.
Rolf Hermichen	26	64	Rk+El. JG 26, 11, 104.
Hermann Staiger	26	63	Rk. JG 26, 1, 7.
Hugo Frey	26	32	Rk post. JG 1, 11. KIA 6.3.44.
Egon Mayer	25	102	Rk+El+Sch. JG 2. KIA 2.3.44.
Werner Gerth	25	c 30	Rk. JG 3. KIA 2.11.44.
Kurt Bühligen	24	112	Rk+El+Sch. JG 2.
Ernst Börngen	24	45	Rk. JG 27. WIA 19.5.44.
Walter Loos	22	38	Rk. JG 3, 300, 301.
Hans Weik	22	36	Rk. JG 3.
Heinz Bär	21	220	Rk+El+Sch. JG 51, 71, 1, 3, JV 44
Siegfried Lemke	21	96	Rk, nom. El. JG 2.
Fritz Karch	21	47	Rk. JG 2.
Rüdiger von Kirchmayr	21	46	Rk. JG 1,.11,.JV 44.
Adolf Glunz	20	71	Rk+El. JG 26.
Hans Ehlers	20	52+	Rk.nom. El. JG 1. KIA 27.12.44.
Willy Kientsch	20	52	Rk+El. JG 27. KAS 29.1.44.
Anton-R Piffer	20	26	Rk post. JG 2. KIA 17.6.44.
Hans-H König	20	24	Rk post. JG 11. KIA 24.5.44.

NB Herbert Rollwage of JG 53 has often been erroneously credited with 44 Viermot victories. The true figure was 14.

Rk = *Ritterkreuz*, El = *Eichenlaub*, Sch = *Schwerter*, KIA = Killed in Action, MIA = Missing in Action, WIA = Wounded in Action, KAS = Killed on Active Service.

The problem with the use of large units was the difficulty of getting an unwieldy formation of ninety to a hundred fighters into a good enough position for an effective head-on pass. USAAF escorts ranged ahead and on the flanks of the bombers, and there was little chance of an entire *Geschwader* remaining undiscovered. Once this happened, escorts were drawn like wasps to a jam pot.

Manoeuvring a *Gefechtsverband* in behind a bomber formation was even more tricky, and rarely was it achieved successfully. When it did, it cut great swathes through the bombers. Heavily armoured in front against return fire from the bombers, the unhandy *Sturmböcke* remained vulnerable to fighter attack from astern, and losses were high. In all, only three *Sturmgruppen* were formed; a fleabite against raids of more than 1,000 bombers and several hundred fighters. As usual; it was too little, too late!

On the Back Foot at Night

From the outset, the *Nachtjagdflieger* suffered from German neglect of electronic aids for defensive purposes. From 1943 the situation deteriorated even more, as the British increased their already commanding lead in electronic warfare. Not only could they now find and bomb area targets in poor visibility but advanced electronic countermeasures, allied with clever tactics, made the task of the defenders even more difficult. The one apparent gleam of light was a new night-fighter, the Heinkel He 219A *Uhu*.

The *Uhu* was fast, with a brochure speed of 416 mph (670 kph), had an absolute ceiling of 41,669 ft (12,700 m), and was heavily armed with six forward-firing cannon plus two upward-firing. It made its operational debut in June 1943 in the hands of leading *Experte* Werner Streib. He and Fischer, his sparker, shot down five Lancasters in the space of half an hour. While this was a promising start, the effect was ruined when Streib wrote it off in a crash landing at the end of the sortie.

The obvious next step was to rush the He 219 into mass production, but for various reasons this was not done. The first was political; Chief Designer Ernst Heinkel was not the most popular man with the OKL. Second, the *Uhu* failed to live up to its brochure claims; production aircraft performance fell well short. Finally, a wing loading almost half as much again as its contemporaries made it a very hot ship, suitable for only the most experienced pilots. Only 268 were built.

Meanwhile, the enemy sought to exploit their already commanding lead in electronic warfare (EW). Having established that the Luftwaffe air defence system was heavily reliant on radar systems which used similar wavelengths, they introduced a single countermeasure to jam them all. Codenamed Window,* this consisted of bundles of aluminised strips, each of which gave a radar return similar to that of a bomber.

The blow fell on the night of 24 July 1943. A force of 800 bombers approaching Hamburg suddenly appeared as 10,000 contacts on German radar screens, swamping the ground control. In the air matters were no

---

* In modern parlance, chaff.

better; the *Nachtjagdflieger* vainly chased bogus contacts around the sky. At a stroke, the carefully built night air-defence system lay in ruins. The answer lay in new radars, but these were not immediately available.

Even before the Hamburg debâcle, two expedients had been suggested, both less reliant on radar. The first was *Wilde Sau*, proposed by former bomber pilot Hans-Joachim 'Hajo' Herrmann. Having noticed that the huge fires started by area raids provided a backdrop against which bombers could be seen, Herrmann proposed using Bf 109s and FW 190s over the targets. To avoid the problems encountered three years earlier, these would be flown by former bomber and transport pilots with instrument flying experience.

Initially *Wilde Sau* was a success, in part aided by the light nights of late summer, and three *Jagdgeschwader* were formed for this mission. But it flattered only to deceive; instrument-rated pilots were in short supply; many had already been snapped up by the *Nachtjagdgeschwader*. Perhaps surprisingly, the Bf 109 had been found better suited to night operations than the FW 190. Whereas on landing the former could be wheeled on to the ground, the latter called for a precise three-pointer. In a Bf 109, a misjudged landing usually swiped off the flimsy main gear, leaving the pilot shaken but unhurt. The more robust FW 190 usually went straight over on to its back, often with fatal consequences. With the onset of winter weather, the accident rate became unsustainable.

The doyen of the *Wilde Sau* pilots was Friedrich-Karl 'Nasen' Müller, so-called because he had the biggest nose in the entire Luftwaffe. A pre-war Lufthansa pilot, he had previously served with bomber and transport units. In mid-1943 he became instrument flying instructor to Kommando Herrmann, and scored his first *Wilde Sau* victory on 4 July 1943. Six weeks later, he claimed three in a single sortie over Berlin. His final total of thirty victories included twenty as a *Wilde Sau* pilot.

The second expedient was *Zahme Sau*, proposed by former bomber pilot Viktor von Lossberg. This exploited the fact that no amount of countermeasures could conceal the presence of the bomber stream. When a raid was detected, night-fighters were vectored towards it, there to fight a running battle until fuel or ammunition were expended. If their radars were jammed, they headed for where the jamming was heaviest and searched visually.

For the *Nachtjagdflieger*, all was not lost. Three new devices were introduced before the end of the year. Two were passive homers, able to detect British bomber emissions. The third was Lichtenstein SN-2, an airborne radar unaffected by Window. Once again the battle was on, with *Zahme Sau* increasingly more important than *Himmelbett*.

Fifteen *Ritterkreuze* were awarded to *Nachtjagdflieger* during 1943; two of them posthumously. For the first time, sparkers were honoured: Gerhard Scheibe, who flew with Manfred Meurer, on 10 December, and Walter Kubisch, Lent's back-seater, on the final day of the year.

At the start of 1943, Helmut Lent led the field with forty-nine night victories. He was trailed by Ludwig Becker and Reinhold Knacke with forty each, but both were killed in February. Knacke received the *Eichenlaub* posthumously, his final score being forty-four.

Helmut Lent received the *Schwerter* on 2 August for sixty-six night and eight day victories. At the end of the year, Lent still led, with seventy-five at night, but just behind and closing were two 'late starters'. The 'royal coachman', as his crew called him, Heinrich Prinz zu Sayn Wittgenstein, was in second place with sixty-eight, followed by Manfred Meurer with sixty-two. Two other contenders for the top spot had both fallen in September: Hans-Dieter Frank collided with a night fighter, his total was fifty-five, and August Geiger was shot down by a British night-fighter ace Bob Braham two days later on a score of fifty-three. Both received the *Eichenlaub* posthumously.

The race continued. By the night of 21 January 1944, Lent had claimed seventy-nine victories, Wittgenstein seventy-eight. That night Lent claimed another two, Wittgenstein five. But while the former survived, Wittgenstein was shot down and killed by a British night-fighter. For the *Nachtjagdflieger* it was a double tragedy. A few miles away, Manfred Meurer had been brought down by a crashing bomber.

For the *Nachtjagdflieger*, 1944 commenced as a year of victory, but ended in defeat. Often the ground controllers were misled by course changes, feints, and diversionary raids. But just occasionally, fortune smiled on the defenders. Notable was the Nuremberg raid of 30/31 March when about 220 night-fighters made contact with a bomber stream over 750 strong. On a clear moonlit night, the stage was set for a massacre.

What happened was rather less, although bad enough for the bombers. The *Nachtjagdflieger* claimed just seventy-nine victories, plus two shared with the *Flak*. While this was certainly a German victory, it was not good enough. Given the known multiple victories scored that night, three quarters of the *Nachtjagdflieger* to make contact had failed to register a single claim.

The most successful *Experte* that night was Martin 'Tino' Becker (no relation to Ludwig). His first sortie, a *Zahme Sau*, yielded six victories; his second, a *Himmelbett*, added one more, bringing his score to twenty-six, for which he received the *Ritterkreuz*. Previously a reconnaissance pilot, he was a relative newcomer to night-fighting, but soon proved a master of mass destruction. He had previously claimed six on 23 March 1944, and on 14 March 1945, he claimed nine, to bring his final score to fifty-eight. He was awarded the *Eichenlaub* six days later.

For the *Nachtjadgdflieger*, Nuremberg was the high water mark. For a few months they had a respite as Allied forces pounded Normandy as a prelude to the invasion, but when the bombers returned to the Reich, they used new tactics and new electronic gadgetry. Outclassed in the electronic war, the *Nachtjagdflieger* were hounded by intruders even over their own airfields. Although losses to this cause rarely reached five a night, casualties mounted. By December, British bomber losses had shrunk to a minuscule 0.7 per cent. By now only a handful of *Experten* could continue to fly interception sorties.

December 1944 saw RAF bomber losses at their lowest. In this month 114 German night fighters went down, of which RAF Mosquito intruders claimed thirty-eight, losing just two of their own. Assuming that return fire from the bombers accounted for five, while friendly fire and accidents accounted for another five, sixty-six (fifty-eight per cent) were un-accounted for. Why and how?

There was no mystery about this. From mid-November onwards, fuel permitting, many *Nachtjagdflieger* were committed to night strafing attacks on Allied ground forces. Almost certainly this accounted for the balance, although the only leading *Experte* lost in this way was Heinz-Horst Hißbach, shot down by anti-aircraft fire while strafing American forces near Gelnhausen. His final score thirty-four; he was awarded a posthumous *Ritterkreuz*.

In all, thirty-seven *Nachtjagdflieger* received the *Ritterkreuz* in 1944. Of these, seven were sparkers and one was a gunner. Eight failed to survive the war. Nine received the *Eichenlaub*, while a further three were nominated for it, one of whom was a sparker. One notable *Eichenlaub* recipient was Günther Radusch, the only Spanish Civil War veteran to become a leading night-fighter *Experte*. He survived the war with a tally of sixty-five victories, sixty-four of them at night. The top award, the *Brillanten*, went to Helmut Lent on 31 July, for his hundredth night victory (108 total). He died as the result of a daylight landing accident on 5 October. With him died his sparker, Walter Kubisch, who had participated in eighty-eight of his victories, eighty of which were at night.

The star of the year was however Heinz-Wolfgang Schnaufer. Having opened his account in June 1942, he scored steadily. His first sparker was Dr Baro, with whom he scored twelve victories. He then flew with Erich Handke, who later flew with with Martin Drewes (forty-three night and eight day victories). The turning point came when Schnaufer teamed with Fritz Rumpelhardt, with whom he achieved an almost telepathic rapport.

From then on his score climbed rapidly. On the final day of 1943, he lay fourteenth in the list with a score of forty-two, for which he received the *Ritterkreuz*. By 24 June 1944 his score had reached eighty-four, for which he received the *Eichenlaub*. His example was quickly recognised with the *Schwerter* five weeks and five victories later. The *Brillanten* for 100 victories followed on 16 October. By the end of the year he was the leading *Nachtjagdflieger* with 106 night victories. He ended the war with 121.

Some idea of his achievements are given by the fact that he claimed seventy-nine victories between 1 January 1944 and the end of the war. His closest rivals during this period were Heinz Rökker and Gustav Francsi with fifty-six apiece, followed by 'Tino' Becker with fifty-two.

For Schnaufer, it was teamwork. His sparker, Rumpelhardt, who was nominated for the *Eichenlaub* in March 1945, shared in a hundred victories. His gunner, Wilhelm Gänsler, whose night vision was legendary, shared in ninety-eight. Gänsler had previously shared in seventeen night victories with Ludwig Becker; his *Ritterkreuz*, awarded on 27 July 1944, was hard-earned.

One final point. Schnaufer, unlike most of the other top scoring night *Experten*, flew only the inferior Bf 110.

The top fifteen *Nachtjagdflieger* are shown below:

Name	Units	Score	Notes
Heinz-Wolfgang Schnaufer	II/NJG 1	121N	Rk, El, Sch, Br.
	Stkap 12/NJG 1		
	Kdr IV/NJG 1		
	Kdre NJG 4		
Helmut Lent	I/ZG 76	102N	Rk, El, Sch, Br. KAS 5.10.44.
	Stkap 6/NJG 1	8D	
	Kdr II/NJG 2,		
	then IV/NJG 1		
	Kdre NJG 3		*contd*

Name	Units	Score	Notes
Heinrich Prinz zu Sayn-Wittgenstein	Stkap 9/NJG 2		Rk, El, Sch. posthumous.
	Kdr I/NJG 100	83N	KIA 21.1.44
	Kdr II/NJG 3	(29 Russia)	
	Kdre NJG 2		
Werner Streib	I/ZG 1	65N	Rk, El, Sch. *Inspekteur der*
	Stkap 2/NJG 1	1D	*Nachtjagdflieger* from March 44.
	Kdr I/NJG 1		
	Kdre NJG 1		
Manfred Meurer	ZG?; 1/NJG 1	65N	Rk, El. KIA 21.1.44. He 219.
	Kdr special dets		
	Kdr II/NJG 5		
	Kdr I/NJG 1		
Günther Radusch	Stkap 2/ZG 1	64N	Rk, El. 1 day victory Spain.
	Kdr I/NJG 1		
	Kdr I/NJG 3		
	Kdr II/NJG 3		
	Kdre NJG 5, 2 and 3		
Rudolf Schönert	4/NJG 1	64	Rk, El.
	II/NJG 2	(35 Russia)	
	Stkap 4/NJG 2		
	Stkap 5/NJG 3		
	Kdr II/NJG 5		
	Kdr I/NJG 100		
	Kdr NJG 10		
	Kdre NJG 5		
Heinz Rökker	I/NJG 2	63N 1D	Rk, El. Several in Med.
	Stkap 2/NJG 2		
Paul Zorner	II/NJG 2	59N	Rk, El. Former transport pilot.
	IV/NJG 2		
	Stkap 2/NJG 3		
	Stkap 8/NJG 3		
	Kdr III/NJG 5		
Martin 'Tino' Becker	I/NJG 4	58N	Rk, El. Former recce pilot.
	Kdr IV/NJG 6		
Gerhard Raht	4/NJG 3	58N	Rk, El.
	Stkap 1/NJG 2		
	Kdr I/NJG 2		

Name	Units	Score	Notes
Wilhelm Herget	II/ZG 76	57N	Rk, El. One with Me 262.
	NJG 3, 1 and 4	15D	
	Kdr I/NJG 4		
	then JV 44		
Heinz Strüning	5/ZG 26	6N	Rk, El. Intruder. KIA
	1/NJG 2		24.12.1944.
	II/NJG 3		
	3/NJG 1		
	Stkap 9/NJG 1.5		
Josef Kraft	II/NJG 4	156N	Rk, El. Incl. 20 transports over
	II/NJG 5		Hungary.
	II/NJG 6		
	Stkap 12/NJG		
Gustav Francsi	I/NJG 100	56N	Rk, nom El. Mainly East.

Rk = *Ritterkreuz*, El = *Eichenlaub*, Sch = *Schwerter*, B = *Brillanten*; KIA = Killed in Action, KAS = Killed on Active Service; N = Night, D = Day.

This table gives an indication of how various *Experten* were moved around to meet the exigencies of the moment; also to provide both an example and leadership. Strüning was the only one of the above who started out as an NCO.

The following one shows the successful night crewmen (shared victories):

Name	Pilot(s)	Victories	Notes
Wilhelm Gänsler	Ludwig Becker	17N	Rk. WO/gunner
	Schnaufer	98N	
		115 Total	
Fritz Rumpelhardt	Schnaufer	100N	Rk, nom. El. Sparker
Walter Kubisch	Lent	80N, 8D	Rk. WO/Sparker.
			KAS 5.10.1944.
Hannes Richter	Rudolf Schönert	68N	Rk. Sparker
Carlos Nugent	Heinz Rökker	61N, 1D	Rk. Sparker
Gerhard Scheibe	Manfred Meurer	60+N	Rk. Sparker KIA 21.1.44.
Erich Handke	Schorch Kraft	14N	Rk. Sparker
	Schnaufer	8N	
	Martin Drewes	37N	
		Total 59N	

Name	Pilot(s)	Victories	Notes
Karl-Ludwig Johanssen	Martin Becker	58N	Rk. Sparker
		Total 59N	
Heinrich Wilke	Paul Zorner	58N	Rk. Sparker
Hans Liebherr	Wilhelm Herget	57N, 11D	Rk. WO/gunner Sparker
Hans-Georg Schierholz	Rudolf Frank	Total 57N.	Rk. Sparker Baled out four
	Werner Husemann		times.

Rk = *Ritterkreuz*, El = *Eichenlaub*, Sch = *Schwerter*, B = *Brillanten*; KIA = Killed in Action, KAS = Killed on Active Service; N = Night, D = Day.

Whereas most of the above indicate an early affinity between pilot and radar operator, others show that it was a while before they found a compatible partner. Of course, most never did.

CHAPTER 8

THE NET CLOSES

Out of Africa

North Africa had always been the Cinderella front, and by the beginning of 1943 it was crumbling fast. Following the heavy defeat at El Alamein, the fast-retreating Axis forces were heading westwards, only to find themselves faced with the new Anglo-American army advancing from Algeria. The scene was set for a North African reprise of Custer's last stand.

During the previous year, Marseille had so far outstripped his rivals that competition had become meaningless. His death, resulting from mechanical failure, coupled with the loss of other high-scoring *Experten*, had demoralised the exhausted JG 27, which was withdrawn in November 1942. This left I/JG 53 as the sole desert 'old hands' unit. Reinforcements poured in, mainly from the East. The Bf 109G-equipped JG 77 arrived, led by Kommodore Jochen Müncheberg, containing such luminaries as 'Pritzl' Bär, 'Toni' Hackl, and Ernst-Wilhelm Reinert. It was closely followed by II/JG 51 with Hartmann Grasser, also with Bf 109Gs. Then in November, the FW 190 made its first appearance in North Africa with II/JG 2, led by Adolf Dickfeld, and containing high-scoring *Experten* Erich Rudorffer and Kurt Buhligen.

Heavy fighting against odds followed. Müncheberg was killed on 23 March when he collided with a Spitfire, his 135th victim. He was replaced by 'Macky' Steinhoff, a 150-victory *Experte* from the Eastern Front and previously *Kommandeur* of II/JG 52. Shot down by a Spitfire on his first day in action, Steinhoff quickly learned that North Africa was a much harder school.

It is a truism that awards tend to reflect success, and few *Ritterkreuze* were awarded in the dying days of the North African campaign. Just three were given, all on 14 March 1943. Otto Schulz, *Staffelkapitän* of 6/JG 51, had scored fifty-one victories, of which twenty were over Tunisia. Of the others, only a handful of the fifty-three victories of Herbert Kaiser of III/JG 77, and of the forty-three gained by Günther Rübell, *Staffelkapitän* of 5/JG 51, were attained over North Africa.

Of those who flew over Tunisia, the highest scorer was Heinz Bär, *Kommandeur* of I/JG 77, with forty-five victories. Next came Jochen Müncheberg with forty-one, followed by FW 190 pilots Kurt Bühligen with forty and Erich Rudorffer with twenty-seven. Adolf Dickfeld claimed eighteen, but was seriously injured on 8 January when he fell victim to the take-off quirks of the FW 190. Raising the tail a tad too much, his propellor hit the ground and he somersaulted onto his back. He was not the only one; two more FW 190 pilots did the same in the next three days.

The German presence in North Africa became unsustainable, and the Axis capitulated in May 1943. Steinhoff, with experience in emergency evacuations from Stalingrad and the Kuban, managed to extricate JG 77 to Sicily in better order than most, with the mechanics crammed into the space behind the cockpits.

Sicily then came under attack by overwhelming forces and fell within a matter of weeks, after which the Italian mainland was invaded. But this was good defensive country, and Allied progress was slow on the ground. It did however put the vital Romanian oilfields within reach of US strategic bombers.

Just three *Ritterkreuze* were awarded during the defence of Sicily and Southern Italy. Jürgen Harder, brother of Spanish Civil War *Experte* Harro, reached forty victories on 5 December 1943 with JG 53. Heinz-Edgar Berres, *Staffelkapitän* of 1/JG 77, was killed by Spitfires over the Straits of Messina on 25 July; his tally fifty-three, of which forty-seven were against the West. His award was posthumous. Franz Schieß, *Staffelkapitän* of 8/JG 53, gained the award on 21 June for fifty-four victories. Missing near Ischia on 2 September, his total of sixty-seven included fourteen in Russia and thirteen in Tunisia.

There were however three awards of the *Eichenlaub* during this period, all to members of JG 27 which, based in Sicily and Italy, had returned to the fray. Gustav Rödel, who had succeeded Edu Neumann as *Kommodore*, received his on 26 June for seventy-eight victories, many of which were scored over North Africa and the Mediterranean. Werner Schroer, *Kommandeur* of II/JG 27 and the second highest scorer in North Africa, was decorated on 2 August for 84 victories. Both Rödel and Schroer survived the war with scores of ninety-eight and 114 respectively. Finally there was a posthumous *Eichenlaub* to Wolf Ettel. Transferred to 8/JG 27 from 4/JG 3 in the East in May, he claimed two Viermots and two Spitfires before falling to flak on 17 July, his total score being 124.

Countdown to Overlord

On the Channel coast, it was business as usual throughout 1943, albeit at a gradually increasing tempo, while faced with frequent USAAF heavy bomber incursions, the distinction between tactical and strategic defence became increasingly blurred.

It was generally acknowledged that the Channel Front was the toughest theatre of all, contested by large numbers of well-trained British and American fighter-pilots. Fighting continually on the defensive and against heavy odds, survival was difficult enough; building a score was even more so, even for the veterans.

In 1940 Gerhard Schöpfel had been one of the most successful *Experten* of JG 26. Appointed *Kommandeur* of III/JG 26 in August, he had claimed twenty victories by 11 September. But his next twenty took another twenty-eight months, even though he had succeeded the hard-driving Adolf Galland as *Kommodore* in December 1941.

Why the difference? Operating offensively over England, the Jagdwaffe more often than not had the advantages of altitude, position, and numbers. The surprise bounce, culminating in a short-range no-deflection shot, was their preferred tactic. The defensive battles over northern France were quite the reverse. Heavily outnumbered, surprise became increasingly difficult to obtain, and most shooting opportunities were fleeting, at high-deflection crossing targets. To this defensive scenario, Schöpfel appears to have been less well-suited.

Josef 'Pips' Priller, who twice succeeded Schöpfel, firstly as *Kommandeur* of III/JG 26, then on 11 January 1943 as *Kommodore*, proved rather more equal to the defensive role. He attained his twentieth victory thirty-eight days later than Schöpfel, but his next twenty-one (and the *Eichenlaub*) came in just nine months. He continued to score steadily, reaching his century on 2 July 1944, for which he received the *Schwerter*.

Both Schöpfel and Priller were experienced professionals, having been fighter-pilots since 1936. For a wartime-trained pilot, pitched straight into battle with minimal hours on type, things were far more difficult. Just three won the *Ritterkreuz* on the Channel Front in 1943.

Adolf 'Addi' Glunz was not the average beginner. He had been an aerobatic pilot in his youth, and he had been blessed with exceptional distance vision. Later, he became proficient at flying the FW 190A on instruments; a far from easy undertaking.

Glunz joined 4/JG 52 on the Channel in March 1941, and went to Russia with them in June where he claimed three victories. He then returned to the West to join II/JG 26. His score mounted steadily rather than spectacularly, and by 29 August 1943 he had claimed thirty-eight victories, for which he received the *Ritterkreuz*. Commissioned, he went on to win the *Eichenlaub* on 24 June 1944, his score now sixty-five. By January 1945 his score had risen to seventy-one, but he was then transferred to JG 7.

Remarkably, in the course of 238 combats he was never once shot down or wounded. In part this may have been due to good flying and situational awareness, but his tally included twenty Viermots, and against these, survival depended largely on luck.

Wilhelm-Ferdinand 'Wutz' Galland was one of four brothers, three of whom became fighter-pilots. Inspired by the deeds of Adolf, he transferred from the *Flak*, retrained as a fighter-pilot, and joined II/JG 26 in July 1941. He quickly proved a gifted flyer, some thought better than Adolf, although he lacked the latter's flair for dynamic leadership. Scoring considerably faster than Glunz, he was appointed *Kommandeur* of II/JG 26 in January 1943. His *Ritterkreuz* came on 18 May, by which time he had claimed forty-one victories. On 17 August he was shot down and killed by Thunderbolts while attacking USAAF bombers; his tally was fifty-five, including nine Viermots.

The third man was Kurt Goltzsch of 5/JG 2. With forty-three victories against the West, including fourteen over Tunisia, he was shot down by Spitfires over the Channel in November. Seriously injured in the ensuing crash-landing, he received the *Ritterkreuz* on 5 February 1944, but died of his injuries eight months later.

A single hard-earned *Eichenlaub* was awarded in the West in 1943. It went to Egon Mayer, *Kommandeur* of III/JG 2, on 16 April, for his sixty-third victory. Mayer had pioneered head-on attacks against the Viermots. Whereas the standard Jagdwaffe scarf was yellow, a colour useful for attracting attention when shot down in the sea, Mayer affected a white one. This distinguishing feature was spotted by his opponents, to whom he became known as 'the man with the white scarf!'

In 1944, with a cross-Channel invasion imminent, Allied air activity increased. Inevitably, Jagdwaffe losses rose, but while replacement pilots were available, these were hastily trained and of little worth. Far more critical was the loss of experienced leaders, who were for all practical purposes irreplaceable.

In the first four months of the year, JG 2 suffered a double blow. On 2 March, Egon Mayer, now the *Kommodore*, was shot down and killed by Thunderbolts near Montmedy. He had been the first man to achieve 100 victories entirely on the Channel Front, and his total of 102 included twenty-five heavy bombers, making him the leading Viermot slayer at that time. His award of the *Schwerter* on the day he was killed was little compensation for his unit.

Mayer's replacement was Kurt 'Kuddel' Ubben, formerly *Kommandeur* of III/JG 77, with ninety victories in the East, and others over North Africa and Italy. Alas, he lasted barely eight weeks before he also fell to Thunderbolts. A holder of the *Eichenlaub*, his final score was 110. On a lesser scale, the *Kommandeur* of IV/JG 3 Franz Beyer, had been chased into the ground by Spitfires on 11 February. Beyer had eighty-one victories, of which seventy were in the East. Many other Eastern Front *Experten* signally failed to cope with conditions in the West; among them 108-victory *Experte* Emil Bitsch, *Staffelkapitän* of 8/JG 3, shot down by British fighters over Volkel on 15 March, only four of whose victories were in the West, and Franz Schwaiger, *Staffelkapitän* of 1/JG 3, killed by Mustangs on 24 April. His tally of sixty-seven victories contained fifty-five in the East.

In the final two months prior to the invasion, the Allies flew three counter-air sorties for each one by the Jagdwaffe. For the *Experten* it was a target-rich environment. But only for those who could survive long enough to exploit it!

Few could. And on 11 May, the Jagdwaffe suffered another devastating blow when Walter 'Gulle' Oesau, *Kommodore* of JG 1, holder of the *Schwerter*, with 123 victories including eight in Spain and seventy-one in the West, fell to Lightnings over the Eifel. Worse still, it was rumoured that Gulle left his sick bed to fly after Göring had suggested that his absence was due to cowardice! Colleagues have stated that at the time he was at the end of his physical and mental strength.

Overlord, the Aftermath

Between 1 April and 30 August, 4,773 German fighters were lost to all causes, with pilot losses in proportion. After the invasion, matters worsened as the adverse fighter sortie ratio doubled to six to one. This was disastrous. A full year earlier, General der Jagdflieger Adolf Galland had commented that the shortage of experienced leaders had become so extreme that many *Geschwader Kommodoren* were barely qualified to lead a *Gruppe*, while most *Kommandeure* were little more than glorified *Staffelkapitäne*!

One of the first to go down was Karl-Heinz Weber, *Kommandeur* of II/JG 1, who was shot down by fighters south of Rouen on 7 June. A *Ritterkreuzträger*, he had failed to add to his Eastern Front score of 136, but was awarded a posthumous *Eichenlaub*. Two days later he was followed by sixty-nine-victory *Experte* Eugen-Ludwig Zweigart of III/JG 54, who had at least managed fifteen victories in the West. On the same day, two more *Experten* fell. Herbert Huppertz, *Kommandeur* of III/JG 2, was shot down by Thunderbolts near Caen; his total was sixty-eight, of which thirty-three were in the East. Like Weber, Huppertz was awarded a posthumous *Eichenlaub*. Siegfried Simsch, *Kommandeur* of I/JG 11, fell to Mustangs near Rennes; his tally was fifty-four, only fourteen of them in the West.

One notable exception was 'Sepp' Wurmheller, now *Kommandeur* of III/JG 2. A brief sojourn in the East with I/JG 53 had brought him just nine victories. The remainder of his total of 102 were all in the West, including fourteen Viermots. In a furious dogfight over France on 22 June, he collided with his *Kacmarek*. He was awarded the *Schwerter* posthumously on 24 October.

The slaughter among the Eastern Front veterans drafted in continued. Friedrich Wachowiak, who had been nominated for the *Eichenlaub*, was killed on 16 July having claimed eighty-six victories in the East. August Mors, of I/JG 5, was shot down over France on 6 August. His total of sixty victories, forty-eight of which were gained in the East, earned him a posthumous *Ritterkreuz* on 24 October. Kurt Ebener, *Staffelkapitän* of 5/JG 11 was wounded and taken prisoner on 23 August; his tally was fifty-seven victories, only five of them in the West. Karl Kempf had sixty-five victories, of which forty-nine were in the East. Flying with 2/JG 26, he was shot down by Mustangs on 3 September.

On that same day, the man widely regarded as the boldest in the Jadgwaffe fell. Buck-toothed Emil 'Bully' Lang, with 148 victories in the East, holder of the *Eichenlaub*, was appointed *Kommandeur* of II/JG 26. Over the next thirty-six days he added another twenty-five victories, but was then shot down and killed by Thunderbolts near St Truiden with a his final score of 173.

Also killed that month was Klaus Mietusch, *Kommandeur* III/JG 26, who fell to a Mustang. The longest serving member of the *Geschwader*, his final score was seventy-two, of which fifty-seven were in the West, including ten Viermots. Mietusch was a survivor, having been shot down ten times and wounded four times. On 26 March he had been awarded the *Ritterkreuz* for about sixty victories. A posthumous *Eichenlaub* followed on 18 November.

By the end of the year, three more high scoring *Experten* had gone to Valhalla. On 26 November Horst Haase, *Kommandeur* of I/JG 3, collided with his *Kacmarek* on take-off; he scored fifty-six, of which fifty were in the East. Heinrich Bartels of IV/JG 27 went missing over Bonn after combat with Thunderbolts with his score at ninety-nine, of which fifty-seven were in the East. Finally, Robert 'Bazi' Weiß, *Kommandeur* of III/JG 54, was shot down by Spitfires near Lingen; his score was 121, of which about ninety were in the East.

These were only the *Ritterkreuzträger*. To them must be added the loss of even greater numbers of experienced *Experten* who for various reasons, had not been thus decorated. So serious did the situation become that by 5 July, notwithstanding his constant harangues about cowardice and lack of aggression, Reichsmarschall Göring ordered that no leader was to fly with less than a minimum number of aircraft in his formation. Even though the minimum number specified was less than fifty per cent of establishment, there were times when units were unable to meet this requirement and were grounded. And by now, the standard of training of replacement pilots had sunk to an all-time low. They were little more than cannon fodder.

For the *Experten* who did survive the bloodletting of 1944, it was business as usual. Kurt Bühligen, *Kommandeur* of II/JG 2, raised his score to ninety-six, and was awarded the *Eichenlaub* on 2 March. Late in April he succeeded 'Kuddel' Ubben as *Kommodore*, then having added a further eight victories, he received the *Schwerter* on 14 August. He survived the war with 112 victories, all against Western-flown aircraft, including forty in Tunisia, and twenty-four Viermots.

The indestructible Georg-Peter Eder, *Staffelkapitän* of 6/JG 1, received the *Ritterkreuz* on 24 June for forty-nine victories scored mainly with JG 2. His *Eichenlaub* came on 25 November, by which time he was flying jet fighters with III/JG 7. We shall meet him again in the next chapter.

Siegfried 'Wumm' Lemke had flown with 1/JG 2 on the Channel coast from Autumn 1942. His *Ritterkreuz* came with his forty-seventh victory on 14 June 1944. In the following month he was appointed *Kommandeur* of III/JG 2. By the end of the war his score had risen to ninety-six; ninety-five in the West including twenty-one Viermots, and he was nominated for, but did not receive, the *Eichenlaub*.

Of the final five *Ritterkreuze* awarded in the West during 1944, four went to members of JG 26. Wilhelm Hofmann got his on 24 October for forty victories. Gerhard Vogt, *Staffelkapitän* of 5/JG 26, was decorated on 25 November for forty-six victories. He was killed on 14 January 1945, his final tally forty-eight. Decorated on the same day for forty-one victories, Karl Borris was *Kommandeur* of I/JG 26, having first joined the *Geschwader* in December 1939. He survived the war with a total of forty-three. Johannes 'Focke' Naumann had been transferred to II/JG 6 as *Kommandeur* at the time of his award, but most of his thirty-four victories had been scored with II/JG 26.

The final recipient was Julius Meimberg, *Kommandeur* of II/JG 53. He also was a 'first to last' flyer, starting with II/JG 2. His war total of fifty-nine victories were all against Western-flown aircraft, of which eleven were scored over Tunisia.

The Long Road Home

In the East, the disaster at Stalingrad was followed by further defeats at Orel and Kursk. For the Wehrmacht it was the beginning of the end. On the ground and in the air, the Russians threw in overwhelming numbers. Overstretched, the Jagdwaffe was used as a fire brigade, switched incessantly from one crisis point to the next. The tide could not be stemmed; by the end of 1944 Soviet forces threatened the very borders of the Reich.

Conditions in 1941 and the early part of 1942 had been a 'Happy Hour' for the Jagdwaffe; a target-rich environment against tactically poor opponents in inferior aircraft. It could not last. The target-rich environment remained; if anything it became even richer as the years passed, but with experience the Soviet fighter arm improved its tactics, and introduced new fighters which were at least as good as their German opponents.

Fighting on the Russian Front was almost entirely tactical; unlike the battles in the West, most engagements took place at medium and low altitudes. Man for man, the Soviet pilots were less well-trained and less tactically aware than their opponents. Like the French in the First World War with the Cigognes, the Russians tended to group their better pilots in elite Guards Regiments, to the detriment of the line units, which were often of middling worth. Raised in a totalitarian society even more restrictive than the Third Reich, the average Soviet pilot lacked initiative, although his courage was unquestionable. But the best of them were very good indeed.

The Russians compensated for their tactical shortcomings in three ways. First, they adopted the *Rotte* (*pary*) and *Schwarm* (*zveno*) system of their opponents. Second, when out in force, which was usual, individual sections flew in a seemingly unco-ordinated manner, with no apparent pattern, swirling like a flock of starlings. This made a surprise attack on them very difficult to achieve, as there were few obvious blind spots. Third, they flew everywhere at full throttle.* The term energy-manoeuvrability had yet to be coined, but this was the general effect; they could attack, manoeuvre or defend very quickly. It did nothing for engine life, but as Soviet fighters were built to last only about 80 hours, this was not a problem; few lasted that long anyway. And with the huge Soviet manufacturing capacity now fully harnessed, replacements were readily available.

The Jagdwaffe pilots in the East never lost their sense of innate superiority. Posted to the Mediterranean as Kommodore of JG 77, Macky Steinhoff commented that by comparison, air fighting on the Eastern Front was little more than a harmless game!† But this sense of superiority made many Jagdwaffe pilots careless. In the East, they could take chances and survive. But combat is the ultimate, and the unkindest judge. The West was a much harder school, and all too many *Experten* fell when transferred from the East, often for a meagre return. Others survived, but achieved little. Only an elite few were successful on both fronts.

Having said that, the day-fighter's war against the Soviet Union was one of superlatives. It was an arena in which victories were numbered in tens of thousands, where all-time record scores were set, where the annals of mass destruction were unsurpassed, where the race to become top scorer lingered longer than anywhere else and where, most importantly for the Jagdflieger, the greatest glory was to be won.

In 1943, thirty-four *Ritterkreuze* were won in the East. In the first five

---

* Just full throttle; not emergency power.
† Steinhoff, *The Straits of Messina*, London, 1977.

months, scores for the award varied between forty-six (Wolfgang Böwing-Treuding, *Staffelkapitän* of 10/JG 51), shot down by ground fire on 11 February, and sixty-seven (Gustav Denk of II/JG 52), who also fell to ground fire two days later. But from June, criteria for the *Ritterkreuz* became inconsistent. Of thirteen awards made between 1 June and 12 November, nine recipients had passed the hundred mark. Highest of all was Erich Hartmann of 9/JG 52, who by 29 October had amassed 148 victories, followed by Otto Kittel, of JG 54, with 123. At the other end of the scale, Albert Brunner of 6/JG 5 received a posthumous award for fifty-three victories, while Hans Döbrich of the same *Staffel*, with sixty-five victories, had been wounded severely enough to be withdrawn from front line duty.

Scores for the remaining eight *Ritterkreuze* awarded from 12 November on, varied between ninety-five (Joachim Brendel of I/JG 51) and sixty-six (Maximilian Mayerl, *Staffelkapitän* of 9/JG 51). Four were posthumous, while Werner 'Quax' Quast of 4/JG 52 had been taken prisoner after being rammed by a Soviet Il-2. One posthumous award went to Günther Scheel of 3/JG 54. In the course of just seventy sorties, he claimed seventy-one victories, giving him by far the best strike rate in the entire Jagdwaffe.* He was killed over Orel on 16 July when he collided with a Yak-9.

Seven *Eichenlaub* were awarded in the East during 1943. By 11 January, battling Gerd Barkhorn of II/JG 52 had brought his tally to 120. In August, Heinrich Ehrler and Theodor Weißenberger, respectively *Kommandeur* of III/JG 5 and *Staffelkapitän* of 6/JG 5 both reached 112, while Joachim Kirschner, *Staffelkapitän* of 5/JG 3, brought his tally to 170 on 2 August. Kirschner did not survive the year; appointed *Kommandeur* of IV/JG 27 in Greece, he was shot down by Spitfires over Croatia on 17 December. He baled out safely, but was captured and executed by communist partisans.

September saw the Austrian top-scorer Walter 'Nowi' Nowotny, *Kommandeur* of I/JG 54 – he of the 'lucky trousers' – reach 189 victories, while on 25 November, Dietrich Hrabak, *Kommodore* of JG 54, and Wilhelm Lemke, the recently appointed *Kommandeur* of II/JG 3, were rewarded for 118 and 125 victories respectively. Hrabak survived the war with 125 victories, of which 109 were in the East, but Lemke was killed

---

* Many high-scoring *Experten* needed a lengthy 'running in' period. Not so Scheel, who started scoring from the outset.

over Nijmegen on 4 December.

Just two awards of the *Schwerter* were made in the East during 1943. Günther Rall, *Kommandeur* of III/JG 52, attained his 200th victory (three in the West) on 12 September; 'Nowi' Nowotny reached 218 just ten days later. Then on 19 October, he was awarded the *Brillanten* for 250 victories. His war total was 258, of which 255 were in the East.

During 1944, the Soviet armies advanced relentlessly. No sooner were they halted in one area, often for no other reason than they had outrun their supplies, than they began a new offensive elsewhere. Already heavily outnumbered, the *Jagdflieger* were increasingly weakened by the loss of units recalled to the West. Most unit leaders now realised that the war was irrevocably lost. Nor did it help matters that many knew what was happening in the extermination camps. To them, this was unthinkable, and they simply closed their ears to it, there being 'no alternative in the pursuit of ultimate victory'.* Not that they could believe in ultimate victory, but the alternative was too frightful to contemplate. With no other choice, they fought on with the fury of despair.

In all, fifty-two *Ritterkreuze* were won by *Jagdflieger* primarily for operations in the East during 1944, although five of these were belated posthumous awards for actions in the previous year. Five others were also posthumous. A total of thirteen were killed in action, four in flying accidents; two were captured and five had been too severely wounded to continue flying. Of these, Josef Haiböck, formerly of I/JG 52 (seventy-seven victories, sixty in the East), was a 'hospital' award after he had been shot down in the West.

The inconsistency of the final weeks of 1943 continued into 1944. Whereas in the second half of 1943, nine out of thirteen (sixty-nine per cent) *Ritterkreuz* winners had claimed a hundred victories or more, in 1944 only six of forty-seven (thirteen per cent) had done the same. In fact, many scores were in the sixties and seventies, although curiously, Oberfeldwebel Fritz Tegtmeier of I/JG 54 had reached ninety-nine.

Some very high scorers began to emerge in this year. Former flying instructor Wilhelm Batz of II/JG 52 scored his seventy-fifth victory on 26 March. In the next 120 days he claimed another hundred for the *Eichenlaub*, and as *Kommandeur* of III/JG 52 he brought his Eastern tally up to 232. Five more against Western-flown aircraft with II/JG 52 saw him awarded the *Schwerter* on 21 April 1945.

---

* Steinhoff, *The Last Chance*, London, 1977.

Another double centurion in the East was Helmut Lipfert of II/JG 52, who built his ninety victories by 5 April 1944 to 203 by 17 April 1945, including two Viermots, for which he received the *Eichenlaub*. He was shot down fifteen times in all. Lipfert was closely followed by Walter Schuck of 7/JG 5, who had notched up eighty-four victories for the *Ritterkreuz* on 8 April. His *Eichenlaub* came with his 171st victory on 30 September. When he left the East early in 1945 to join JG 7, with whom he scored a further eight, his total was 198.

One of the most remarkable records of all was that of Günther Josten of I/JG 51. Awarded the *Ritterkreuz* on 5 February for eighty-four victories, and the *Eichenlaub* on 28 March 1945 for 161, his final total was 178, which included more than sixty Il-2m Shturmoviki. The heavily armoured Shturmovik was not only very difficult to shoot down, but carried a rear gunner. Given this, it is almost incredible that in 420 sorties Josten was never once shot down or wounded.

Many other *Ritterkreuz* winners in 1944 went on to top the 100 victory mark in the East. To mention but a few, Heinrich Sturm of 4/JG 52 recorded 157; 152 of Gerhard Thyben's total of 157 came in the East with 6/JG 3 and 7/JG 54. The previously mentioned Fritz Tegtmeier reached 146; Gerhard Hoffmann of 4/JG 52 gained 125, and Hans-Peter 'Dackel' Waldmann of 6/JG 52 with 134 (121 in the East). Also notable was attack pilot August Lambert, *Staffelkapitän* of 8/SG 77. Tasked with providing fighter protection to the rest of his *Schlachtgruppe* over the Crimea, in spring 1944 he claimed seventy victories in less than three weeks, to bring his score to ninety, for which he was awarded the *Ritterkreuz*. In all he was credited with 116 victories and had been nominated for the *Eichenlaub*. It was not to be. On 17 April 1945 he was bounced by Mustangs on take-off and killed.

Established *Experten* were also scoring well in the East that year. The boyish Erich Hartmann of 9/JG 52 was awarded the *Eichenlaub* on 2 March for 200 victories; the *Schwerter* on 4 July for 239 (someone had finally noticed him), and after a purple patch of seventy-eight victories in less than four weeks, the *Brillanten* for 301 on 25 August. His progress did not keep pace with his record; not until October was he appointed *Staffelkapitän* of 4/JG 52, and he became *Kommandeur* I/JG 52 on 1 February 1945. His final total was 352.

Recognition had also come late to Otto Kittel of JG 52. His *Eichenlaub* arrived just twenty-nine victories but nearly six months after his *Ritterkreuz*, bringing his score to 152. The next seven months saw another seventy-eight for the *Schwerter* on 25 November. He continued to score, but was shot down and killed by an Il-2 over Courland on 14 February 1945, his final score 267.

A 'wallflower' for years, Walter 'Graf Punski' Krupinski had in 1942 been on the verge of a transfer away from fighters before suddenly discovering how it was done. He never looked back. A *Ritterkreuzträger* since October 1942, by 2 March 1944 he had amassed a further 124 victories, for which he received the *Eichenlaub*. Transferred to the West, he scored a further twenty for a total of 197. Other noted *Eichenlaub* winners in the East in 1944 included Horst Adameit, *Kommandeur* of I/JG 54; shot down and killed by ground fire on 8 August with a score of 166, all but one in the East. Meanwhile well-deserved *Schwerter* had gone to Gerd Barkhorn, *Kommandeur* of II/JG 52, for his 250th victory on 2 March. Barkhorn became the second highest scorer of all time, with 301 victories, all in the East.

That the Eastern Front offered more scoring opportunities than others can hardly be denied. Ten or more victories in a single day were claimed no less than eighteen times by thirteen *Experten*, although they generally needed several sorties. Of these, all but one were in the East; the sole exception was in North Africa.

The following table shows the list of single-day multiple victories:

Name	Unit	Score	Date	Notes
Emil Lang	9/JG 54	18	12.43	Total 173, 148 in East. KIA West 3.9.44
Hans-Joachim Marseille	3/JG 27	17	1.9.42	Total 158; 151 in N Africa. KIFA 30.9.42
August Lambert	8/SG 77	17	Spring 44	Total 116, Sebastopol. KIA 17.4.45
Hubert Straßl	8/JG 51	15	8.6.43	Total 67, Orel; KIA 8.7.43
Wilhelm Batz	5/JG 52	15	30.5.44	Total 237
August Lambert	8/SG 77	14	Spring 44	Total 116, Sebastopol; KIA 17.4.45
Emil Lang	9/JG 54	12	21.10.43	Total 173, 148 in East. KIA West 3.9.44
August Lambert	8/SG 77	12	Spring 44	Total 116, Sebastopol; KIA 17.4.45
Franz Dörr	III/JG 51	12	7 June 44	Total 128 (122 East)
Heinz Marquardt	IV/JG 51	12	?1944	Total 121 (120 East)
Walter Schuck	7/JG 51	12	June 44	Total 206 (198 East)
Adolf Dickfeld	III/JG 52	11	May 42	Total 136 (115 East) *contd*

Name	Unit	Score	Date	Notes
Walter Krupinski	7/JG 52	11	July 43	Total 197 (177 East)
Erich Rudorffer	II/JG 54	11	6.11.43	Total 222 (136 East)
Erich Hartmann	9/JG 52	11	23.8.44	Total 352 (all East)
Erich Rudorffer	II/JG 54	11	28.10.44	Total 222 (136 East)
Walter Nowotny	9/JG 54	10	24.6.43	Total 258 (255 East), KIA 8.11.44 in West
Hubert Straßl	8/JG 51	10	6.7.43	Total 67, KIA 8.7.43

KIA = Killed in Action; KIFA = Killed in Flying Accident

In 1940, a rate for the *Ritterkreuz* had been set which was only slightly variable. But as time passed, this changed, and the inconsistencies are often difficult to explain. Some may have been due to ever-longer delays in victory confirmations; at least one pilot had up to seventy-five victories awaiting confirmation at war's end. Another anomaly is that many *Jagdflieger* ran up scores which should have qualified them for an award. At least a dozen scored fifty or more; for example, sixty-seven victories by Robert Fuchs of I/JG 54 who was killed in action in the East on 10 October 1943 or sixty by Kurt Tangermann, who flew with JG 54, JG 52, and JG 7.

Be that as it may, the end of 1944 saw the Jagdwaffe almost cease to be as an effective force. It had plenty of fighters, but little fuel, and too few experienced pilots to fly them. Even the inadequate pilot training had virtually ceased. The all too numerous enemy ruled the skies.

CHAPTER 9

NEW WEAPONS, OLD ERRORS

Towards the Future

As the war progressed, performance increasingly took precedence over manoeuvrability. But even before the war, the limitations of the propeller-driven reciprocating engine had become obvious to forward-thinking designers. One of the most important performance parameters was maximum speed in level flight. While this varies according to altitude, it always occurs when the generated thrust equals drag; drag being the resistance of the air through which the aircraft is flying.

Now the problem is that while drag increases with the square of the speed, i.e. double the speed produces four times the drag, propeller efficiency falls away sharply at high speed. Even pre-war, calculations showed that a performance plateau would one day be reached at about 450 mph (724 kph). To go beyond this, a radically new form of propulsion was needed. Engine designers in England, America, the Soviet Union, and Italy, as well as Germany, were all working on the solution. But Germany won the race into service with two radically different engines; the turbojet and the rocket.

Compared with the reciprocating engine, the turbojet was mechanically simpler and much lighter. Even better, its power output was fairly constant throughout the entire speed range. Freed from the tyranny of the propeller, the turbojet-powered fighter could reach speeds unattainable by conventional aircraft, subject only to sufficient thrust being available.

The liquid-fuelled rocket was even simpler and lighter than the turbojet, and its thrust to weight ratio was enormous. And with no need for atmospheric oxygen for combustion, thrust did not fall away with altitude. In fact, due to falling back pressure on the combustion chamber, it actually increased. Although prodigal with fuel, the rocket gave an incredible rate of climb.

As early as 1938, several German companies were engaged in turbojet research. Of these, BMW Flugmotorenbau and Junkers Flugzeug und Motorenwerke were the most promising. Of the two, BMW was the more advanced, and the company predicted that two engines would be ready for flight trials by late 1939. They were overly optimistic. Even today, with the advantage of half a century of experience, engine development is the driver in every new fighter programme.

Rivalry

Messerschmitt had produced a design study for a suitable research aircraft to carry either the BMW or the Junkers turbojet, although not until 1940 were they awarded a contract to build four examples. But now an outsider had joined the lists.

Ernst Heinkel was a man with a mission. In 1936 his He 112 had been widely expected to be selected as the first Luftwaffe monoplane fighter, but it had been passed over in favour of the Bf 109. Then in 1938, he produced the outstanding He 100 fighter, a modified version of which set a new world absolute speed record. This also failed to attract Luftwaffe orders. But in 1939 he stole a double march on his rival Willi Messershmitt, using two tiny experimental aircraft.

On 30 June 1939, the He 176, made the world's first flight by an aircraft designed solely for rocket power, propelled by a Walter liquid-fuelled motor. This was followed on 27 August by the first flight of a purely turbojet-powered aircraft, the rather larger He 178. What made the latter a tour de force was the fact that the engine was also a Heinkel product. Neither aircraft had the potential for development into a fighter, but Heinkel had gained both experience and prestige.

His next attempt at one-upmanship was a dedicated jet fighter; the He 280. Very sleek, it had straight wings with elliptical trailing edges, and provision for two underslung turbojets. The high-mounted tailplane carried twin endplate-type fins and rudders. To avoid the tailplane being blanketed by the wing wake on takeoff, it was given a tricycle under-carriage with a nosewheel. Heinkel had also done his operational homework. Aware of the difficulties of abandoning ship at high speeds, he had built in a primitive ejection seat powered by compressed air. Unpowered flight trials began on 22 September 1940, but lack of engines delayed the first powered flight until 2 April 1941, when Fritz Schäfer took the world's first jet fighter into the air. This was some fifteen months before the first all-jet flight of the rival Me 262. Handling was described as excellent, but at this stage the He 280 was demonstrably underpowered.

At a later stage in development, the He 280 was fitted with the same Junkers Jumo 004 turbojets as the Me 262, when it proved faster, climbed better, and had a higher ceiling. It handled well, and its characteristics in the spin were benign.

As is now a matter of record, the He 280 was quietly dropped and the Me 262 became the world's first operational jet fighter. It has been suggested that Willi Messerschmitt had more influence at court than Ernst Heinkel, and that the He 280 was shelved for this reason. Whatever the truth of this, the He 280 appears to have had the greater potential.

Several reasons were given for its non-adoption. Its three 20 mm cannon lacked the hitting power of the four 30 mm cannon of its Messerschmitt rival. It was shorter-legged, which was of course a serious handicap, while the empennage was structurally weak. But these shortcomings would all have been corrected in the proposed He 280B, fitted with six 20 mm cannon and increased fuel capacity. Although a slight reduction in performance would have resulted, it still should not have been significantly inferior to the Me 262, and would have outperformed Allied fighters by a convincing margin. And most telling of all, the ejection seat might have saved the lives of many pilots who were lost flying the Me 262!

The *Reichluftministerium* (RLM) showed no great urgency in getting jet fighters into service. This was hardly surprising; for much of the war there was no threat which could justify a new wonder fighter. As late as 1943 it was felt that existing fighter types could cope, even against the massed raids by American heavy bombers, and events that year seemed to bear this out. It was December 1943 before the first armed Me 262 flew.

Then, also in December 1943, the USAAF introduced the P-51B Mustang. The Luftwaffe had always dismissed as impossible the idea of an agile single-engined fighter with the range to reach Berlin. Suddenly they were faced with the reality. No longer would the Jagdwaffe have the luxury of being able to wait until the escort fighters turned back before setting about the bombers. Worse still, weighed down by the heavy armament needed to destroy bombers, the German fighters were disadvantaged against their new opponents. Heavily outnumbered, the Jagdwaffe could only hope to redress the balance by a quantum leap in quality. And only the new jet fighters offered the possibility of this.

Messerschmitt Me 262

Even had more urgency been given to the Me 262 programme in its early stages, it is improbable that progress could have been advanced by much. Engine development was hampered by an almost complete lack of the materials needed for high-temperature steel alloys, and the expedients used were less than satisfactory. More delay was caused by difficulties in mass-producing the engines. Not until June were there enough complete aircraft to form trials units; Erprobungskommando 262 (Ekdo 262) with fighters and Kommando Schenk with fighter-bombers.* Like its Heinkel rival, the Me 262 was twin-engined. Its wing leading edge was swept back, and while this gave it a pleasing appearance, the angle was insufficient to delay the onset of compressibility more than marginally. Unlike the He 280, it had a conventional single fin and rudder. Provided that the turbojets kept running, handling was fairly benign, but as we shall see, it was no aircraft for a beginner.

The Jumo 004 turbojets which gave it the overwhelming speed which was its greatest strength, were also the source of its greatest weakness. Short-lived and unreliable, the slightest mishandling of the throttles would cause them to flame out or even catch fire. All too often an aircraft was forced to return on one engine. While it would fly perfectly well on the other, problems arose when it slowed down to land, when asymmetric thrust made handling tricky.

Another adverse factor was poor deceleration. Lacking air brakes, the sleek Messerschmitt reduced speed very slowly. Consequently it needed a long straight landing approach. This had to be perfectly judged, as even if the throttles were opened, the aircraft was likely to hit the ground before enough thrust became available to allow it to go around for another attempt.

Acceleration was equally poor. Thrust built slowly, which made for a lengthy take-off run, and an even longer climb out before it reached fighting speed. It was equally a problem in combat. Hard turning greatly increased drag, and this bled off speed at an alarming rate. Whereas conventional fighters could quickly regain fighting speed, the Me 262 could not. Once lost, speed could only slowly be regained, and until it was,

---

* Despite assertions to the contrary, Hitler's demand for the Me 262 to be used exclusively as fighter-bombers caused minimal delay to the service entry of the fighter variant.

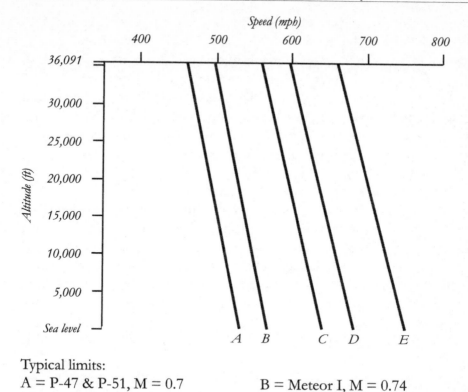

Typical limits:
A = P-47 & P-51, M = 0.7   B = Meteor I, M = 0.74
C = Me 262, M = 0.84   D = Spitfire, M = 0.9
E = Mach 1

Limiting Mach Numbers: Me 262 vs Allied Fighters

Mach 1, the speed of sound, is shown here using the ICAO standard atmosphere, with a theoretical rate of change of density of about two per cent per 1,000 ft. With Machmeters not yet invented, German jet pilots worked on a rule of thumb based on indicated air speeds at various altitudes. V_{max} for the Me 262 was 541 mph at 19,686 ft; little more than 40 mph less than the Mach limit of 0.84. Only the thin-winged Spitfire had a higher Mach limit.

the Me 262 was vulnerable to enemy fighters.

There were other problems. In 1944, the phenomenon of compressibility was imperfectly understood. Even in level flight, the sheer speed of the Me 262 took it very close to its limiting Mach number* of 0.84, and

---

* The Mach number is the speed of the aircraft in relation to the local speed of sound. As this varies with altitude, Me 262 pilots were forced to rely on a rule of thumb.

the Machmeter had yet to be invented. In even a shallow dive, the Mach limit could be inadvertently exceeded very quickly. When this happened, the result was a strong nose-down trim change. This put the aircraft into an ever-steepening dive, from which recovery was very difficult.

In clear skies with visual cues, this could usually be avoided, but clear skies are not the norm in northern Europe. Often the Me 262 pilot was forced to let down through thick cloud, and unless he was well versed in instrument flying, he could all too easily stray into the area of lost control, often with fatal results.

It was for these reasons that pilots selected for Ekdo 262 were mainly drawn from *Zerstörer* units. Not only did they have extensive experience on twin-engined fighters, including engine-out situations, but they were instrument rated. Most were drawn from III/ZG 26, an Me 410 *Gruppe* then engaged in the Reich air defence. The *Kommandeur*, twenty-seven-victory *Experte* and *Ritterkreuzträger* Werner Thierfelder, also came from this unit. There was however a leavening of experienced single-engined pilots.

Based at Lechfeld, near Munich, Ekdo 262 cut its teeth on intercepting lone high-altitude reconnaissance aircraft. With little success. Thierfelder himself was killed in mysterious circumstances on 18 July, probably because he strayed into the area of lost control. He was replaced by Horst Geyer, an eighteen-victory *Experte* from JG 51. Over the next month, Geyer's pilots claimed five victories; an errant B-17 and four reconnaissance aircraft, of which two were Mosquitos.

Into Service at Last

Der Gröfaz now conceded that the Me 262 could be used as a fighter. On 27 September detachments of Ekdo 262 were deployed to Achmer and Hesepe, near Osnabrück, to form an *Einsatzkommando*. The remainder of Ekdo 262 remained at Lechfeld to become III/EJG 2 (*Ergänzungjagdgeschwader*); a conversion unit for the Me 262. Alas, the reality was far from the ideal; by November, III/EJG 2 had sixty-nine pupils, twelve instructors, but only two Me 262s!

Achmer and Hesepe had been chosen for two reasons; both had long concrete runways, and they were near the main USAAF bomber approaches to targets in central Germany. The theory was that they could demonstrate the innate superiority of the Me 262 by engaging the American escort fighters and forcing them to drop their external fuel tanks. Deprived of their long-range capability, the escorts would have to turn back, leaving the unprotected bombers to be dealt with by conventional fighters.

To lead the *Einsatzkommando*, one of the most distinguished fighter-pilots in the Jagdwaffe was appointed. Walter Nowotny, one of only nine fighter-pilots to be awarded the *Brillanten*, had been credited with 255 victories in the East with JG 54. He was then appointed *Kommodore* of JG 101; a training unit near the Franco-Spanish border. Gladly he left a boring training job to lead what was to become Kommando Nowotny.

A few *Experten* that had flown with Nowotny in the East had converted to the Me 262, and they now joined him. Men like Karl 'Quax' Schnörrer who had flown with the famous 'Nowotny *Schwarm*'. But not all were successful. Alfred Teumer, once *Staffelkäpitan* of 7/JG 54, *Ritterkreuzträger* with seventy-six victories, sixty-six of them in the East, flew to join his new unit on 4 October after the briefest of conversion courses. Arriving with one engine out, he was killed while attempting an asymmetric landing.

Inevitably the Allies took a keen interest in the new jet fighter, and their ever watchful reconnaissance aircraft quickly identified the jet bases. In truth this was not difficult. Runways and hardstandings on Luftwaffe airfields were typically surfaced with tarmacadam. Prior to ignition, the turbojet was spooled up. During this process, unburnt fuel tended to collect in the tailpipe. Then when the engine lit up, this ignited and spilled onto the tarmac, which promptly caught fire. The answer was concrete, scorch marks on which showed up clearly on reconnaissance photos.

With the jet bases known and watched, the vulnerability of the Me 262 during the lengthy acceleration and deceleration phases was soon apparent, and Allied fighters began to patrol in their immediate vicinity.

The first action by Kommando Nowotny took place on 7 October, when five Me 262s were scrambled. In an ominous portent for the future, three jets were lost, with one pilot killed, for three B-24 bombers shot down, one by Nowotny himself. Over the next month, things were little better. Four Viermots, twelve fighters, and three reconnaissance aircraft were claimed, for six Me 262s lost in combat; one of which collided with the reconnaissance Spitfire it was attacking. This less than promising beginning was made worse by an appalling accident rate, in which seven more Me 262s were destroyed and nine damaged.

To offset the vulnerability of the Me 262 on climb-out and the landing approach, flak lanes were set up, and the area was covered by conventional fighters. But the Allies had fighters enough and to spare to deal with these.

To complete a disastrous spell, two Me 262s were lost on 8 November; one of them flown by Nowotny, who was probably hit by 'friendly' flak. The other was flown by Franz Schall, formerly of JG 52, who with 117 victories mainly in the East had been awarded the *Ritterkreuz* on 10 October. Schall, who was destined to become one of the leading jet *Experten*, claimed victories over three Mustangs during this sortie before baling out safely.

To General der Flieger Adolf Galland, who was on a visit of inspection at that time, the facts were clear. The deployment of Kommando Nowotny so close to the front, with undertrained pilots and a new and unreliable aircraft, was a major error of judgement.

Nowotny was replaced by the indestructible Georg-Peter Eder, previously *Kommandeur* of II/JG 26, who had been earmarked for command of the projected third *Staffel* of Kommando Nowotny. Eder's first jet victory was a reconnaissance Lightning, with which he collided on 13 November; fortunately he landed safely. Six days later, Kommando Nowotny was withdrawn to Lechfeld, to become III/JG 7 on 24 November.

The first and only jet *Jagdgeschwader*, JG 7 Hindenburg had been formed in August to fly the FW 190A, then the Bf 109G-14. For various reasons these plans fell through. Then in the middle of November, Reichs-marschall Göring finally gave permission for the first jet *Jagdgeschwader* to be formed. More or less by default, it was JG 7. 'Macky' Steinhoff, the vastly experienced *Kommodore* of JG 77, who had already flown the jet, was appointed to lead Jagdgeschwader Nowotny, as it was now renamed.

Commanded by Erich Hohagen, III/JG 7 was the first jet *Gruppe* to become operational. He had been awarded the *Ritterkreuz* on 5 October 1941 for thirty victories, twenty of them in the East. Since then he had flown in the West with JG 2 and JG 27, but had been off operational flying for some time after a bad crash in an FW 190. Theodor Weißenberger was a *Zerstörer* pilot who had claimed twenty-three victories before transferring to JG 5, where he had brought his tally up to 200. Holder of the *Ritterkreuz mit Eichenlaub*, he was appointed *Kommandeur* of I/JG 7 in November. II/JG 7 was a latecomer; it was not activated until 24 February 1945.

At the end of the year, JG 7 was still not operational, despite the fact that some of its pilots, notably those of the IIIrd *Gruppe*, were engaging the enemy with a degree of success.

Rocket Fighter

Even before the ground-breaking flight of the He 176, an experimental programme was in place to produce a rocket-powered high speed research aircraft. It would obviously require an advanced airframe, the design of which was entrusted to Alexander Lippisch of the DFS. This was basically a research facility for gliders. Then in January 1939, Lippisch and his assistants were seconded to Messerschmitt, and the project was designated Me 163.

The Me 163 was unusual, in that it had no horizontal tail surfaces. Control was provided by elevons, which operating differentially, served either as ailerons or elevators. It is often described as tiny, but this is misleading. Wingspan was only a little less than that of the Bf 109E, while its wing area was more than twenty per cent greater. Only in length was there an appreciable difference. And where the fuselage of the Bf 109 was sleek; that of the Me 163 was squat; a deep oval. The wing leading edge was raked back, but like that of the Me 262, not enough to materially delay the onset of compressibility. To keep weight to a minimum, a jettisonable trolley was used for take-off, while landings were made on a retractable skid.

The first, unpowered gliding flights were made from Augsburg in the late spring of 1941, but for security reasons, testing under power was moved to the research centre at Peenemünde on the Baltic coast. The first 'sharp' start was made on 13 August with test pilot Heini Dittmar at the controls.

It soon became clear that the Me 163 was exceptionally fast, and on 2 October the magic figure of 1,000kph(621mph) was exceeded in level flight; the only blemish being that it then hit the compressibility buffers and pitched violently downwards. Within three weeks, an order was placed for seventy Me 163s, modified to operational standards. The plan was to have an operational *Gruppe* of rocket fighters by the spring of 1943, but this was not to be. The Me 163 was at first a solution in search of a problem, and as such it was accorded a low priority.

It was June 1942 before the fighter prototype, the Me 163B, was ready for flight trials, but these were unpowered, as the new Walter rocket motor was not yet ready. During the previous month an operational trials unit, Erprobungskommando 16, had been formed at Lechfeld. It was commanded by Wolfgang Späte, holder of the *Ritterkreuz mit Eichenlaub*, with seventy-two victories in the East, and consisted of just four other pilots, including Eastern Front *Ritterkreuzträger* Josef 'Joschi' Pöhs, with forty-three victories, and test pilot Rudolf 'Pitz' Opitz.

Späte had been a gliding champion pre-war, and the founding members of Ekdo 16 were also experienced glider pilots. They had been chosen deliberately; the endurance of the new rocket fighter was measured in minutes. Once all fuel had been expended, it was expected to glide back to its base.

In combat, this sounds positively suicidal, but in practice it was less hazardous than it seems. As would be expected of a Lippisch design, the Me 163 had excellent gliding characteristics with a ratio of twenty to one. Unpowered, it could be dived at speeds exceeding 525 mph (845 kph), while with all fuel expended, its low wing loading of barely 22 lb/sq.ft, combined with its modest aspect ratio, made it exceptionally man-oeuvrable. Low-drag fixed slots on the wing leading edges made it spinproof. Provided the pilot saw them coming, the unpowered Me 163 was no sitting duck for enemy fighters. Hanna Reitsch, the famous German aviatrix, reported that handling was better than any conventional fighter; a conclusion also endorsed by Wolfgang Späte. The only drawback was that the landing approach speed of 137 mph (220 kph) was dispro-portionately high, calling for very fine judgement.

As with the Me 262, the greatest problems of the Me 163 were caused by the propulsion system, although for different reasons, of which lack of acceleration was not one. The main propellant was HTP (High Test hydrogen peroxide in eighty-four per cent solution). Highly unstable, it was also extremely corrosive, especially to organic material.* This included the pilots, who had to wear protective overalls of synthetic material.

HTP was used in conjunction with a catalyst. Initially this was the fairly benign calcium permanganate, but problems with this, and the need to develop more power, caused Walter to switch to the rather nastier hydrazine hydrate in a solution of methyl alcohol. The clever bit was combining HTP with the catalyst in the correct proportions to give controlled thrust. Getting it wrong resulted in a large and lethal explosion. The other, equally difficult, problem was varying the thrust. This was finally overcome by using an idle plus three-stage system.

What was never achieved was sufficient endurance. At full power, the rocket motor burned all its fuel in just four minutes, although judicious

---

* So corrosive was it that bulk deliveries were made in glass-lined rail tank cars, some of which were used post-war by the British SR 53 mixed-power fighter programme. Dick Stratton, the engineer on the SR 53, once walked through a puddle of HTP, only to have his leather boots start smoking!

power management could just about double this. After a full year's delay, the first powered flight of the Me 163B took place on 23 June 1943 at Peenemünde. For test pilot Rudolf Opitz, it was rather too exciting. He barely scraped off the ground after his take-off trolley became detached; then the cockpit filled with stinging HTP fumes from a cracked pipe. He landed safely, but it was a near thing.

In July, Ekdo 16 began to expand when a batch of volunteers arrived at Bad Zwischenahn. The first task was to convert them onto type, using the Me 163A. Ground school* was followed by towed unpowered flights. Only when these were completed, and the pupils had demonstrated that they could land safely, were they allowed to make powered flights.

Casualties began. On 30 November, Alois Wörndl misjudged his landing and was killed when his aircraft overturned and exploded. A month later, the dangers of HTP were gruesomely brought home to the pilots of Ekdo 16. When 'Joschi' Pöhs released the trolley after take-off, it rebounded and hit the underside of his Me 163A. The motor immed-iately cut out. Too low to bale out, he made a desperate attempt to land, but his overweight machine grazed a flak tower and dropped heavily to the ground. Amazingly there was no explosion, but by the time the rescue services reached him, it was too late. Seeping through the seams of his overalls, HTP had already done its ghastly work!

Other accidents were common. Hard landings caused severe back injuries, something that removed Heini Dittmar from the programme. HTP leaked into the cockpit, causing eyes to stream. And sometimes, for no apparent reason, an aircraft would explode even before it left the ground.

With the long-threatened American heavy bomber raids now a reality, attempts were made to get the Komet, as it was now called, operational. *Ritterkreuzträger* Robert Olejnik, formerly *Kommandeur* of III/JG 1, had joined Ekdo 16 in November to convert on to type. In January 1944, 20/JG 1 was formed under Olejnik's command, but was redesignated 1/JG 400 in February, and deployed to Wittmundhafen in March. Shortly after, he was badly injured while escaping from a Komet moments before it blew up.

The truth was that the Komet was still far from being ready for service. It had the speed to evade enemy fighters with ease, and its sparkling climb

---

* Ekdo 16 pilot Mano Ziegler was typical of the classically educated German officer caste when he commented, 'I had never heard of anybody learning to ski from a knowledge of the manufacturing methods of skis... I cannot say that I took kindly to this new stage [how the motor worked] in our training.'

would take it up to the altitude of the bombers in little more than two minutes. But when it levelled out after the climb, negative g often caused the motor to cut out, a fault that was never cured. Nor could it be quickly restarted. And its brief endurance made precision interception essential. Unless scrambled at the right moment, and vectored in exactly the right direction, there was little chance of success, even in clear visibility. And all was further compromised by shortages; aircraft, trained pilots, and finally the exotic fuels.

It was 13 May before the first actual interception was attempted, when Wolfgang Späte scrambled against a pair of P-47s, only to have his motor cut. Amazingly his Komet, painted bright red, remained unseen. Having restarted his rocket, he set out in pursuit, only to hit the Mach limit and pitch down before he could bring his sights to bear.

Späte's experience was fairly typical. By the end of 1944, a single understrength *Gruppe* of Komets was operational, with a low rate of serviceability. To the Allies their potential was worrying, but Komet pilots were even more worried, and with far greater reason. The number of victories they scored was still in single figures. Not so their losses. The Me 163 killed far more of its own pilots than it ever did of the enemy.

Crisis

By 1944 the daylight bomber incursions over the Reich were seemingly unstoppable. The Führer blamed the Reichsmarschall, and Göring, in turn, passed the kicks downwards, mainly to the fighter leaders engaged in Reich defence. Constant accusations of defeatism and cowardice, coupled with threats of courts martial, and even of summary execution, badly undermined morale. Even though his threats were not carried out, it was an appalling way to treat men who were risking their lives every day.

In mid-November, Göring called a meeting of senior Luftwaffe commanders and leaders at Gatow to discuss remedial measures. In line with the classical education of the majority of German officers, he called it an Areopagus.* Discussion of shortages and possible means of improvement were permitted; then Göring's monstrous ego took over. He categorically banned any criticism of himself as commander-in-chief, with the words traditionally used to announce the election of a new Pope.

---

* A judicial tribunal council in ancient Athens, which cast potsherds to decide sentences on offenders.

'*Habemus pappam*. (We have a father)!' He then departed, leaving the General of Bomber Pilots as the moderator.

The heads of fighter, bomber and reconnaissance commands reported briefly on their particular situations, shortages, failures etc., but the really critical subject, the daylight air defence of the Reich, seemed so hopeless as to be scarcely worth mentioning. Objections by Jagdwaffe officers were brushed aside; the others seemed keen to disassociate themselves from failure. The final flight from reality came with the idea of the Luftwaffe Creed. Victory was now to be won by 'cold hatred and fanatical dedication!' inspired by the works of Adolf Hitler. To the despair of the Reich air defence commanders present, who wanted effective leadership above all. It was clear that unless Göring could be deposed, there was no hope. This was the start of the so-called Jagdwaffe mutiny.

Der Grosse Schlag

Was there in fact any hope at all, or was it all too late? Generalmajor Adolf Galland had earlier conceived a daring plan, which he called *Der Grosse Schlag* (the great blow). In 1943 the two American attacks on Schweinfurt had sustained such heavy casualties that deep penetration raids virtually ceased until long-range escort fighters became available. If insupportable losses could be inflicted on the raiders, the American bombing offensive would be halted, at least temporarily, and this would give Germany as a whole a breathing space. Insupportable losses were assessed as 400 to 500 bombers; something like fifty per cent of the raiding force. Galland's plan was extremely ambitious, but how realistic was it?

While the total number of American escorts on each raid was impressive, tactical considerations demanded that they operated in relays. Consequently they could not be everywhere all the time. Their usual method was to range out ahead and to the sides of the bombers, ready to break up inbound Jagdwaffe formations. To Galland, the problem was the age-old one of concentration of force. If enough fighters could be brought into action, the ensuing battle might just be decisive.

With this in mind, he started to husband his forces. Several fighter *Gruppen* were withdrawn to central Germany to reform and retrain. With the shortage of experienced leaders now critical, these were expanded, often to double their normal establishment of pilots and aircraft. In the initial onslaught, more than 2,000 fighters would intercept the inbound raid. They were then to land to refuel and rearm, after which it was expected that roughly 500 would take off again to catch the raid as it headed homewards. Nor was this all. Bombers damaged and forced out of formation often sought sanctuary in neutral Sweden or Switzerland. These would be headed off by about a hundred night fighters.

Extrapolated from known statistics, predicted German losses would be about 400 fighters. This was no problem; German fighter production was at record levels. Even the projected loss of between 100 and 150 pilots was less serious than it sounded. In the first four months of 1944, Jagdwaffe losses ran at an average of more than 250 a month. If the Viermot raids could be halted for a while, the deficit would quickly be made good. But pilots were the weak link.

Fuel was short, and pilot training less than adequate. From October 1944, basic training had all but ceased to exist. As 'Macky' Steinhoff, *Kommodore* of JG 77 commented, 'We were assigned young pilots who were timid, inexperienced, and scared... It was hard enough leading and keeping together a large combat formation of experienced pilots; with youngsters it was hopeless.'

This boded ill for the future. But with his country under heavy attack daily, what other choice did Galland have? On 12 November, his preparations were complete. The final requirement was clear weather, without which such a huge operation could not be carried out.

It was not to be. Hitler cancelled the proposed *Grosse Schlag* and switched the available forces to support his offensive in the Ardennes, which began in mid-December. In the event, bad weather ensured that the Jagdwaffe contributed little.

As the Ardennes offensive commenced, it had been planned to launch a simultaneous attack on many Allied airfields. This was prevented by bad weather, and Operation Bodenplatte, as it was called, was finally carried out at dawn on New Year's Day, by which time it was irrelevant. About 900 fighters and fighter bombers took part. Surprise was achieved and just over 200 Allied aircraft were destroyed or damaged beyond repair, mainly on the ground. This was a mere bagatelle, as they could quickly be replaced. The much harder to replace Allied pilots suffered minimal casualties.

For the Jagdwaffe, Operation Bodenplatte was an unmitigated disaster. They lost about 300 aircraft, roughly a third of the force. Far more damaging was the loss of 237 pilots killed, missing, or taken prisoner, with eighteen more wounded. Worse still, twenty were experienced leaders: three *Kommodoren*, six *Kommandeure*, and eleven *Staffelkapitäne*. It was a blow from which the Jagdwaffe would never fully recover.

CHAPTER 10

FIVE MINUTES TO MIDNIGHT

In ancient Teutonic mythology, Wotan and his fellow gods, supported by the inhabitants of Valhalla, had gone down to utter defeat at the hands of their enemies in *Götterdammerung*, the final battle, the Twilight of the Gods, in part due to their own failings. For example, Wotan had traded one of his eyes for a dubious ability to foresee the future. It was therefore poetic justice that the Luftwaffe, nurtured on myths and legends, and led by a metaphorically one-eyed commander-in-chief, should suffer a similar fate.

By mid-January 1945, the end was in sight. Luftflotte 1 was cut off in the Courland Peninsula in Latvia, its two *Gruppen* of FW 190s too short on fuel and spares to mount more than small-scale operations. Evacuation was forbidden as Hitler, in his infinite wisdom, saw Courland as a springboard from which to launch a counterattack with troops that no longer existed. With the defection of Finland, Luftflotte 5, with two *Gruppen* of Bf 109s, had withdrawn to Norway.

Luftflotte 6, based in East Prussia and Poland, faced the might of the Soviet Air Force with just five *Gruppen* of Bf 109s and two of night-fighters, while further south, Luftflotte 4 had been forced back into a now hostile Hungary and Jugoslavia, where its three *Gruppen* of Bf 109s had to contend with Russians to the East and Americans from Italy.

For the Jagdwaffe, the Italian front had ceased to exist; only night attack and reconnaissance aircraft remained with Luftflotte 2, leaving fighter defence in the hands of the Aeronautica Nazionale Republicana.

The vast majority of conventional fighters were concentrated in western Germany with Luftflotte 3; FW 190s and Bf 109s in thirty-two *Gruppen*, backed by Luftflotte Reich with seven *Gruppen* of Bf 109s and FW 190s. The Jagdwaffe was understrength throughout, but Luftflotten 3 and Reich, still recovering from the losses of the disastrous Operation Bodenplatte, were more so than most. The Me 262 had not yet been declared fully operational as a fighter, while the handful of Me 163 rocket fighters of I/JG 400 were of very limited value.

Luftflotte Reich contained the bulk of the night-fighter force; 723 operational fighters, mainly Ju 88s and Bf 110s, with a sprinkling of He 219s. Numerically formidable, this force was by now largely grounded through lack of fuel, the day-fighters having been given priority for what little there was.

The once all-conquering Luftwaffe now stared defeat in the face. The bomber units had almost all been disbanded, leaving only reconnaissance and *Schlachtgruppen* to support the *Heer*, while the fighter-pilots, out-numbered by thirty or forty to one, had lost control of the air. How had this happened?

The Crisis of Leadership

That the early Luftwaffe was largely Hermann Göring's creation is undeniable. But once the new service was up and running, he relaxed his efforts. Not that he surrendered control; it was 'his' Luftwaffe, shedding reflected glory on its commander-in-chief. Nobody could be allowed to encroach on what he regarded as his personal fiefdom. Suggestions that ran counter to his own preconceptions were unwelcome.

His defence against these was to surround himself with cronies and yes-men, who not only confirmed that he was the *deus ex machina*,* but served to counter unwelcome advice. As a spin-off, it undermined his more capable subordinates, notably his deputy, Erhard Milch, whom he suspected of hogging the limelight.

The figuratively one-eyed Göring made three major errors in the pre-war period. Owing to his inability to comprehend the value of intelligence, he failed to provide an effective intelligence service. Mesmerised by numbers rather than capability, he failed to develop a strategic bomber force. Then blind to the value of logistics, he failed to establish a dedicated transport force. This last resulted from sheer prejudice. Transport pilots, who neither shot down aircraft nor dropped bombs, were openly scorned. This 'bloody bus-driver' attitude, common enough in the lower echelons of every air force, was disastrous in a commander-in-chief.

Dazzled by success in Poland, Scandinavia, and Western Europe, his bombastic style of leadership was defeated by the cerebral approach of

---

* The whizzbang out of the works!

RAF fighter commander 'Stuffy' Dowding. Even then, Göring confidently expected a short war, and left aircraft production and pilot training at peacetime levels throughout 1941. The result was that both production and training were hard-pressed to keep pace with losses, thus ensuring that expansion was close to impossible when it was most needed.

There are none so blind as those who refuse to see. In 1942, Göring refused to believe intelligence projections about the potential of USAAF heavy bomber raids. Nor in the following year could he believe that single-engined US escort fighters could reach the Reich, even though some had been shot down within its borders. As for them reaching Berlin, which they did in March 1944; this was impossible!

Göring's follies were compounded by his failure to stand up to Hitler in 1942 by refusing to countenance the supply of 6th Army at Stalingrad by air. Finally, and perhaps most seriously of all, he fatally undermined the morale of the Jagdwaffe over a period of years.

His obsession with the Richthofen Legend (tied closely in with his own assiduously fostered myth) was the root cause. When all went well, his fighter-pilots were heroes. The successful ones were showered with decorations. They were featured in the Luftwaffe magazine *Der Adler* and the Swiss magazine *Interavia*, and shown on the newsreels. Postcards of them were on sale across the nation. But when in 1943 the tide of war flowed against Germany, the German fighter-pilots were blamed for not preventing it. More or less by default, the Jadgwaffe became duty scapegoat.

The years of decline had begun in 1943: Tunisia and Sicily in the south, the American daylight bomber raids in the West and to a lesser degree, Kursk and the Soviet offensive in the East. In all theatres the Jagdwaffe was heavily outnumbered and increasingly outclassed technically. Even the Soviets, who had improved out of all recognition since 1941, had fighters which could match them.

Strongly criticised by Hitler, Göring passed the buck downwards. Whereas he had once used the Richthofen legend to inspire the Jagdwaffe, he now used it as a stick with which to beat them, attributing their failures to cowardice and even malingering. He further impugned their honour by suggesting that they had falsified their victory scores. That these were incorrect was beside the point. While their claims had been made in good faith, the error was in intelligence.

Göring, by now living in a fantasy world in which he often wore a toga, turned to ancient Rome for motivation. Unsuccessful legions were punished by decimation; the execution of every tenth man. Göring's version was to threaten to have selected pilots court-martialled and shot! Not that this was ever implemented, but 128 victory *Experte* and leading Viermot slayer Walther Dahl, at that time *Kommodore* of JG 300, was just one of many who came under this interdict.

Like all demagogues, in his own eyes Göring could do no wrong. Richthofen and his illustrious successor had solved all the problems of fighter combat. There was nothing else to be learned. The Areopagus of November 1944 was carefully angled to allow the rest of the Luftwaffe, the bomber, reconnaissance and attack pilots, to side with him against their fighter comrades.

The final straw came in January 1945, when General der Jagdflieger Adolf Galland was sacked, to be replaced by the ambitious, humourless, and less than charismatic Gordon Gollob.

Whatever his faults, Galland had the unqualified respect and trust of the fighter community, but his bitter criticism of the Luftwaffe High Command, and the Reichsmarschall in particular, had increasingly caused him to be sidelined. His removal triggered what became known as the fighter-pilot's mutiny.

Long disaffected by the Reichsmarschall's behaviour, a group of distinguished Jagdwaffe commanders banded together to present their grievances direct to Göring. Given that it took place in a totalitarian state increasingly controlled by Himmler's SS, it was an extremely bold under-taking. As Macky Steinhoff wrote:

> For most of us, the step to insubordination was quite literally appalling, but we had to take it; subordination had become more than we could bear'.*

Franzl Lützow was their spokesman, with Macky Steinhoff, Hermann Graf, Edu Neumann, Gustav Rödel, Hannes Trautloft and Heinz Bär. Galland, now under surveillance by the Gestapo, could take no active part.

All they wanted was effective leadership. Göring was to relinquish his authority and become a mere figurehead, at the same time ceasing his tirade of abuse against his fighter-pilots. The sycophantic bomber Mafia surrounding him must be removed, and Galland reinstated. Finally, the entire efforts of the Luftwaffe (not just the Jagdwaffe) and German

---

* Steinhoff, *The Last Chance*, London, 1977.

industry, should concentrate on halting the Allied bombing offensive.

It failed. Against an egomaniac like Göring, it could hardly have done otherwise. By the end of January the ringleaders of the Jagdwaffe 'mutineers' had been scattered. Lützow was exiled to Italy as *Jafü Oberitalien*, a non-job, as the only fighter units left in the area were Italian. Trautloft was sent to a training unit, also a non-job, as training had virtually ceased. Sacked from the command of JG 7, Steinhoff had been consigned to limbo, fearing arrest at any moment.

Göring, the supposed paladin of knightly chivalry, now indulged in an Olympic-class display of petty spite. Galland was to be appointed *Staffelkapitän* of 4/JG 54, a unit penned up in the Courland pocket. A *Generalleutnant*, holding the highest decoration that Germany had to offer, to command a mere *Staffel*! Gollob, his successor as *General der Jagdflieger* from 31 January 1945, ratified the posting. But before it could be implemented, Hitler learned of this shameful situation and ordered that Galland should be allowed to form a small jet fighter unit. Although obstructed at every turn, notably by Gollob, this he succeeded in doing.

Jagdwaffe at Bay

The war was irretrievably lost, yet the Jagdwaffe fought on. In truth, what alternative did they have? Apolitical like most soldiers, they had gone to war believing their cause to be just. Others had been seduced by the siren song of glory.

Their cause tainted, their motives were mixed. Too many of the surviving *Alte Hasen* were flown out, utterly exhausted, with their nerves in shreds. A mere shadow of their former selves, they tried to avoid flying where possible; when it was forced upon them they often turned back. Oil pressure dropping, radio failure, any excuse would do. Or they avoided combat. The accent, particularly in the West, was on personal survival; going through the motions. Often they were men of unquestioned courage and ability; for example 'Pips' Priller, Kommodore of JG 26 with 101 victories in the West. In the final months of his command, he flew little. His 307th and last sortie was during Operation Bodenplatte, when he seems to have gone astray.[*]

Even at this late stage, there were still a handful of 'throatache' sufferers who desperately tried to win a *Ritterkreuz* before it was too late.

---

[*] Caldwell, *JG 26*, New York, 1993.

Often they were killed in the attempt. On the rare occasions when they succeeded it often came as a blessed relief to their hard-pressed underlings, who were no longer led into impossible situations.

Honour remained the driving force of a few, which usually, but not entirely, consisted of regular officers from 'good' families, who fought on with the courage of despair. Chief among these was Adolf Galland, at the head of his jet fighter unit.

Night Air Defence

In the first quarter of 1945, just 240 RAF bombers were lost to all causes; virtually all to established *Experten*, a handful of whom claimed multiple victories. On 23 March, Martin 'Tino' Becker, *Kommandeur* of IV/NJG 6, was credited with nine, three of which fell to his gunner, Karl-Ludwig Johanssen. Nine Lancasters were claimed by Schnaufer in the course of two sorties on 21 February. Then on the night of 21/22 February, Johannes Hager of II/NJG 1 claimed eight, while Günther Bahr of I/NJG 6 claimed seven. On 7 February, Gerhard Raht, *Kommandeur* of I/NJG 2, was credited with six.

The clever bit was in evading the Mosquitos. Consider then the experience of the 23-year-old *Kommandeur* of III/NJG 6 Wilhelm Johnen, based at Leipheim.* On 16 March, the British raided Würzburg. Scrambled to intercept, hardly had Johnen's wheels left the ground when the first Mosquito arrived. After nerve-wracking minutes of low flying over the blacked-out countryside, he succeeded in shaking off his pursuer, and climbed to altitude. He soon gained a radar contact over Würzburg, but as he closed on it, a Mosquito forced him to break off. Again and again that night he gained radar contacts, but each time he tried to reach a firing position, so he in turn became the hunted. Twisting and turning in the night sky over the blazing city, he evaded for dear life. Only once was he able to shoot. Quite by chance he blundered across a bomber; his thirty-fourth and final victory.

Immediately beset by enemy fighters, his Naxos warning device lit up constantly. Under attack from one Mosquito, he evaded straight into the path of another. Hard-hit and streaming petrol, he dived steeply to low level and headed homewards. To no avail – his pursuers followed and began to circle the airfield. Low on fuel, Johnen had no alternative but to

---

* Johnen, *Duel under the Stars*, London, 1957.

land, but a lit flarepath would make him a sitting duck. Instead he called for two small and dim lamps to give him some orientation. Having coaxed his stricken bird on to the ground, he taxied to a hangar in darkness. As he reached it, a mechanic briefly showed a light. It was enough. As Johnen and his crew hurriedly abandoned ship, two Mosquitos strafed, destroying his Bf 110 and two others.

The hedghopping flight out after take-off, and the low level cross-country return to base, became a standard method of evading intruders. Grimly called '*Ritterkreuz* Height', it was hazardous, especially in bad weather, and many *Nachtjagdflieger* came to grief in accidents. This was the fate of twenty-five-victory *Experte* Alfons Köster, *Kommandeur* of IV/NJG 3, who hit a farm building on 7 January 1945 while returning at low level. Friendly flak was a further hazard. But either way, it was considered safer than being hunted home by a Mosquito!

Fuel shortage was a major factor. Wilhelm Johnen recorded that his unit often pumped the remaining fuel from several machines in order to get just one in the air5. But how well did the *Experten* fare against the Mosquitos?

Only three *Experten* were killed by Mosquitos during these final months. Hans-Heinz Augenstein, *Staffelkapitän* of 12/NJG 1 was lost on 6 December; his final total was forty-six. Heinz Strüning, *Eichenlaubträger* and *Staffelkapitän* of 9/NJG 1 went down on 24 December, his final score fifty-six. Finally, Walter Borchers, *Kommodore* of NJG 5, was shot down over Leipzig on 5 March. Borchers, who had been nominated for the *Eichenlaub*, had scored twelve victories as a *Zerstörer* pilot with II/ZG 76; he had three Viermots by day, and about forty-eight victories by night. Then there was former bomber ace Ernst Andres. Retrained for night fighting, he succumbed to a Mosquito while taking off from Gütersloh on 11 February.

Mosquitos were not the only hazard. Paul Semrau, *Kommodore* of NJG 2, fell to Spitfires when landing at Twente in Holland on 8 February. A successful intruder in 1941, his final score was forty-six. He received a posthumous *Eichenlaub*. On 16 March, Gerhard Friedrich, *Kommandeur* of I/NJG 6, made the ultimate *Nachtjagdflieger* error. Attacking his thirtieth victim, a Lancaster, his fire detonated the bomb load, the explosion of which destroyed him. Given the handicaps under which the *Nachtjagdflieger* operated, they did extremely well.

There was however a threat with which they were unable to cope. Mosquito light bombers raided Berlin with such regularity that the

Nachtjagdflieger dubbed them the 'Berlin Express', and coded their usual approach routes *Bahnsteige Ein, Zwei* and *Drei* (platforms one, two, and three).

Conventional night-fighters were too slow to catch them, even the Heinkel He 219 *Uhu*. Single-engined fighters using visual methods had only limited success. In desperation, the speedy Me 262 was impressed as a makeshift night-fighter.

A jet night-fighter evaluation unit was formed on 2 November 1944 with just two Me 262s, commanded by the successful former *Wilde Sau* pilot Kurt Welter. Lacking onboard radar, he relied on searchlights to illuminate RAF bombers. The overwhelming speed of the jet would then close the range rapidly. The difficulty then became aiming and firing before overshooting. But as he gained experience, his victories started to mount.

More aircraft and pilots arrived, and by the end of February 1945 Kommando Welter, which now became 10/NJG 11, had a strength of six. It was then joined by six two-seater Me 262Bs fitted with radar. Although the drag of the antennae and the longer canopy made them appreciably slower than the single seater, overshooting was still a problem, especially against Lancasters. This was partially solved by approaching from below, then attacking in a steep climb to bleed off excess speed.

Kommando Welter was credited with forty-eight victories, of which more than twenty were claimed by its commander, awarded the *Eichenlaub* on 18 March. Of his pilots, Karl-Heinz Becker downed six Mosquitos in the final ten days of March to add to a solitary P-38 by day, to become the second-highest-scoring jet night-fighter-pilot of the war.

Eastern Front

In the East, the Jagdwaffe fought against increasingly heavy odds. Fuel shortages meant that rarely could large-scale operations be mounted; mainly they flew in pairs and fours. When they encountered Soviet fighters, they were often outnumbered by thirty or forty to one, and sometimes more. While this provided a target-rich environment for the Jagdwaffe, survival became ever more difficult. The latest Soviet fighters were the equal of their German opponents, while Soviet fighter-pilots had improved immeasurably, notably those in the elite Guards Regiments.

With no chance of gaining even brief local air superiority, most sorties were flown against the Red Armies. Just eight *Ritterkreuzträger* were lost in the East during 1945, and of those, four went down to ground fire, while 125-victory *Experte* Gerhard Hoffmann of JG 52 went missing near Görlitz to unknown causes on 17 April. He had only just returned to operations after a lengthy spell as an instructor.

Only two fell to fighters. Friedrich Haas, *Staffelkapitän* of 5/JG 52 was shot down and killed over Vienna on 9 April, his final score being seventy-four, all in the East, while Erich Leie, now *Kommodore* of JG 77, collided with a Yak-9 on 7 March. Leie, who had been nominated for the *Eichenlaub*, had flown with Helmut Wick in 1940, then later with Walter Oesau. He had amassed a score of 118, forty-three of them in the West. But the most grievous loss of all was Otto Kittel of JG 54, who was shot down by Il-2s over Courland on 14 February. Holder of the *Schwerter*, Kittel's tally of 267 made him the fourth-highest scorer of all time.

In all, nine *Ritterkreuze* were awarded to fighter-pilots on the Eastern Front in 1945. They were hard-earned; three posthumous while a fourth was killed by ground fire shortly after. The unfortunate Hans-Joachim Kroschinski of JG 54, having shot down five Pe-2s in one sortie, himself became a victim. He survived, blind and minus his right leg.

Western Front

Poor weather limited Jagdwaffe operations in the West until mid-January. This was just as well; many units were still shaken by their losses during Bodenplatte. Not until 14 January did they rise in force to oppose more than 900 USAAF bombers escorted by hundreds of fighters. Their losses were horrendous; 181 fighters lost, with 109 pilots killed and forty more wounded. Their reward was meagre; only eight bombers and thirty-four escorts. From this point on, large-scale defensive operations were no longer possible.

Most of their efforts were now directed to providing cover for the ground troops, intercepting Allied fighter-bombers or trying to attain a brief measure of local air superiority. Yet another task was protecting the jet airfields. It was a vain hope; the German army had a grim saying: 'If they're silver they're American; if they're camouflaged they're British; and if they're not there at all, they're ours!' Be that as it may, on every occasion that they flew, the Jagdwaffe could expect to encounter British Spitfires and Tempests and American Mustangs and Thunderbolts, all spoiling for a fight.

The casualty list of *Experten* continued to rise. Ten *Ritterkreuzträger* were lost during these final months while flying conventional fighters. Jürgen Harder, the one surviving brother of Spanish Civil War *Experte* Harro, had risen to become *Kommodore* of JG 11. Awarded the *Eichenlaub* on 14 February, he crashed three days later as the result of oxygen failure, his score being sixty-four, of which forty-seven were in the West. Then Franz Hrdlicka, *Kommandeur* of I/JG 2, was shot down on 25 March just two days after receiving the *Eichenlaub*. More tragically, Wilhelm Hofmann, *Staffelkapitän* of 5/JG 26, was shot down in error by his own *Kacmarek* on 26 March. Hofmann had lost the ability to focus his left eye in a stupid ground accident on in October 1944, but continued to fly. His final score was forty-four, all in the West.

As in the East, fuel shortages increasingly curtailed fighter operations, but by now the new jets were entering service in numbers. And not only were jets given a degree of priority; their J2 fuel was less refined and therefore easier to produce than that used by conventional reciprocating engines.

Jets in Service

Beset on all sides, the Luftwaffe had little choice but to rush the Me 262 into service. Quality offered the only hope of offsetting the huge Allied quantitative advantages. But such haste brought problems. Essentially this boiled down to training.

No matter how experienced in conventional fighters, Me 262 pilots had to relearn air combat from scratch. It was a truism that an orthodox fighter could be effective in the hands of a slow-thinking but quick reacting pilot. For the Me 262, the opposite was true; quick thinking in order to stay ahead of the game, was best combined with slow and considered reactions – care when using the throttles, refusal to be suckered into hard manoeuvring and most of all, fine judgement of time and space were what really counted.

Finding tactics to exploit the new fighter's overwhelming speed advantage was a major problem. Macky Steinhoff, *Kommodore* of JG 7 in January 1945, was still unable to finalise these, even though he had the experience of the former Kommando Nowotny, now III/JG 7, to draw upon.

As we saw in the previous chapter, blind-flying experience, so essential for the new jet, was at a premium in the Jagdwaffe. A school of thought now arose that the Me 262 should be flown by former bomber pilots, all of whom were well versed in instrument flying. Among those in favour

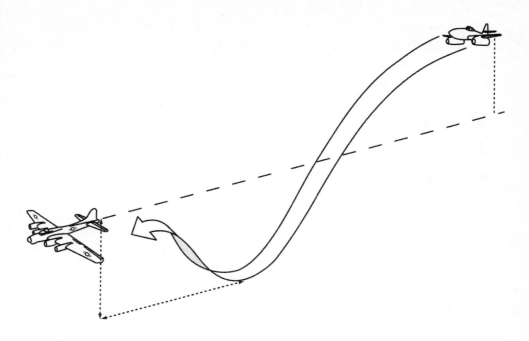

The Roller-Coaster

Against the USAAF Viermots, the huge speed advantage of the Me 262 could be embarassing, as it gave too little time to aim and shoot. To overcome this, the initial approach was made from high astern, followed by a high-speed dive through the escorts to a point about one mile astern and below the bombers. They then pulled up to mush off excess speed, attacked then accelerated away downwards before the escorts caught them.

were Gordon Gollob, currently on the operational staff for jet fighters and soon to succeed Adolf Galland as *General der Jagdflieger*; Generalmajor Dietrich Peltz, a bomber commander with an obvious axe to grind; and the Reichsmarschall himself.

The theory was simple; fighter combat per se was not required. All the jet pilots had to do was to bore straight in and attack the bombers at close range.

And so it proved. KG(J) 54 Totenkopf started to convert to the Me 262 late in November 1944. Bomber pilots were great at blind flying, but were used to having an observer to handle the navigation. As the cruising speed of Me 262 was almost three times greater than that of the Ju 88, the mental gymnastics needed to keep track of their progress came hard.

Manoeuvring was another problem. Bomber pilots were more used to making gentle turns while staying right side up. Nor was that all. Turning a stolid bomber chauffeur into a dashing aggressive fighter-pilot was not a practical proposition, as Galland rightly pointed out.

The proof came on 9 February 1945, when I/KG(J) 54 sent about ten Me 262s against a huge USAAF bomber raid. They damaged a solitary B-17, but lost six of their own to Mustangs. Among the dead was the *Kommodore*, bomber ace Volprecht, Freiherr von und zu Eisenbach Riedesel. Just 16 days later, the II Gruppe lost a dozen aircraft in one day; six in air combat, two in accidents, and four destroyed on the ground.

In its early days, the Me 262 conversion unit III/EJG 2, was unable to achieve much. That all changed when a truly exceptional man was appointed to command it; Heinz 'Pritzl' Bär. It was an inspired choice.

Bär was arguably the most versatile German fighter-pilot of the war. As we saw in earlier chapters, pilots who had done well on one front were seldom successful when transferred to another. Bär was a rare exception. He had scored well on every front; West, East, and North Africa. On Home Defence, he became a leading Viermot specialist. Equally at home in the Bf 109 or the FW 190, he had risen from *Unteroffizier* to *Oberstleutnant*, from a *Rottenflieger* in I/JG 51 to *Kommodore* of JG 3 Udet. Awarded the *Ritterkreuz* and *Eichenlaub*, he had gone on to win the *Schwerter* (only the third awarded to the Jagdwaffe) on 16 February 1942.

Since then no further honours had come his way, even though his score had now risen to 204. Outspoken to a fault, he had antagonised the top brass. This was the man who now arrived to command III/EJG 2, and lead it from the front.

It says much for the character of 'Pritzl' that he did not at once seek refuge from his almost impossible task in the sky. Instead, he worked to establish a worthwhile training regimen. Only then, on 29 January 1945, did he make his first jet flight. Even for a training unit, it was impossible to avoid the omnipresent Allies, and III/EJG 2 was frequently in action. Bär himself flew between eighty and ninety jet sorties. His first victory was a P-47 in early March, scored with an Me 262C-1a. Intended to catch high flying Mosquito reconnaissance aircraft, this unusual bird had a rocket motor in the rear fuselage which gave it a tremendous rate of climb. It was however destroyed on the ground shortly after.

Using the call-sign Buzzard 1, Bär continued his career of jet mayhem in late March, with ten victories in six days: four P-51s, two P-47s, two B-24s, and two B-26s. It was not done easily; as he recorded:

It was a petrifying experience to be low on fuel, preparing to land, and suddenly discover that Allied fighters had followed you home!

The brief life of III/EJG 2 ended on 23 April when Bär led the unit to join Adolf Galland's JV 44 at Munich Riem. His unit had been credited with forty victories, of which he had claimed thirteen.

The 500 Club; JG 7 Hindenburg

By January 1945, Macky Steinhoff,* *Kommodore* of JG 7, was feeling optimistic. Under the leadership of Erich Hohagen, the Third *Gruppe*, which was now at full strength, looked ready to be declared operational, and had already started to pick up the occasional victory. The first successes had been scored on 28 November, by Rudolf Sinner and former *Schlacht* pilot Hermann Buchner, while on 2 December, Joachim Weber claimed three Mosquitos.

At this point, Steinhoff embarked on a tour to find suitable bases from which to defend Berlin. When he returned, it was to find that he had been sacked. His association with the mutineers could not be forgiven. His replacement was 200-victory *Experte* Theodor Weißenberger, previously *Kommandeur* of I/JG 7, who had spent most of his time with JG 5 in the Arctic. It is perhaps indicative of the atmosphere within the Jagdwaffe at this time that Weißenberger, who had been nominated for the *Schwerter*, avoided any contact with Steinhoff.

The only man in the entire *Geschwader* to act honestly was Erich Hohagen, who left off his *Ritterkreuz* in protest (Galland had already done so), and followed Steinhoff into limbo. Only a bad head wound, not yet healed from the previous summer, made this possible without repercussions.

Command of I/JG 7 was given to Erich Rudorffer, possibly the only man in the Jagdwaffe whose record was comparable to that of Bär. Rudolf Sinner took over III/JG 7 from Hohagen, while Georg-Peter Eder became *Staffelkapitän* of 9/JG 7. By March JG 7 was able to operate in strength; on the 18th, thirty-seven jet sorties were flown, and for the first time, the R4M unguided rocket was used. Salvoed in batches of twelve or twenty-four, the R4M could be used from well outside the range of the defensive fire of the bombers. This often succeeded in breaking up their

---

* Steinhoff, *The Last Chance*, London, 1977.

formations, after which the jets closed for a gun attack. But it was too little, too late. Of the twenty-six pilots who scored five or more victories with the Me 262 in daylight, twenty-four had flown at least some of the time with JG 7. Nine had previously flown with either Ekdo 262, Kommando Nowotny, or both, while just four had later gone from JG 7 to JV 44. The final victory tally of JG 7 was about 500, making it by far the most successful jet-fighter unit of its time.

It is a strange quirk of human nature that solid achievement is often overshadowed by celebrity, justified or not. This was the fate which befell JG 7.

Formed by Adolf Galland, with Macky Steinhoff as his head of training, Jagdverband 44 was destined to become the most famous Luftwaffe unit of the entire war. In the normal way of things, it would have been named Kommando Galland, but continuing official spite had forbidden this. Galland, whose first command had been a *Staffel* of J 88 in Spain, selected the number forty-four, half 88, to cock a snook at OKL.

Its fame was less to do with its achievements – it was credited with a mere fifty-six victories in its short life – but rather with its glamorous personnel. One of the first was Erich Hohagen, complete with a repair to his skull consisting of Plexiglas. He was followed by a galaxy of fighter-pilots: Lützow, Barkhorn, Krupinski, the diminutive night-fighter ace Willi Herget who flew in with his Me 262 special armed with a 50 mm cannon, Hans-Ekkehard Bob, Hans 'Specker' Grünberg, Alfred Heckmann, Heinz Sachsenberg, cousin of the First World War ace Gotthard, and many others. As Galland later commented, the *Ritterkreuz* was the badge of his unit. Heinz Bär, at the head of the remnants of III/EJG 2, was a late arrival.

There were a few notable exceptions. Erich Hartmann, already the top-scoring fighter-pilot of all time, declined jet training, preferring to remain with his unit in the East. Günther Rall, grounded through wounds until November 1944, was retained in a staff position until March 1945, by which time he was too late to begin conversion training, while Hermann Graf preferred to stay as *Kommodore* of JG 52 to the end.

Be that as it may, JV 44, nominally a *Staffel* in strength, eventually contained sixty to seventy pilots, and as other units threw in the towel, even more aircraft. But low serviceability rates and continual raids on their airfields prevented all but the best pilots from flying. Even then, some took to jet combat better than others. Eduard Schallmoser never quite adjusted to the speed of the Me 262, and all too often collided with his victim. He earned the name of 'The Jet Rammer'.

Waldemar 'Hein' Wübke, a 15 victory Experte from III/JG 54, carried the legend 'I fly for the Reichsbahn' on his aircraft. Shot down four times in a row, he habitually returned by train. Franzl Lützow, who had not flown operationally for three years, also had problems in handling the jet. Having claimed a B-26 on 24 April, which was unconfirmed, that afternoon he tried to evade P-47s by diving, only to fall foul of the Me 262 Mach limit. Pursued by Thunderbolts, he dived straight into the ground near Munich.

Too little, too late! JV 44 did not enter service until the final weeks of the war, by which time it was totally outnumbered in the air. Steinhoff was badly burnt in a take-off accident on 18 April, with six jet victories to his credit. Eight days later, Galland, with seven jet victories, was wounded. Command was then assumed by Heinz Bär, who destroyed a P-47 on 29 April, his third victory with JV 44, to bring his war total to 220.

The Jet *Experten* were:

Name	Unit(s)	Jet Victories	Total	Remarks
Kurt Welter	Instructor, II/JG 301, 10/NJG 11	20+	63	Rk, El.
Heinz Bär	I/JG 51, I/JG 77, 1, 3, III/EJG 2, JV 44	16	220	Rk, El, Sch, 13 with III/EJG 2.
Franz Schall	I/JG 52, Kdo Nowotny, 10/JG 7	14	137	Rk. KIFA 10.4.45.
Hermann Buchner	8/SG 1, 6/SG 2, III/EJG 2, III/JG 7	12	58	Rk.
Georg-Peter Eder	JG 51, JG 2, 6/JG 1, 6/JG 26, II/JG 26, Kdo Nowotny, III/JG 7	12	65	Rk, El.
Erich Rudorffer	I&II/JG 2, II/JG 54, II/JG 7	12	222	Rk, El, Sch.
Karl Schnörrer	1/JG 54, Ekdo 262, Kdo Nowotny, JG 7	11	46	Rk. WIA 30.3.45.
Erich Büttner	Ekdo 262, Kdo Nowotny, JG 7	8	8	KIA 20.3.45.
Helmut Lennartz	Ekdo 262, Kdo Nowotny, JG 7	8	13	Fw.
Rudolf Rademacher	3/JG 54, 1/JG 54, I/JG 1, 11/JG 7	8	102	Rk.

contd

Name	Unit(s)	Jet Victories	Total	Remarks
Walter Schuck	JG 5, 3/JG 7	8	206	Rk, El. 30 unconfirmed.
Günther Wegmann	Ekdo 262, 9/JG 7	8	14	WIA 18.3.45.
Hans-Dieter Weihs	3/JG 7	8	8	
Theodor Weißenberger	JG(Z) 77, 7/JG 5, 6/JG 5, II/JG 5, I/JG 5, I/JG 7, Kdre JG 7	8	208	Rk, El.
Alfred Ambs	III/JG 7	7	7	
Heinz Arnold	11/JG 7	7	49	Ofw
Karl-Heinz Becker	10/NJG 11	7	7	Fw.
Adolf Galland	Stab/JG 27, III/JG 26, Kdre JG 26, JV 44	7	104	Rk, El, Sch, B.
Franz Köster	III/EJG 2, JG 7, JV 44	7	7	Uffz.
Fritz Müller	JG III/JG 7	6	22	
Johannes Steinhoff	10/JG 26, 4/JG 52, II/JG 52, Kdre JG 77, Kdre JG 7, JV 44	6	176	Rk, El, Sch. WIA 18.4.45.
Helmut Baudach	Kdo Nowotny, JG 7	5	20	KIA 22.2.45.
Heinrich Ehrler	6/JG 5, III/JG 5, Kdre JG 5, Stab/JG 7	5	206	Rk, El, nom. Sch. KIA 6.4.45.
Hans Grünberg	5/JG 3, 2/JG 7, JV 44	5	82	RK.
Herbert Heim	I/JG 7	5	5	Gef. KIA 10.4.45.
Klaus Neumann	JG 7, JV 44	5	37	
Alfred Schreiber	ZG 26, Ekdo 262, Kdo Nowotny, JG 7	5	5	KIA 26.11.44.
Wolfgang Späte	5/JG 54, IV/JG 54, Ekdo 16, IV/JG 54, Kdre JG 400, I/JG 7, JV 44	5	99	Rk, El.

Rk=*Ritterkreuz*, El=*Eichenlaub*, Sch=*Schwerter*, B=*Brillante*.
KiA=Killed in Action, KiFA=Killed in Flying Accident, WiA Wounded in Action and withdrawn from active service, PoW=Prisoner of War, Ofw=*Oberfeldwebel*, Fw=*Feldwebel*, Uffz=*Unteroffizier*.

As can be seen, while most pilots were *Experten*, a few were novices.

Others

The Me 163-equipped JG 400 recorded just ten victories, losing considerably more pilots in action and to accidents in the process. On 10 April Fritz Kelb downed an RAF Lancaster with the upward-firing SG 500 Jagdfaust, triggered by a shadow passing over a light-sensitive cell. Fifteen days later, flying an Me 262 of JG 7, he downed a B-17, to become the only pilot to score with both jet and rocket fighters. He was posted missing on 30 April.

The other jet type to enter service was the Heinkel He 162. Of simple construction for rapid mass-production, it was a single-engined fighter armed with two 20 mm cannon. The dorsally mounted engine almost completely blocked the view to the rear, and had it not been for the Heinkel-designed ejection seat pioneered on the He 280, escape from the cockpit during flight would have been totally impossible.

The diminutive He 162, variously called the *Volksjäger* or Salamander, was tricky to fly. It was issued to JG 1, commanded by 130-victory *Experte* Herbert Ihlefeld in mid-March. In just eight weeks, nine pilots were killed and five injured, mainly in accidents. Only one claim was made; an RAF Typhoon by Rudolf Schmitt of 1/JG 1 on 4 May, but it was disallowed.

The end came in May 1945. Within days, Germany was completely occupied, and the skies were quiet for the first time in more than five and a half years.

CHAPTER 11

THE EXPERTEN (1)

The leading Luftwaffe Experten outscored the aces of every other nation by a wide margin. On this evidence, it has been suggested that Germans are inherently better as fighter-pilots than those of any other nation. This theory is easily disproved. In the First World War, Manfred von Richthofen was the top scorer with eighty, by the tiny margin of five victories. The Frenchman René Paul Fonck was second with seventy-five. But whereas Richthofen had virtually no unconfirmed victory claims, Fonck, due to his penchant for flying solo deep in enemy territory, had no fewer than fifty-two! If just a small fraction of these had been confirmed, the Red Baron would have come second. The following table lists the top scorers of that conflict.

Name	Nationality	Score	Remarks
Manfred von Richthofen	German	80	KIA 21.4.18.
René Paul Fonck	French	75	plus 52 unconfirmed
Billy Bishop	Canadian	72	
Edward Mannock	Irish	68	KIA 22.7.18.
Ernst Udet	German	62	
Raymond Collishaw	Canadian	60	plus 2 in Russia
Jimmy McCudden	British	57	KIFA 9.7.18.
Proccy Beauchamp-Proctor	South African	54	
Georges Guynemer	French	54	KIA 11.9.17.
Erich Löwenhardt	German	53	KIA 10.8.18.
William Barker	Canadian	52	
Roderic Dallas	Australian	51	KIA 19.6.18.

KIA = Killed in Action, KIFA = Killed in Flying Accident.

As can be seen, just three of the twelve top scorers (twenty-five per cent) are German, occupying places one, five and ten and holding twenty-six per cent of the victories listed. In all 451 pilots of all nations were credited with between ten and forty-nine victories. Of these, thirty-six per cent were German.*

So why the difference in the second conflict? Simply put, it was opportunity. Whereas Allied pilots were rested at frequent intervals, and few flew more than 300 sorties, Jagdwaffe pilots were rarely rested. Literally dozens flew more than 500 sorties, while a handful exceeded the 1,000 mark. In addition, in most campaigns the Jagdwaffe flew against heavy odds, but this in turn meant a target-rich environment, with high scores for those who survived and shot straight.

Theatre of war was a major factor. In the East, the Soviet air force provided comparatively low-grade opposition, and the highest scores were achieved on this front. In the West, the British and Americans were far more formidable opponents, and the relative scores suggest that one victory in the West was roughly equivalent to three in the East, with the Mediterranean and the Western Desert, where Allied aircraft quality was lacking, somewhere in the middle. Another factor was the battle against the Viermots from 1943. In these, with attacks made in the teeth of massed firepower from the bombers, survival hinged more on chance than skill. Readers may care to compare overall scores in the light of these comments.

One final point. There is sufficient statistical evidence to indicate that given equal opportunities, a handful of Allied pilots would have done at least equally well as the Jagdwaffe *Experten*.

The Experten

The profiles that follow have been selected to encompass the broadest possible cross-section of the Jagdwaffe; the choice is, however, necessarily arbitrary.

Ace of Aces

The greatest *Experte* was Erich Hartmann. The son of a doctor, he learned to fly the Bf 109 in early 1942. In October of that year, he joined 7/JG 52 in the Caucasus. By the end of the war, he had racked up 352 victories in the East, including seven USAAF Mustangs over Romania,

---

* Figures taken from Spick, *The Complete Fighter Ace*, London, 1999.

making him the top-scoring fighter-pilot of all time, by a considerable margin. Yet compared to Richthofen, he is little known.

There is another mystery. He was not awarded the *Ritterkreuz* until 29 October 1943, by which time he had amassed no less than 148 victories. This was far more than anyone else. Why?

What follows is purely conjecture. A bad start takes time to live down, and Hartmann's start was as bad as could be. On his first enemy contact, led by 'Paule' Rossmann (ninety-two victories), he first obstructed his leader, then lost him. He panicked, mistook his leader for an attacking Russian whom he tried to evade, and ended up belly-landing out of fuel and far from base. Naturally this took time to live down, and in the next three months he claimed only two victories.

Nor was this all. Aggression, only partly tempered with caution, was part of the fighter-pilot ethos. Many high-scoring *Experten* survived multiple shoot-downs, or escaped from apparently hopeless situations. Generally admired, these men quickly became leaders, and served as role models for newcomers.

The innately cautious Hartmann developed his own methods, which were to a degree at variance with accepted practice. He regarded the multi-bogey dogfight as far too risky, and avoided it where possible. His tactics were, in his own words, 'see, decide, attack, break and coffee break'. He only attacked when he had all the advantages, then he disengaged to see what other opportunities might be on offer.* This enabled him to keep the situation controllable.

This rather clinical approach paid off; in more than 800 combats he was shot down only twice, was never wounded, and never lost a wingman. However, it is possible that his more aggressive colleagues may have regarded his methods as over-cautious, which would not have endeared him to them.†

There is in fact a historical precedent. In the First World War, René Fonck had developed what virtually amounted to a slide-rule approach to combat, only be regarded as lacking the correct warrior ethos. 'Too much like a successful commercial traveller booking his orders' was the comment of one fellow pilot. While there is no suggestion that Hartmann was as unpopular as the arrogant Frenchman, the attitude of his peers

---

* In a post-war interview.
† That criticism existed is speculative. If it did, it was silenced by Hartmann's later record. His philosophy of maximum harm for minimum risk was entirely justified.

may just have been a factor in the long delayed award of his *Ritterkreuz*.

Hartmann's career of mayhem really took off in the second half of 1943. In seventy-five days from 7 July, he claimed seventy-nine victories, bringing his tally to one hundred. He never looked back. The next forty-eight for the *Ritterkreuz* took only thirty-nine days. The *Eichenlaub* came on 2 March 1944 for his 200th victory. At the time this was the highest score for which it had been awarded.*

Whatever had been amiss previously, he was no longer ignored. His *Schwerter* arrived on 4 July for 239 victories and the *Brillanten* on 25 August for 301. His 352nd and final victory was a Soviet fighter shot down on the last day of the war.

One area in which he was certainly not cautious was his 'stick your nose in the enemy cockpit and you can't miss' shooting technique. Although often credited with being a long-range marksman, he has denied this, stating that he only fired when his entire windshield was black with the enemy aircraft!

It was extremely risky; he force-landed sixteen times when his fighters were damaged by debris from his victims. In fact, on 20 August 1943, he belly-landed in Soviet-held territory. Taken prisoner, he escaped after a few hours, only to be nearly shot by a 'friendly' sentry as he returned to the German lines.

Hartmann's rise to leadership was also slow. On 23 August 1943 he replaced Berthold Korts (113 victories) as *Staffelkapitän* of 9/JG 52; in October 1944 he became *Staffelkapitän* of 4/JG 52; then *Kommandeur* of I/JG 52 in February 1945. In March he was posted to convert to the Me 262, but declined and returned to his unit in the East. Postwar he became an *Oberst* and *Kommodore* of JG 71.

His incredible total of 1,425 sorties was made possible by three factors. Unlike most high scorers, he was never wounded and out of the line for lengthy periods. Nor until the final months was he burdened with command duties which might have restricted his flying. Finally, his amazing stamina ensured that he never became 'flown out', as so many of his comrades were.

His cautious approach to combat was undoubtedly correct in a protracted war against heavy odds, although it resulted in the relatively modest strike rate of about two victories in every five sorties. It is possible

---

* It was exceeded just once. By 17 April 1945, Helmut Lipfert, then *Kommandeur* of I/JG 53, had scored 203 victories.

that many pilots with better strike rates would have outscored Hartmann had they remained in the line for longer. But lacking his survival skills, they didn't!

The Runner-Up

Gerhard Barkhorn was an even slower starter than Hartmann. He joined 6/JG 52 in August 1940, but success over England eluded him. He was shot down twice. The dates are not known for certain, but it seems probable that Barkhorn crash-landed his badly damaged Bf 109E at his Peuplingues base on 27 September: then on 29 October he was forced to bale out into the icy waters of the Channel. These salutary experiences taught him caution, and respect for a tough foe.

During 1941, Barkhorn operated as a *Schwarmführer* in tip-and-run raids over south-east England, but still without success. Then in early June, JG 52 was transferred to the East. Hostilities against the Soviet Union commenced on 22 June, but it was twelve days before Barkhorn opened his account, on his 120th sortie.

Appointed as *Staffelkapitän* of 4/JG 52 on 23 August, he scored steadily rather than spectacularly. More than a year passed before he was awarded the *Ritterkreuz* on 23 August 1942, for fifty-nine victories. The *Eichenlaub* followed on 11 January 1943, for 120 victories. Appointed *Kommandeur* of II/JG 52 in June 1943, on 13 February 1944 he was the third *Jagdflieger* to reach 250 victories, for which he was awarded the *Schwerter*.

It was not done without cost; he was downed seven times in the East and once badly injured. In the midst of the slaughter, he retained his humanity, more than once flying alongside a stricken Soviet aircraft to signal its pilot to bale out.

By May 1944, Barkhorn led the field with 273 victories. But tired and careless, he fell victim to a Soviet fighter-pilot, and fractured his spine in a crash-landing which put him out of action for four months. During this period, his score was overtaken by Hartmann.

Post-war, Macky Steinhoff chose Barkhorn as the greatest fighter-pilot of all; no mean compliment. Many aces have been credited with giving away victories to others, but rarely was this true. But Barkhorn's generosity of spirit was such that he really did. His 301st and final victory was scored on 5 January 1945.

Two weeks later he was appointed *Kommodore* of JG 6, flying the FW 190D-9. But conditions in the West were totally foreign, and in the six weeks of his command, no further success came his way. In early April he joined Galland's JV 44, but on only his second sortie, engine failure forced him to crash-land. Badly injured, he was out of the war. In all he flew 1,104 sorties.

Post-war he became a Major-General in the *Bundesluftwaffe*.

The Third Man

The son of a merchant, Günther Rall joined the army from school in 1936, but transferred to the Luftwaffe two years later. Flying with 8/JG 52, he shot down a French Hawk 75 on 12 May 1940, but over England that summer further success eluded him, even though he had been appointed *Staffelkapitän* in late July. Losses were heavy, and his *Gruppe* was withdrawn to re-equip in October. He next saw action but no air combat over Crete in 1941.

From late June, he flew in the southern sector against the Soviet Union. By dusk on 28 November his score had risen to thirty-six, but he then made the classic error of watching a burning victim go down. While thus distracted, he was seriously attacked by a Soviet fighter and crashed, suffering multiple spinal injuries which left him paralysed. He was given no hope of ever flying again.

With the help of a lady doctor whom he later married, he made a full recovery, but not until 28 August 1942 did he return to his unit. It was now that he fully developed an intuitive flair for deflection shooting. By 3 September his score had risen to sixty-five, bringing him the *Ritterkreuz*. The *Eichenlaub* arrived with his 101st victory on 26 October, the *Schwerter* on 12 September 1943 for his 200th, while on 28 November he became second to reach 250, for which Walter Nowotny had been awarded the *Brillante* just weeks earlier. Meanwhile in April of that year, Rall had become *Kommandeur* of III/JG 52.

His score continued to rise, but at 272, he was transferred to the West in March 1944 as *Kommandeur* of II/JG 11; his task to draw off American escort fighters while other units tackled the Viermots. Only three more victories came his way, before on 12 May he was shot down by a Thunderbolt which removed his left thumb in the process. While he baled out safely, his wound became infected. Not until November could he resume flying, only to command a school for junior leaders. In March 1945 he became *Kommodore* of JG 300, flying the FW 190D-9, but no further success came his way.

With 275 victories amassed in just 621 sorties, Günther Rall was one of the greatest marksmen of the war. His shooting, which often made his

Kacmarek Friedrich Obleser (120 victories) shout with surprise, was perhaps only matched on the Allied side by the Canadian ace 'Screwball' Beurling. In all he was downed five times; once after a mid-air collision with an La 5 in 1943. Post-war, he became *Inspekteur General* of the *Bundesluftwaffe*.

Fourth Place

Feldwebel Otto Kittel joined 2/JG 54 Grünherz in the autumn of 1941. Short, quiet spoken and hesitant, he was far from the glamorous image of a fighter ace. Like many others, he was a slow starter, with only fifteen victories in his first eight months. In May 1942 he converted to the FW 190A, but added only twenty-four victories in the nine months to February 1943.

Gradually he found his 'shooting eye', and his scoring rate increased. On 29 October he was awarded the *Ritterkreuz* for 123 victories, and the *Eichenlaub* followed on 14 April 1944 for 152, by which time he had been commissioned. As *Staffelkapitän* of 3/JG 54, he received the *Schwerter* on 25 November for about 230. It was not done without cost. Twice he was shot down. Captured by the Russians, he escaped after two weeks and returned to the fray. His luck ran out on 14 February 1945, when he was killed by return fire from Il-2m3 Shturmoviks, his final score at least 267. He was distinguished on two counts; as the highest scoring *Experte* to have risen from the ranks, and the highest scorer to be killed in action.

The Fighter Generals

Three *Jagdflieger* rose to the appointment of *General der Jagdflieger:* Werner Mölders, Adolf Galland and Gordon Gollob. Of these, only Galland was actually promoted to General Officer rank, while Gollob's tenure, at a time when the war was utterly lost, was too brief to be significant.

Mölders and Galland were utterly dissimilar. While Mölders was set on a military career, Galland wanted to be a commercial pilot. When Mölders decided to transfer from the *Heer* to the Luftwaffe, at first he was plagued with motion sickness severe enough to have daunted a lesser man. Only by a tremendous effort of will did he conquer it. By contrast, Galland seems to have taken to the air as readily as a bird. Mölders was serious-minded, devout and unsmiling. Galland on the other hand was fond of the good things of life, with a passion for hunting. Mölders' legendary care for his men caused him to be dubbed '*Vati*' (Daddy), whereas even

'*Onkel* Adolf' would have been unthinkable for the more ruthless Galland. Mutual respect tinged with rivalry allowed them to be friends, despite their different temperaments.

As fighter-pilots, Mölders, although a full year younger than Galland, had a head start. In Spain, Mölders was not only credited with formalising a new and superior tactical system, but emerged as the top-scoring German fighter-pilot, while Galland had flown exclusively in the close air support role. This situation continued in the early months of the Second World War; while Galland flew close air support in Poland, Mölders was scoring over France.

Regarded as a close air-support expert, Galland's ambition to fly fighters appeared stillborn. But not averse to suborning doctors, something the more correct Mölders would probably not have done, Galland feigned rheumatism to get himself banned from flying in the open cockpit Hs 123.

It worked. In April 1940 he was posted to JG 27 as adjutant. On 12 May, in company with fellow *Stab* member Gustav Rödel (ninety-eight victories), he sneaked away from his desk and claimed his first victory, an RAF Hurricane. The career of the man that many came to regard as the greatest fighter-pilot of all, was under way.

When France capitulated, Mölders had become the Jagdwaffe's top scorer. He was appointed *Kommodore* of JG 51 on 27 July 1940, replacing the elderly Osterkamp, only to be shot down and wounded on the following day, and was out of action for three weeks.* Meanwhile Galland had increased his score to thirteen. Against England he became *Kommandeur* of III/JG 26, before being appointed *Kommodore* of JG 26 on 22 August.

With both men *Kommodoren*, an interesting contrast in styles of leadership emerged. Mölders' first victory, in Spain on 15 July 1938, had been marked by over-eagerness which led to mistakes which could have been, but fortunately for him were not, lethal. By contrast, Galland's first victory was so easy that it left him with twinges of conscience.

In air combat, it was accepted that to succeed, risks had to be taken. Both men were aggressive, and both survived three shoot-downs. On 8 September 1939, Mölders force-landed with engine damage after a dogfight with French Hawk 75s. Then on 5 June 1940, he was shot down and taken prisoner by the French, but released at the Armistice. Then as

---

* Believed to be by South African ace 'Sailor' Malan of No 74 Squadron RAF.

previously related, he was outfought by a Spitfire in July and wounded.

Galland was at first more fortunate. A leader, he had a penchant for steep plunging attacks to very close range, relying on his *Kacmarek* to cover him. This worked well enough until 21 June 1941, when he was shot down twice on the same day, wounded and in flames on the second occasion. Then on 2 July he was wounded once again.

Unlike Mölders, Galland was very aware of his image, and fostered the legend as a morale booster. He smoked cigars in the cockpit; something no sane man would do; and had his personal Bf 109s fitted with cigar holders.* His personal insignia was a cigar-smoking Mickey Mouse with a hatchet in one hand and a six-gun in the other. His trademarks were an impossibly misshapen hat, and a liking to wear his collar closed up to the neck, the better to show off his *Ritterkreuz*! When on leave in Berlin, he associated with the 'film' set.

He flew constantly, and the stress took its toll. By 1941, his breakfast consisted of a couple of raw eggs beaten up in red wine. Nothing else would stay down before nightfall.

By mid-1941, it had become a two-horse race. Helmut Wick, Wilhelm Balthasar and others had fallen by the wayside, leaving Mölders and Galland to battle it out for top spot. Mölders' humanitarian side had nearly been his undoing; on 11 November 1940 he left his sick bed to make a futile search for a shot-down friend. He was therefore potentially less effective than the ruthless Galland. And ruthless he was, as can be seen from the many decisions he made as *General der Jagdflieger*. As Galland wrote, 'Only the spirit of attack borne in a brave heart will bring a success to any fighter aircraft…'† This is the Red Baron legend revisited, and is in direct contrast to the dictum 'fly with the head as well as with the muscles.'

Be that as it may, Mölders, the first man to surpass the Red Baron's score of eighty, and the first man to reach one hundred victories, was appointed *General der Jagdflieger* in July 1941. He died in a flying accident on 22 November, to be replaced by Galland, who went on to command the universal respect of the Jagdwaffe at the expense of the favour of Commander-in-Chief Hermann Göring. Sacked as *General der Jagdflieger*, he ended the war commanding the jet unit JV 44, scoring seven victories before he was wounded on 22 April 1945. In about 425 sorties, he was credited with 104 victories, all against the West, including four Viermots.

---

*   A parallel with Douglas Bader and his pipe!
†   Galland, *The First and the Last*, London, 1955.

In the course of over 300 sorties, Mölders claimed 115 victories: eighteen French, fifty British, thirty-three Russian and fourteen in Spain.

The Young Turks

These were the younger breed of *Kommodoren* introduced in 1940 to replace unsuccessful leaders. Not that in general they were that much younger than the men they replaced; just two or three years on average. However, they were all battle-proven leaders. Not all were successful. The youngest, Helmut Wick, overreached himself in the race for the top spot and was killed within weeks of taking over JG 2. There were however three major successes: Günther Lützow of JG 3, Hannes Trautloft of JG 54 and Günther Freiherr von Maltzahn of JG 53.

Günther Lützow

Born in Kiel in 1912, Günther 'Franzl' Lützow was the scion of a military family. His father was a retired admiral from the family for whom the pocket battleship *Deutschland** was renamed, and who for years commented on the war at sea for German radio. Although not an aristocrat, Franzl was a Prussian gentleman, decent and honest. Educated in a Protestant cloister school, he upheld the proud warrior tradition of his family. Upright and immaculate, he usually wore his 'fore and after' rather than the peaked cap favoured by most of his contemporaries. His haughty demeanour was misleading; it concealed a keen sense of humour and a mercurial temperament. As tutor and leader he was exceptional; Adolf Galland nominated him as the outstanding fighter leader of the Luftwaffe.

March 1937 saw him commanding 2/J 88 in Spain, equipped with the first Bf 109Bs. Low serviceability forced him and his fellow *Staffelkapitän* Joachim Schlichting,† to experiment with *Rotten* (pairs) rather than *Ketten* (threes), thus paving the way for Mölders to develop the new Jagdwaffe tactical system. With five victories in Spain in the undergunned Bf 109B, Lützow returned to Germany to become training leader at the *Jagdflieger-schule* at Schleissheim, under the command of Theo Osterkamp. In July 1938, the *Schule* was redesignated IV/JG 132 to cover the occupation of the Sudetenland.

---

* The sinking of the *Deutschland* would have been a propaganda gift to the British. It was therefore renamed.
† *Ritterkreuzträger* wounded over England and taken prisoner on 6 September 1940.

In the war Franzl became *Kommandeur* of I/JG 3. With his score rising, he was appointed *Kommodore* in August 1940, and received the *Ritterkreuz* on 18 September 1940 for fifteen victories, the fourteenth *Jagdflieger* so honoured, and awarded in part for exceptional leadership. Just three more victories came his way before he left the West.

For Operation Barbarossa, JG 3 was assigned to Luftflotte 4 in the south. Franzl's career of mayhem really took off against the Russians. He was awarded the *Eichenlaub* on 20 July for forty-two victories, and the *Schwerter* on 11 October for ninety-two. Just thirteen days later he downed three MiG-3s to to raise his score to 101; only the second pilot (after Mölders) to reach a century.

At the time, he was the most successful *Jagdflieger* in the East. Between late June and November, *Stab* JG 3 claimed 106 victories. Of these Lützow was responsible for eighty-three! Like Mölders, he was then banned from flying operationally, though he remained as *Kommodore* until August 1942. Like Mölders, and for that matter Galland, he managed to engineer a couple of 'accidental' encounters in the interim.

From August 1942 onwards, he served on the staff of the *General der Jagdflieger* in a variety of positions. While this work was not particularly to his liking, he recognised that the Luftwaffe was short on combat-experienced staff officers, and did what he saw as his duty. Among other posts, he was *Jafü Sizilien* in 1943, then *Inspekteur der Jagdflieger (Süd)*, before commanding Jagddivisions 1 and 4. As spokesman for the *Jagdflieger* mutiny, he was exiled to become *Jafü Oberitalien*, before returning to fly the Me 262 with JV 44. He was killed on 24 April 1945. In about 300 sorties, he claimed 108 victories.

Hannes Trautloft

The son of a forester, Trautloft learned to hunt at an early age. Enamoured of flying, he attended Schleissheim in 1931, then took the final course at Lipetsk in the following year. By 1934 he had returned to Schleissheim as an instructor.

In August 1936, Trautloft arrived in Spain as part of what first became Jasta Eberhardt, then 1/J 88. Flying the Heinkel 51, he opened his account with a Breguet XIX, but just days later, having accounted for a Potez, he was shot down by a Dewoitine. Then from December he evaluated a prototype Bf 109. He returned to Germany in February 1937 with four confirmed victories.

Huge by fighter-pilot standards, the 6 ft 4 in Trautloft almost overflowed the cramped cockpit of the Bf 109. Despite this, he became an outstanding pilot and instructor at the fighter school at Werneuchen commanded by Theo Osterkamp. How outstanding was recognised by his inclusion in the successful Dubendorf team in July 1937. In July 1938, the school reformed to become IV/JG 132 to cover the occupation of the Sudetenland, followed by the rest of Czechoslovakia in March 1939.

In the wholesale changes that followed, IV/JG 132 became I/JG 77. Trautloft, formerly *Staffelkapitän* of 10/JG 132, now found himself commanding 2/JG 77. In September he flew briefly against Poland, but lacked opportunities to open his score. He did not remain with this unit for long; on 19 September 1939, he was appointed *Kommandeur* of III/JG 51 under Osterkamp. This *Geschwader* bore the brunt of the early fighting over England, sustaining heavy casualties, twenty-four in July alone. One of these was Trautloft himself, who on 19 July was shot up by his Defiant victim, and belly-landed his stricken bird at St Inglevert. The fact that his *Gruppe* had virtually annihilated No 141 Squadron was some compensation.

When in mid-August the assault on England really started, he gained a reputation for effective close-escort of the bombers, although this essentially defensive fighting restricted his scoring opportunities.

It was for his experience, leadership and the ability to instruct youngsters how to survive that Trautloft was appointed *Kommodore* of JG 54 on 25 August, thus rather undermining the oft-quoted statement that success in combat was the main criterion for the new generation of *Kommodoren*. Trautloft had been born in Thuringia, the 'Green Heart' of Germany, and this became the badge of JG 54.

Like many others, the Grünherz Geschwader arrived in the East in June 1941, after a brief spell flying against Yugoslavia. On arrival, Trautloft had claimed just eight victories in the West. A further twelve brought him the *Ritterkreuz* on 27 July, but compared with many, his scoring rate was pedestrian. He remained as *Kommodore* of JG 54 until 5 July 1943, but claimed only forty-five victories over Soviet aircraft. He then became *Inspizient Ost* under Galland. His part in the so-called mutiny was rewarded with a non-job – *Kommandeur* of the 4th Flieger Schul Division.

Trautloft's strike rate of fifty-seven victories in 560 sorties, including Spain, was unexceptional, but his reputation as a teacher and leader is unchallenged. Post-war he became a *Generalmajor* in the *Bundesluftwaffe*.

Günther Freiherr Von Maltzahn

Generally known as Henri, Günther von Maltzahn was born in Pomerania

to a family of minor aristocrats. Having first joined the *Heer*, he transferred to the Luftwaffe at an early stage. A born leader, he became
Kommandeur of II/JG 53 in August 1939, and led this unit over France;
then against England in 1940. He was appointed *Kommodore* of JG 53 *Pik
As* (Ace of Spades) on 10 October 1940; the oldest of the new breed of
Kommodoren. His *Ritterkreuz* was awarded on 30 December, as much for
outstanding leadership as for his thirteen victories. In this, and with the
combination of being an outspoken critic of the high command although
never a high scorer, his career paralleled that of Trautloft.

When transferred to the East for Barbarossa, his score had risen to
twenty. On the first day of fighting against the Soviets, Maltzahn was
often frustrated by the agile Polikarpov fighters, which could quickly reef
through 180 degrees, turning the classic stern attack into a head-on pass.
Against heavily-armed I-16s, this was not a good place to be. But he
learned, and he survived. By 22 July 1941, he had shot down twenty-two
Soviet aircraft for the *Eichenlaub*. Another eleven followed; but at the end
of that year, JG 53 was posted to Sicily to fly against Malta.

Barely had they arrived there when II/JG 53 was sent to Libya. Then in
March, Spitfires arrived on the beleaguered island. This made life much
more difficult, but slowly Maltzahn's score rose. But in late May, he was
shot down into the sea and spent a most uncomfortable night in his
dinghy. Such was the regard in which he was held that both I and III
Gruppen turned out next morning to look for him, much to the
embarrassment of Spitfire pilots Reade Tilley and Tiger Booth, who
survived being outnumbered by about thirty to one!

'Henri' von Maltzahn claimed thirteen victories over Malta, making his
war total sixty-eight, amassed in more than 500 sorties. After two months
in Germany in 1943, he returned south on 13 December as *Jafü Oberitalien*.
As one of the mutineers he was sidelined for the final months of the war.
Post-war, he dedicated himself to recruiting for the *Bundesluftwaffe*, but
died in June 1953.

The Playboys

To a degree, all fighter-pilots were almost by definition playboys,
inasmuch as they tended to excess in extra-curricular activities. It went
with the glamour image, as did the studied disrespect for decorations they
affected. To them, the *Deutsches Kreuz* was the 'fried egg', while the
Eichenlaub mit Schwerter became the 'cabbages, knives and forks!' It was all

a safety-valve for the stresses of life and death combat.

> Our unconditional self-sacrifice in the service of the Third Reich is too well documented... so are our dissipation and debauchery, the boozing with which we stupefied ourselves, the sheer youthful lust for life that spent itself in fornication.'*

A considerable number of *Jagdflieger* could have qualified for the playboy category; with Adolf Galland not the least of them. But two pilots really stood out from the pack: Marseille, the 'Star of Africa', and 'Graf Punski' Krupinski.

Hans-Joachim 'Jochen' Marseille

Son of an army officer, Marseille was born in Berlin in 1919. Having joined the Luftwaffe in 1938, he qualified as a fighter-pilot. Although selected as an officer candidate, his irresponsibility and indiscipline were such that he spent longer awaiting his commission than any other cadet.

He joined I(Jagd)/LG 2 on 10 August 1940, and claimed his first victim, a Hurricane, shortly after. Later that month he was transferred to 4/JG 52, commanded by 'Macky' Steinhoff. He soon proved to be a *Kriminal*,† plunging headlong into a dogfight without considering the tactical situation. While he claimed another five victories over England in 1940, he was himself shot down into the Channel four times.

The fact that he knew (in the biblical sense) glamorous women was important to Marseille, but his comrades were less than impressed. Far more important to his *Staffelkapitän* was that his strenuous horizontal exploits all too often rendered him unfit to fly! To Steinhoff, this was totally unacceptable, and Marseille was transferred to I/JG 27 at the end of 1940.

'Edu' Neumann, *Kommandeur* of I/JG 27, took a much more relaxed view of Marseille's lifestyle. This was aided in April 1941 when the *Gruppe* deployed to Libya. An area with a distinct lack of women helped Marseille to keep his mind on his work. Not that his arrival was auspicious; within days he was shot down by a Hurricane flown by an elderly Free French pilot.

Gradually the young pilot honed his skills, becoming a devotee of the 'stick your nose in the enemy cockpit and you can't miss' school. His

---

* Steinhoff, *The Last Chance*, London 1977.
† *Kriminal* was Jagdwaffe slang for 'fangs out, hair on fire'.

deflection shooting became legendary; at the height of his powers he used an average of just fifteen shells and bullets on each victim.*

Finally commissioned, his fiftieth victory brought the *Ritterkreuz* on 22 February 1942, his seventy-fifth the *Eichenlaub* on 6 June and his 101st the *Schwerter* just twelve days later, by which time he had become *Staffelkapitän* of 3/JG 27; and his 126th brought the *Brillanten* on 2 September, the day after his greatest success of seventeen victories in three sorties.

He was killed on 30 September when his Bf 109G caught fire. Blinded by smoke, he rolled inverted to bale out, but failed to notice that his Gustav had adopted a steep nose-up attitude. He hit the tail, and stunned, was unable to open his parachute.

Jochen's final score was 158, all against Western-flown aircraft. It must however be considered that of these, only about twenty were Spitfires; most of the others were inferior P-40s and Hurricanes, plus four twin-engine types.

Walter (Graf Punski) Krupinski

Born in East Prussia, Krupinski flew with 4/JG 52 against England in the summer of 1940 as a nineteen-year-old cadet. With little talent for fighter combat, he failed to score. Even in the East, where victories were easier, he remained a wallflower. Steinhoff, his *Staffelkapitän*, and from February 1942 his *Kommandeur*, was on the point of transferring him away from fighters.

Then in August 1942, he shot down an I-16 near Maikop in a daring low-level attack. It was the turning point. He became a *Kriminal*, hurling himself into the thick of the fray, somehow surviving against all odds. By 29 October his score reached fifty-three and he was awarded the *Ritterkreuz*. His tally continued to rise, but on sixty-six he was wounded, and away from the front.

He returned on 2 March 1943 as *Staffelkapitän* of 7/JG 52. His first *Kacmarek* was Hartmann, then a novice with just four victories, who learned the benefits of getting in close under Krupinski's tutelage while adding another six to his score. It was possibly at this time that Hartmann developed his aversion to the 'bar-room brawl' style of dogfighting!

Krupinski's biggest day came during the battle for Kursk. On 5 July 1943, he downed eleven Russians during the day, but was badly wounded during the final combat; his tally was ninety. It was six weeks before he

---

* At least three instances exist of Allied pilots equalling or exceeding this.

returned to the front to continue his meteoric rise, his 150th victory coming on 1 October. He was awarded the *Eichenlaub* on 2 March 1944, his tally at 177. Shortly after, he was posted to the West as *Staffelkapitän* of 1/JG 5, then *Kommandeur* of II/JG 11, and from 2 October *Kommandeur* of III/JG 26.

Although a great fighting pilot, his leadership left much to be desired. On the ground, his devotion to wine, women, and song (the order depending on availability) had earned him the soubriquet of '*Graf* Punski'. As a *Kommandeur* he made no attempt to lick III/JG 26 into shape, even though this was badly needed. The *Gruppe* was disbanded on 24 March 1945, having achieved little. Krupinski left for the fighter-pilot's Rest Home near Munich, from where he was recruited to fly the Me 262 with JV 44.

In all, Graf Punski flew 1,100 sorties, and was credited with 197 victories, 177 of them in the East. Perhaps surprisingly given his wartime reputation, he rose to become a *Generalleutnant* in the *Bundesluftwaffe*.

CHAPTER 12

THE EXPERTEN (2)

The Pin-Ups

Virtually all leading *Experten* were glamourised by the media during their often brief lives; they were widely featured in the press and in magazines, and quite frequently in cinema newsreels. Awards of the *Ritterkreuz* and above were often marked by an official photograph. For this they were carefully posed in their best uniforms with full decorations, hats, when worn, tilted at a rakish angle.* The propaganda effect sought was one of heroic intensity. This was not always achieved. Their expressions varied between studiedly nonchalant, apprehensive, bored or even embarrassed. These portraits, often heavily retouched, were sold as postcards throughout the Reich, providing inspirational heroes to the populace.

Joachim 'Jochen' Müncheberg

Like 'Henri' von Maltzahn, Müncheberg was a Pomeranian. As adjutant of III/JG 26, he flew with the *Stab*. His first victory was an RAF Blenheim on 7 November 1939. Still flying with the *Stab*, he claimed four victories over Dunkirk on 31 May. When Adolf Galland became *Kommandeur*, he flew as his *Kacmarek*, picking up a further four victories and learning the advantages of the steep diving attack from astern. In August 1940 he was appointed *Staffelkapitän* of 7/JG 26. By 14 September his score had risen to twenty, for which he was awarded the *Ritterkreuz*. By the end of 1940, his score had risen to twenty-three. Then on 9 February 1941, his *Staffel* was detached to Gela in Sicily, to fly against Malta.

The photogenic Müncheberg, chunky, blond and blue-eyed, was the epitome of Aryan manhood, and he attracted rather more than his share

---

* In No. 2 dress, it was unusual to wear more than the highest decoration awarded plus the pilot's badge.

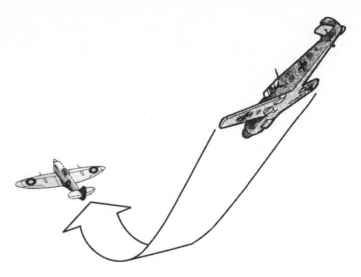

The Up-and-Under Attack

Most victories were scored when the victim was taken by surprise. The 'up-and-under' attack was favoured by Galland, Münchberg and many others. A swift dive into the blind spot below and astern was followed by a pull-up to mush off excess speed. Preferably this was made from slightly to the right, as the average pilot, with his right hand on the stick and his left on the throttle, could look more easily over his left shoulder than his right.

of media attention. But his glamorous aura once failed him. When film star Carola Höhn visited the troops that spring, Müncheberg was instantly attracted, but lost out to – of all things – bomber pilot, Arved Crüger!

Over Malta it was a different matter. With height and the initiative, 7/JG 26 cut a deadly swathe through the elderly Hurricanes. The *Staffel* claimed forty-one victories. Jochen's share was eighteen, plus an Avia biplane over Podgorica in Yugoslavia on 6 April. His tally now forty-three, he was awarded the *Eichenlaub* on 7 May, before being ordered to Libya on 20 June.

He returned to France on 26 August; his score was now fifty-two. On 19 September he became *Kommandeur* of the FW 190-equipped II/JG 26, where he remained until 22 July 1942. With his score now eighty-three, he was sent to the East to fly with JG 51 as a probationary *Kommodore*. By 9 September his score had risen to 103, for which he received the *Schwerter*. In two months in the East, he claimed thirty-three victories, but was himself downed three times. He was then appointed *Kommodore* of JG 77 in Tunisia. Then on 23 March 1943, he pressed his attack too closely and collided with a USAAF Spitfire. Both went down. It was his 135th and final victory, achieved in 500 sorties.

Hermann Graf

Hermann Graf was the most controversial *Experte* of the war. This was hardly his fault. In the early years, most top-scorers were officers of high educational standards, and drawn from good middle- and upper-class families. By contrast, Graf's origins were humble. This, coupled with his outstanding prowess in the air, gave Dr Göbbels' propaganda department a unique opportunity to create an authentic National Socialist working class hero. Not, so far as is known, that he ever joined the Party, but to Göbbels this was a minor consideration.

Too poor to afford a secondary education, Hermann became an apprentice blacksmith. This was obviously not to his liking. When his time had expired, he left and became a local-authority clerk.

He began gliding in 1933, and qualified on powered aircraft three years later. At the outbreak of war he joined JG 51 as a *Feldwebel*, but shortly after was posted to the Fighter Training School as an instructor. Then in June 1941 he joined 9/JG 52 in time for Operation Barbarossa.

His first victory came on 3 August 1941. At nearly twenty-nine, he was older than most of his contemporaries, but soon demonstrated a flair for fighter combat. Commissioned, he had scored forty-two on 24 January 1942, and was awarded the *Ritterkreuz*. Over the next 114 days his score climbed to 104 victories, for the *Eichenlaub*. By now he had been discovered, and the *Schwerter* followed on 19 May, just two days and two victories later. Then on 16 September he received the *Brillanten* for 172 victories. *Staffelkapitän* of 9/JG 52 since 24 March, he had been the seventh pilot (on 14 May 1942) to reach 100 victories; the second (on 4 September) to reach 150; then on 2 October, after an unprecedented spell of fifty-two victories in just four weeks, he became the first to pass the 200 mark, with 202. Shortly after, he was withdrawn to take part in the defence of the Reich, first as *Kommandeur* of Jagdergänzungsgruppe Ost, then from July 1943, JGr 50, downing two Viermots with the latter unit, which was disbanded after only four months.

Graf's next assignment was as *Kommodore* of JG 11, which he held from November 1943 to 29 March 1944, when he was injured in a collision with an American fighter. He claimed another eight Viermots during this period, bringing his total to 212. On his recovery in October, he returned to the East as *Kommodore* of JG 52. Although he remained with them until the surrender he claimed no more victories. In all, he flew about 830 sorties.

As a prisoner of the Russians, his behaviour was the subject of widespread disapproval by his contemporaries, and after his release in 1950, he was under a cloud for years. In all fairness, his humble background contained no military honour and tradition, and it was perhaps unjust to expect too much of him.

The Ghost of St Trond

The top-scoring night fighter-pilot of all time was Heinz-Wolfgang Schnaufer. Like Hartmann he was a Württemberger; they were the same age to within two months; they were both among the last to receive peacetime-style training; and the dates of their awards right up to the *Brillanten* matched closely.

Schnaufer joined the Luftwaffe in 1939, and trained as a pilot. Having qualified first for *Zerstörer*, then for night-fighting, he was posted to II/NJG 1 early in 1942, flying *Himmelbett* sorties. The most fruitful boxes and the optimum times were reserved for experienced crews, such as his *Kommandeur*, Helmut Lent, then one of the leading night *Experten*. Novices gained experience with the crumbs from the table. It was 2 June before the twenty-year-old Schnaufer gained his first victory.

Over the next fourteen months his tally rose. The key to success at night was teamwork. Although he flew with several different crewmen, the vast majority of his victories were scored with sparker Fritz Rumpelhardt and gunner Wilhelm Gänsler; both fellow Württembergers. By 13 August 1943, Schnaufer's score had mounted to twenty-three. At about this time he was appointed *Staffelkapitän* of 12/NJG 1.

Schnaufer led by example. On 16 December, his unit was grounded by low cloud. Undaunted, he took off into the murk, and emerging into the clear air above, shot down four Lancasters. He then groped his way back to base and landed safely. By the end of the year, he had claimed forty-two victories and was awarded the *Ritterkreuz*. He was now in 14th place.

Schnaufer was the greatest exponent of *Zahme Sau*, the freestyle mode of interception in which the fighter was directed into the bomber stream, where it remained until out of ammunition or low on fuel, before landing at the nearest airfield. While the bomber stream tended to swamp the defences with sheer numbers, it also provided a target-rich environment for the *Experten*. Post-war, he recalled that on clear moonlit nights, he could sometimes have visual contact with up to twenty-five bombers, although on dark nights it was usually three or less. Once sighted, his superb flying skills and marksmanship did the rest. While the majority of his victories were scored with his forward-firing armament, he made between twenty and thirty attacks with *Schräge Musik* – his upward-firing cannon. On three of these occasions he claimed victories, even though the target was corkscrewing, presenting him with the most difficult shot of all.

Schnaufer's greatest year was 1944. His fiftieth victory took until 25 March. At about this time he became *Kommandeur* of IV/NJG 1. But shortly after, he was a mite too clever for his own good. On the night of 30/31 March 1944, RAF bombers raided Nuremberg and suffered their heaviest losses of the war. Without Schnaufer! Determined to get into the bomber stream at the earliest possible moment, he flew towards the coast, missed the bombers completely, and never caught up with them.

With the coming of better weather, the tempo increased. Thirty-four victories in the next thirteen weeks brought him the *Eichenlaub*; the *Schwerter* followed on 30 July, his score now eighty-nine. His century on 16 October brought him the *Brillanten*. In November he became *Kommodore* of NJG 4, and he ended the year with a tally of 106.

Schnaufer was now the leading scorer at night. Of his rivals, Helmut Lent (102 night, eight day) had been killed in a flying accident in October. Wittgenstein (eighty-three) and Meurer (sixty-five) had both gone down on the same night in January 1944; Streib (sixty-six) was now in a staff job. The rest were trailing far behind. His record of sixty-four night victories in a year was never approached. In fact, this was the total war score attained by his nearest surviving rivals, Günther Radusch, Rudolf Schönert, and Heinz Rökker. Another fifteen bombers fell to his guns during 1945.

In all, Schnaufer flew just 164 combat sorties for his 121 total, but a high proportion of these came in multiple victories on the same sortie. His best night was 21 February 1945, when he accounted for seven Lancasters in seventeen minutes. Almost a year earlier, on 25 May 1944, he had clawed down five in fourteen minutes. He claimed four victories on five occasions, three victories no less than ten times, plus several doubles. In all, it seems that he returned empty-handed between eighty and ninety times.

It was not done without cost. Several times Schnaufer's fighter was damaged by return fire, and at least once he had to abort a mission after being hit by 'friendly' flak.

Remarkably, it appears that he flew only the Bf 110 operationally, although by the end of the war, NJG 4 had almost entirely re-equipped with the Junkers Ju 88. For both his success and his survival, Schnaufer owed much to Rumpelhardt, his gifted sparker, and Gänsler, his owl-eyed gunner, both of whom did much to help him avoid the Mosquito intruders. Rumpelhardt shared in one hundred victories with Schnaufer, Gänsler in ninety-eight, plus a further seventeen with Ludwig Becker. Both men received the *Ritterkreuz* on 27 July 1944, and both were nominated for the *Eichenlaub* on 8 March 1945. Schnaufer died in a road accident in France on 13 July 1950.

The Father of Night Fighting

Born in Baden in 1911, Werner Streib ranks with his day-fighter contemporaries, Lützow, Trautloft and von Maltzahn, as a teacher and leader. At first an avowed pessimist on the subject, his efforts to establish it saw him acclaimed as the father of night fighting.

In the early 1930s he worked for three years as a trainee banker before joining the *Heer* in 1934. Having transferred to the Luftwaffe, he became first an observer, then a pilot. When war broke out, he was with I/ZG 1, flying the Bf 110. On 10 May 1940 he shot down a Blenheim, his first and only daylight victory.

In June he became *Staffelkapitän* of 2/NJG 1, the first true German night-fighter unit to be formed. His first night victory, a Whitley bomber, came on 20 July. Astonishingly, given the almost complete lack of technical aids, he claimed another six bombers in the next ten weeks, including three Wellingtons on 1 October. This outstanding performance, at a time when it was exceptional even to make a sighting, was rewarded on 6 October with the *Ritterkreuz*.

Appointed *Kommandeur* of I/NJG 1, Streib was based in Venlo in the Netherlands, astride the British route to the Ruhr. His status allowed him to select his own patrols, thus increasing his chances of intercepting. It obviously worked; by the end of May 1941, his tally had risen to twenty-six, making him the leading 'catseye' night fighter. But with the advent of *Himmelbett*, his scoring slowed. His next sixteen victories took him nine months, but brought him the *Eichenlaub* on 26 February 1943.

One of his more memorable moments was the combat debut of the Heinkel He 219. On 11/12 June, Streib shot down five Lancasters in half an hour, but then rather spoiled the effect by writing off the aircraft on landing. On 1 July, Streib became *Kommodore* of NJG 1. He ended 1943 with sixty-three victories, with only Lent (seventy-five) and zu Sayn-Wittgenstein (sixty-eight) ahead of him. But he was never to regain the lead. On 11 March 1944 he was awarded the *Schwerter* and appointed to Galland's staff as *Inspekteur der Nachtjäger*. His final score was sixty-six, all but one at night. Post-war he became a *Generalleutnant* in the *Bundesluftwaffe*.

Princes of Darkness

There were in fact two princes who became high-scoring *Experten* in the *Nachtjagdflieger*, Heinrich zu Sayn-Wittgenstein, and Egmont zur Lippe-Weissenfeld. Neither survived the war.

Heinrich Prinz zu Sayn-Wittgenstein

Born in Copenhagen in 1916, and raised in Switzerland, Wittgenstein was one of the most complex characters in the entire Luftwaffe. Descended from a martial line of aristocrats including a General in Russian service against Napoleon, Prinz Heinrich appears to have had what the Scots would call 'a guid conceit o' himsel!' With an expatriate's fervour, he became an admirer of the Führer, and in Davos in 1932, with a total disregard for Swiss law, he joined the infamous Hitler Jugend. Only later did he become disenchanted with the Nazi regime.

He became a cavalryman in 1936, but transferred to the Luftwaffe in the following year. At the outbreak of war, he was a bomber pilot with KG 1 Hindenburg. Over the next two years he flew 150 sorties over Belgium, France, England and finally the Soviet Union. But bombing was not to his taste; his ambitions lay elsewhere. In August 1941 he attended the night-fighter school, then joined the Ju 88-equipped 9/NJG 2 as *Staffelkapitän*.*

Aloof and humourless, Wittgenstein was not an easy man to know and he made few friends. He was driven by ambition to be the top-scoring *Nachtjagdflieger* to the exclusion of all else, even to the point of bending the rules to his own advantage. For example, having established which *Himmelbett* boxes were likeliest to be busy, he would poach one, telling the incumbent in no uncertain terms to clear off. This selfish attitude was hardly likely to inspire devotion. As Oberst Wolfgang Falck observed of

---

* Although a bomber pilot, he was experienced on the Ju 88.

him, 'He was definitely not the type to be the leader of a unit. He was not a teacher, educator, or instructor'.

Slowly his score mounted. His twenty-second victory on 2 October 1942 won him the *Ritterkreuz*. He then went to the East as *Kommandeur* of IV/NJG 5, later I/NJG 100. There he lived a nomadic existence until September 1943, operating from ad hoc airfields, supported by a train which housed air and ground crews, radar, control, spares and supplies.

Wittgenstein was unhappy in the East, continually fretting that his rivals in the West (as he considered them) had greater opportunities to score. While he was probably right, he continued to score steadily, mainly Ilyushin Il-4 medium bombers. On 23/24 July he shot down seven in a single night! By 31 August his tally had risen to forty-seven, and he was awarded the *Eichenlaub*. After four more victories, he returned home as *Kommandeur* of II/NJG 3.

Back in the West, the obsessed Prince scored rapidly. At the end of 1943, he was in second place to Lent with sixty-eight victories. Appointed *Kommodore* of NJG 2, he celebrated by downing six Lancasters on 1/2 January. More victories followed, but still Lent remained ahead. A triple victory on 20 January was nearly the end of him; his Ju 88 was badly damaged when his third victim plunged down and collided with him. He barely escaped. Then on the following night, he claimed five bombers, which took him into the lead for the first time. But he never knew. He fell to the guns of a Mosquito; his final score eighty-three.

Prinz Heinrich was awarded the *Schwerter* posthumously on 23 January 1944. His two main sparkers were Herbert Kümmritz, who shared in forty-three victories, and Friedrich Ostheimer (sixteen), who survived his final fatal sortie.

Egmont Prinz Zur Lippe-Weissenfeld

Often referred to as 'the other prince', Lippe-Weissenfeld was born in Salzburg in 1918. When in April 1938 the Austrian Air Force was absorbed by the Luftwaffe, he changed uniforms, and later became one of the elite, a *Zerstörer* pilot with II/ZG 76.

As an experienced and instrument-rated pilot of twin-engined aircraft, Egmont was a natural choice for night-fighters. When 4/NJG 1 was formed in July 1940, he was a charter member. He bore patiently the trials and tribulations of the early 'catseye' days and was rewarded on the night of 17 November 1940, when he shot down a twin-engined British bomber. But victories were few and far between at this time. By 1 July

1941 his score was just seven, although this was far above the average. At this point, Helmut Lent, with whom Egmont formed a close friendship, became his *Staffelkapitän*.

Weissenfeld's command abilities were first tested when he led a small detachment at Bergen on the Dutch coast, apparently successfully, as when on 3 November Lent formed II/NJG 2 as *Kommandeur*, the Prinz went with him as *Staffelkapitän* of 5/NJG 2. Barely a week later he scored his first triple victory, three Wellingtons. Then on 26/27 March 1942, he claimed four victories, three Wellingtons and a Manchester. By 16 April his score had risen to twenty-one and he was awarded the *Ritterkreuz*.

The formation of IV/NJG 1 saw Weissenfeld a *Staffelkapitän* in this unit. But not for long; on 1 June 1943 he was appointed *Kommandeur* of III/NJG 1 at Vechta. On 2 August, his score now forty-four, he was awarded the *Eichenlaub*. A proven leader, he next became *Kommodore* of NJG 5 on 12 February 1944. But on 12 March, he was killed when he crashed into high ground in the Ardennes. His final tally of fifty-one night victories placed him twenty-second in the list of *Nachtjagdflieger* Experten, but it must be remembered that of those who outscored him, nearly half failed to survive the war.

The Oldest and the Youngest

In part, the supposition that fighter combat was a young man's game was borne out by the fact that the highest scorers of the war, by day and by night; against East and West, were young men. Hartmann and Schnaufer were just turned twenty-three years old at the end of the war; Marseille, with 158 victories the highest scorer against Western-flown aircraft, had died at the ripe old age of 22. But was it always so?

The Youngest

Berliner Hans Strelow achieved a unique double. At nineteen years and 358 days, he was awarded the *Ritterkreuz* on 18 March 1942 for fifty-two victories. Then six days and fourteen victories later, two days short of his twentieth birthday,* he received the *Eichenlaub*.

Strelow joined II/JG 51 on the Channel coast in the spring of 1941, but his first victory was scored in the East on 25 June 1941. But following the *Eichenlaub*, he claimed only two more in the next two months. On 22

---

* 1942 was a Leap Year.

May he shot down a Petlyakov Pe-2, but damaged by return fire, he force-landed behind Soviet lines. Rather than endure a brutal death at the hands of the Red Army, Strelow shot himself.

The Oldest

'Onkel' Theo Osterkamp, *Kommodore* of JG 51 in 1940, added six victories in the West in 1940 to his First World War tally of thirty-two and received the *Ritterkreuz* on 22 August at the ripe old age of forty-eight, partly for exemplary leadership. But for the oldest high-scoring *Experte* we must look further afield.

Born in 1909 in Thalheim, south of Chemnitz, Emil 'Bully' Lang was a well-known athlete in his youth, and pre-war became a pilot with Lufthansa. A latecomer to fighters, he joined 5/JG 54 *Grünherz* in 1942 at the advanced age of thirty-three, scoring his early victories with the Bf 109.

Later, II/JG 54 converted to the FW 190A, but controversy arose as to its ruggedness. Lang, who really ought to have known better, experimented with a terminal velocity dive from its maximum achievable altitude, followed by a gut-wrenching pull-out. Perhaps surprisingly, the aircraft suffered no damage.

As he gained in confidence, Lang became increasingly aggressive, and this was reflected in a string of multiple victories. During this time he became *Staffelkapitän* of 9/JG 54. On 21 October 1943, he claimed twelve in one day. This was the start of a three-week spell of seventy-two victories. By 22 November his score had risen to 119, which brought him the *Ritterkreuz*. Then in December, he excelled himself with eighteen in one day, a record never equalled. The *Eichenlaub* followed on 11 April 1944, for 144 victories, during which time his fighter had never once been hit.

On 29 June 1944 he arrived in the West as *Kommandeur* of II/JG 26. Unlike many *Experten* from the East, he continued to score, claiming three Spitfires over Caen on 9 July. It could not last. On 3 September, he was bounced by Thunderbolts of the 338th Fighter Squadron near St Trond. An unlucky hit caused his main gear to fall down; thus handicapped he was shot down and killed by P-47 pilot Darren Kramer. In 403 sorties he claimed 173 victories, twenty-five of them in the West. He left behind an unsurpassed reputation for bravery.

The All-Rounders

The conditions on the various fronts at various times were such that few pilots successfully adapted when transferred from one to another. There were however two notable exceptions. Both were born in Saxony. Both started as NCOs and flew from first to last. Both were successful in the West in 1940/41, in the East, in North Africa and in Home Defence. Both survived being shot down many times; both ended the war with more than 200 victories; both won the *Schwerter*, and both became jet aces with the Me 262.

Erich Rudorffer

Slim and scholarly, Erich Rudorffer learned to fly in 1936, but it was 1939 before he entered the Luftwaffe. Having joined I/JG 2 Richthofen as an *Oberfeldwebel* in 1940, his first victory was a French Hawk 75 on 14 May. He scored eight more before France surrendered, but found victories much harder to come by against England. By 1 May 1941, his score had reached nineteen, and he was awarded the *Ritterkreuz*. Commissioned, in June he became *Staffelkapitän* of 6/JG 2. Over the next seventeen months, still in the West, he claimed a further twenty-nine victories, even though in May 1942 II/JG 2 converted to the superb FW 190A. Then in October he was seriously wounded.

Not until mid-December could he rejoin his unit, which by then had redeployed to Tunisia. After a handful of victories, he had two 'Big Days' in quick succession. On 9 February 1943 he claimed six Curtiss P-40s and two Lockheed P-38s in just fifteen minutes. Six days later he claimed another seven. By March, when II/JG 2 returned home, he had been credited with twenty-six victories in Tunisia, bringing his total to seventy-four. Then on 1 August, he was appointed *Kommandeur* of II/JG 54 in the Leningrad area.

Rudorffer continued to score in the East, and on 6 November 1943 he claimed eleven victories in one day. By 11 April 1944 his war total had risen to 130, when he was awarded the *Eichenlaub*. At the end of 1944, Rudorffer had claimed 136 victories in the East, including another eleven in one day on 28 October 1944. A belated award of the *Schwerter* was made on 25 January 1945 for 210 victories, by which time he was converting to the Me 262 jet.

Appointed *Kommandeur* of I/JG 7 in late December 1944, he took over II Gruppe in February, with whom he scored twelve jet victories. His war total was 222, including ten Viermots, amassed in more than 1,000 sorties, with combat on 302 occasions. On the debit side, he was shot down sixteen times, baling out on nine. Post-war he became a civilian flying instructor and businessman.

Heinz 'Pritzl' Bär

The son of a farmer, Bär graduated from gliders to powered aircraft in 1930. While his ambition was to fly for Lufthansa, he could not afford the tuition fees. To gain the licences needed, he joined the Luftwaffe in 1937. An *Unteroffizier* with 7/JG 51, he lost no time in opening his account, with a Hawk 75 on 25 September 1939 as the first of four victories over France.

In 1940, the Jagdwaffe still encouraged dogfighting. While this suited Pritzl's aggressive nature, it was nearly the end of him. Six times he limped home badly shot up. On 2 September he came down in the Channel, but was rescued. Undaunted he continued to score, and by the end of the year was the highest-scoring NCO, with thirteen victories. Commissioned, he claimed four more on the Channel coast before deploying to the East for Barbarossa.

Against the Russians, Bär started like a whirlwind. Ten victories in eleven days, including five on 30 June, brought him the *Ritterkreuz* on 2 July. Thirty-three more in the next forty-three days won him the *Eichenlaub*. Six in a day followed on 30 August. But shortly afterwards he was forced to bale out deep in enemy territory. With a double spinal fracture, he took forty-eight hours to drag himself back to the German lines.

After months in hospital, he returned to operations and recommenced scoring freely. On 16 February 1942 he reached ninety victories and was awarded the *Schwerter*. Six more Soviet aircraft fell to his guns, then he was sent to Tunisia as *Kommandeur* of I/JG 77. Russian pilots, American pilots, it made no difference. Over the next few weeks, he shot down forty-five of them before returning to Germany with malaria, a stomach ulcer and a tally of 141.

On his recovery, 'Pritzl' converted to the FW 190A, then returned to combat as *Kommandeur* of II/JG 1 on Home Defence. A measure of his versatility is that having established an enviable record against enemy fighters and light bombers he was able to shoot down the feared Viermots in this unfamiliar scenario. His 200th victory, a B-24 Liberator, was downed on 22 April 1944.

Bär was a buccaneer by temperament. While he could be charming and witty, he did not suffer fools gladly, and to him, the biggest fool of all was his Commander-in-Chief. His biting criticisms were not well received. The records are unclear, but while it seems that he was briefly *Kommodore* of both JG 1 then JG 3, these appointments were short-lived. What is certain is that at the end of 1944, 'Pritzl' was demoted to become *Kommandeur* of III/EJG 2, the jet conversion training unit. By default, he flew operationally with this unit, recording thirteen victories. At five minutes to midnight, he joined Galland's JV 44, and scored another three, to become the leading Me 262 *Experte* by day. With Galland and Steinhoff injured and Lützow dead, Oberstleutnant Bär became the final commander of this unit.

Like Rudorffer, he flew more than 1,000 sorties. His overall score was two less at 220. He was shot down eighteen times, two more than Rudorffer, but he baled out only four times to Rudorffer's nine. He scored more victories in the West than Rudorffer (ninety-six against sixty), downed more Viermots (twenty-one against ten), and gained more jet victories (sixteen against twelve). In Tunisia, against Western-flown aircraft, he claimed forty-five against Rudorffer's twenty-six. His promotions were also more rapid. He went from *Unteroffizier* to *Oberstleutnant* against *Oberfeldwebel* to Major. Nor did Rudorffer ever become a *Kommodore*. Awards followed a similar pattern. Rudorffer was first to gain the *Ritterkreuz*, but lagged by thirty-two months for the *Eichenlaub*, and almost three years for the *Schwerter*. In all fairness, the opposition in the East was greater in Rudorffer's time.

Without doubt, these two were the greatest of all. Which was the best, the reader must judge. Post-war, Heinz Bär remained in aviation, but died while demonstrating a light sports aircraft on 28 April 1957.

Touching Wood

All too aware that their survival depended on sheer chance, many pilots relied on lucky mascots, or particular rituals before boarding their aircraft. Many avoided the 'unlucky' number 13, but a few, including Heinz Bär (220) and 'Pips' Priller (102, all in the West) favoured it. But the most bizarre touchstone was a pair of faded, salt-stained, torn, and patched trousers.

'Nowi' Nowotny

Born in Austria, Walter Nowotny joined the Luftwaffe in October 1939.

American fighter. His war total was seventy-two, of which fifty-seven were by night. Both he and Liebherr had flown more than 700 sorties.

Dietrich Hrabak

Educated in the humanities, Dieter Hrabak joined the *Kriegsmarine* in 1934 at the age of twenty. Like his friend 'Macky' Steinhoff, he completed his training as a naval officer, before transferring to the Luftwaffe in November 1935 for fighter-pilot training, qualifying a year later. By January 1939, he had become a *Staffelkapitän* in the mainly Austrian-manned I/JG 76, the former Jagdgruppe Wien-Aspern.

Hrabak's combat debut was inauspicious: on his very first sortie over Poland, he was forced to belly-land his stricken Bf109E – fortunately not in Polish-held territory. On 6 April 1940 I/JG 76 was redesignated II/JG 54.

Dieter's first victory was a long time in coming; a Potez 63 on 13 May 1940, which his *Schwarm* then proceeded to beat up on the ground. Just when they had expended all their ammunition, French Hawk 75s arrived. with no means of hitting back, the German fighters ignominiously fled! It was a salutary lesson.

Hrabak flew often against England in the summer of 1940, and on 30 August he was appointed *Kommandeur* of II/JG 54. By 21 October, his score at sixteen, he was awarded the *Ritterkreuz*. Not that it was easy; twice he was badly damaged and barely managed to limp back to a forced landing.

A brief excursion to the Balkans followed in the first half of 1941, then JG 54 moved East for operation Barbarossa. Hrabak continued to score, but on 1 November 1942 he was appointed *Kommodore* of JG 52 in the Caucasus sector of the Eastern Front. Here he developed his dictum 'fly with the head and not with the muscles'. By November 1943 he received the *Eichenlaub* for 118 victories. Four more times he force-landed, but was never injured. He returned to JG 54 as *Kommodore* on 1 October 1944, where he remained until the end of the war, when he led his surviving troops home from the Courland pocket. In all he flew 820 sorties for a total of 125 victories, of which 109 were in the East. Post-war, he joined the *Bundesluftwaffe*, rising to the rank of *Generalmajor*.

Horst 'Jakob' Tietzen

A Neumarker, 'Jakob' Tietzen joined the Luftwaffe at an early stage, and trained as a fighter-pilot. As a *'Kraft durch Freude'* volunteer, he fought with the Condor Legion in Spain. As a member of Jagdgruppe 88, he emerged in eighth equal place with seven victories. of those above or level with him, four failed to make much of an impression in the war that followed.

Tietzen began the Second World War as *Staffelkapitän* of 5/JG 51. He scored over France, then in the summer of 1940 more against England. After Mölders, Galland and Oesau, he became only the fourth *Jagdflieger* to reach twenty victories, but on 18 August his promising career was cut short. He and his *Kacmarek* were shot down and killed over the Thames estuary by two Polish Hurricane pilots of No. 501 Squadron. Awarded a posthumous *Ritterkreuz* on 20 August, his body was washed up near Calais a fortnight later. Tietzen represents the many 'nearly men' who died before they could make a truly lasting mark.

Kurt Welter

A native of Marienbad in the Sudetenland area of the former Czecho-slovakia, little is known about Welter's early career. By late 1943, he was a very experienced *Oberfeldwebel* instructor pilot. Skilled in blind flying, he joined the *Wilde Sau* unit II/JG 301 on its formation in October of that year. With the demise of *Wilde Sau* operations due to an appalling accident rate, in the summer of 1944 he remustered to 2/NJG 11 as a *Leutnant*. Bad weather severely limited his opportunities, and by 18 October 1944, he had flown only forty sorties, all with the FW 190A-8. But in this time, he had claimed thirty-three victories, twenty-nine of them at night, including seven Mosquitos. For this outstanding performance he was awarded the *Ritterkreuz*.

On 2 November, he formed a jet night-fighter Kommando with two Me 262s, to combat the Mosquitos which were raiding Berlin with impunity. Operating with the searchlights, he started to add to his score. By the end of February 1945, Kommando Welter had grown in size, and with the addition of a few radar-equipped two-seaters, was redesignated 10/NJG 11. More victories followed, and Welter was awarded the *Eichenlaub* on 18 March. Then on 30 March he claimed four Mosquitos in a single night.

With the Reich collapsing, and an almost total lack of fuel, night-jet operations tailed off, having claimed forty-eight victories. Of these, almost half fell to Welter, making him the top-scoring jet *Experte* of the war, although lack of records means that his final total cannot be established with any certainty.

Welter died in a freak accident on 7 March 1949, when logs from a passing train fell on his car as he waited at a level crossing.

Karl Borris

A Brandenburger, Karl Borris has been described as dour, superstitious, and humourless, a stickler for regulations, and a strict disciplinarian. He joined JG 26 in December 1939, rose to become *Kommandeur* of I Gruppe, and flew operationally to the final days of the war.

On 13 May 1940, he was shot down over Holland by a Defiant. Having baled out, he evaded capture and returned to his *Staffel* four days later. Borris is believed to have flown with the *Stab* of II/JG 26. On 13 August 1940, as a *Leutnant* with 5 Staffel, he claimed two Hurricanes; the only victories recorded by JG 26 on that day.

In March 1941, Borris, now an *Oberleutnant*, was part of Erprobungsstaffel 190, a detachment tasked with evaluating the FW 190A. In July, with the new fighter cleared for service, Eprst 190 moved to Le Bourget to help II/JG 26 convert onto it. His first victory with the new type came on 19 September 1941, a Spitfire. Then on 6 November, he was appointed *Staffelkapitän* of 8/JG 26.

On 14 May 1942, in a battle against US Viermots with a fighter escort, Borris was shot down again. He baled out, but deployed his parachute at too high a velocity, partially collapsing it. The resultant landing was hard, and he was badly injured. At this point he had twenty-six victories.

Over a year later, he was still only convalescent. But when in June 1943, I/JG 26 returned from the East, he was summoned back to become its *Kommandeur*. Aloof, and a martinet by nature, he rigidly enforced all regulations, even when going by the book resulted in lowered serviceability rates and fewer sorties.

Slowly his score mounted, then another extended absence took him out of the front line. Not until 29 July 1944 did he resume command. He was awarded the *Ritterkreuz* on 24 November 1944, his tally now forty-one, and he celebrated the same day by finishing off a badly damaged B-17.

In December 1944, I/JG 26 began to re-equip with the superb FW 190D, and it was in this type that he led the Bodenplatte attack on an Allied airfield at Grimbergen. His 43rd and final victory was a Spitfire on 14 January 1945.

It was now that his obsession with regulations peaked. His men were forced to share a billet with Luftwaffe girls. In an attempt to prevent undue fraternisation, Borris had a line painted down the hallway which his men were forbidden to cross. But of course, it was invisible in the dark.

Then on 23 January, he was ordered to patrol the jet base at Hansdorf between 16.00 and 16.30, only to encounter hordes of Spitfires and Tempests in the area. When 16.30 came, with the battle still raging, Borris officially changed the mission to a *Freijagd*. As if it mattered! It can only be surmised that such slavish adherence to the correct forms was his touchstone in an uncertain world. At the surrender, he marched his men into captivity, where he continued to impose iron discipline. His tally, all scored in the West, included four Viermots.

Armin Köhler

Experten came from all backgrounds and all walks of life, but one of the most unusual was Armin Köhler. Born to a circus family in 1912, in his youth he was rumoured to have performed with the Rivels, a famous trapeze act. Little is known about his early Jagdwaffe service, but he went through the pre-fighter school at Kamenz during 1941 as a *Feldwebel*. Commissioned shortly after, in March 1942 he was posted to JG 77 in the East. Although relatively elderly at thirty, he was soon off the mark, scoring his first victory on 21 April. Shortly after, I/JG 77 redeployed to Sicily, and from October 1942, the entire Geschwader arrived in Tunisia under Kommodore 'Jochen' Müncheberg.

Köhler, having exchanged one trapeze act for another infinitely more dangerous, had by now proved himself, and was appointed *Staffelkapitän* of 2/JG 77. Despite having contracted malaria, he refused home leave, and pumped full of Atebrin, he continued to fly. Evacuated from Tunisia at the end of April with ground crewmen jammed into the fuselages of their Bf 109Gs, I and II/JG 77 arrived in Sicily.

Flying from inadequate temporary airstrips in Sicily, Köhler endured a hectic time in May, defending Pantelleria. In vain; the island fell, to become a base for Allied fighters. From this point on, Jagdwaffe airfields in Sicily suffered almost constant attacks from Allied fighters and medium bombers.

A new threat then emerged: massed formations of USAAF B-17s and B-24s flying from North Africa, usually with fighter escort, attacking targets both in Sicily and on the Italian mainland.

Against the Viermots, the scenario was essentially different from that over the Reich. First there was little advance warning. Then after bombing, the Viermots often descended to below the inadequate German radar coverage, where low haze masked them from visual detection from above. The pursuing *Jagdflieger* were often drawn far out over the sea, to their extreme discomfort. Köhler's diary for 15 June 1943 reads:

We located the Viermots 150 km off Trapani. They were right down on the water, skimming the crests of the waves, and heading for North Africa. By the time we had expended all our ammunition we found ourselves running low on fuel. This was something that alarmed old hands and new boys alike... I could hear despairing cries: 'My tank's nearly dry – I'm going to drown!'

Their alarm was justified; even if a pilot managed to board his dinghy, his chances of rescue were negligible, as all too many had found to their cost. Nor could he last long under the blazing Mediterranean sun.

The little-known Köhler* was one of the unsung heroes of the Jagdwaffe. His strong Saxon accent, instantly recognisable over the radio, rallied his troops again and again in the battles over Sicily, then later, over Italy. And his score mounted. In August 1944 he became *Kommandeur* of III/JG 77. This *Gruppe* had been detached to the East in May of that year, where it was fought almost to destruction. The quartermaster's returns for 10 January 1945 show its strength as just seven serviceable Bf 109s.

Köhler, by now a Major, ended the war with sixty-nine victories, fifty-five against the West, including thirteen Viermots, in 515 sorties. Given his continuous battle against malaria, this was a remarkable achievement. Taken prisoner by the Russians at war's end, he was sent to Siberia, but escaped en route. Even so, it was 1953 before he returned to Germany.

Josef 'Pepi' Jennewein

It is perhaps surprising that international sportsmen, given their split-second judgement of time and space and their ability to see ahead, rarely become fighter *Experten*. Hermann Graf had been a footballer of repute, while Emil Lang was a field and track athlete. Austrian by birth, 'Pepi' became a world ski champion in 1940, although it must be admitted that with the war under way, the non-Germanic opposition, Switzerland apart, was limited.

Unteroffizier 'Pepi' Jennewein flew against England with 2/JG 26 in the summer of 1940, claiming five victories. In the East, he flew with IV/JG 51, then from early 1943 with I/JG 51. Twice he scored multiple victories, five on 17 January 1943, and seven on 24 February. He was posted missing in action on 26 July near Orel. In 271 sorties he claimed eighty-six victories, eighty-one in the East. Leutnant Jennewein was

---

* Köhler is disguised as Zöhler in Steinhoffs' book, *The Straits of Messina*, London 1971.

awarded a posthumous *Ritterkreuz* on 5 December 1943.

Hermann Buchner

Schlacht pilots were expected to stick to their main task of attacking ground targets, and avoid air combat. However, a few ran up respectable victory scores, Buchner among them. What made him unique was the fact that he successfully made the transition to jet fighters in the air defence role.

A baker's apprentice from Salzburg, Buchner took up gliding in 1934. on 1 October 1937 he joined the *Luftstreitkräfte*, hoping to become a fighter-pilot. But having successfully completed his flying training at the end of 1939, he became an instructor. Not until June 1941 did he escape, to attend the *Jagdfliegerschule* at Werneuchen. There he learned to fly the Bf 109.

Alas for his hopes; he was then sent to II (Schlacht)/G 2 to train as an attack pilot, and in March 1942 to 8/SG 1, later redesignated 6/SG 2. He flew his first operational sortie in the Crimea on 7 May. By now, Soviet strength was growing, and air combat became harder to avoid. In all, Buchner was shot down four times: thrice by fighters, once by ground fire. The first was by an I-16 on 12 September. On the following day he opened his score with an LaGG-3. But the strain of constant operations now began to tell. In October, Buchmann caught a fever, and was out of action until mid-January 1943.

On his recovery he was sent to Leipzig as a factory test pilot, checking out Bf 109G-6s, until an accident put him back in hospital. Not until July was he once more fit to fly, but he then had to convert to the FW 190 before returning to the Front.

On 29 September he claimed a Yak, but was almost immediately shot up and wounded by another. This put him out of action until 12 January 1944. Promoted to Oberfeldwebel, he flew his 500th sortie on 4 March, and his 600th on 4 June. By now his score was mounting, and shortly after he became *Staffelführer* of 4/SG 2.

He claimed his first Viermot, a B-17, on 23 June. On 20 July he was awarded the *Ritterkreuz* for forty-six victories and an equal number of tanks, and was posted home to be an instructor. But he still wanted to be a fighter-pilot!

In November he got his chance. Posted to the newly forming III/JG 7 at Lechfeld, he made his first jet flight on the 19th, and scored his first jet victory, a reconnaissance P-38, one week later. At first he flew with 9/JG 7 commanded by Georg-Peter Eder, then became *Staffelführer* when Eder was shot down and wounded on 22 January 1945.

In March, now a *Leutnant*, Buchner led 10 Staffel, scoring his twelfth and final jet victory on the 31st: an RAF Lancaster, using R4M rockets. Then on 8 April he was caught landing by a Mustang. Nominated for the *Eichenlaub*, he survived unhurt. In 625 sorties, he claimed fifty-eight victories, forty-six in the East (one Viermot) and twelve with the Me 262 (11 Viermots).

Heinrich Ehrler

As the war progressed, Göring's threats of courts martial grew more frequent but ultimately proved empty. There was however a high-scoring *Experte* who was court-martialled and sentenced to death, later commuted to three years imprisonment to be served after the war.

A Swabian from Baden, Ehrler was a flak gunner at the outbreak of war, but remustered to pilot training in 1940. On completion in 1941 he joined an autonomous *Jagdgruppe* in the north, flying against the Soviet Union. In January 1942, this became II/JG 5 Eismeer, part of a newly formed *Jagdgeschwader* which uniquely faced both east and west, from Finland to Norway.

Flying conditions, especially above the Arctic Circle, were terrible. For much of the year the hours of daylight were brief and snowstorms alternated with freezing fog. Despite this, flying against the Russians, Ehrler's score started to mount. Appointed *Staffelkapitän* of 6/JG 5 in August 1942, with forty-two victories he was awarded the *Ritterkreuz* on 21 October. In June 1943 he became *Kommandeur* of III/JG 5, and with 112 victories, he received the *Eichenlaub* on 2 August. Similarly decorated on the same day, with an identical score, was Theodor Weißenberger, then *Staffelkapitän* of 7/JG 5. In May 1944 Ehrler was appointed *Kommodore* of JG 5. By November his tally had risen to 204, all in the East, and he had been nominated for the *Schwerter*.

Now came disaster. On 12 November RAF bombers eluded the fighter defences and sank the German battleship Tirpitz in Tromsö Fjord. A huge outcry followed, and as *Kommodore* of JG 5, Ehrler became duty scapegoat. At his court martial, evidence established that his fighters had failed to respond to radio messages, and he was duly convicted of dereliction of duty.

Having previously flown only the Bf 109, he now converted to the Me 262, flying in the *Stab* of JG 7. Somewhat ironically, the *Geschwader Kommodore* was now his former subordinate and one time rival Weißenberger. His first jet victory was a B-17 on 21 March 1945. A second B-17 followed on the next day, and a third two days later. On 31 March he tangled with the escorts, claiming a P-51 damaged. He flew his final sortie on 6 April, knocking down two more B-17s before falling to the guns of the Mustang escorts. In about 400 sorties, he claimed at least 209 victories, including five Viermots with the Me 262.

Herbert Ihlefeld

Another Pomeranian, Ihlefeld belongs in that distinguished company of pilots who flew from first to last. In fact, he began earlier than most, with seven victories in the Spanish Civil War as an *Oberfeldwebel* in 1937. Commissioned shortly after his return, he was appointed to the Operational Test and Evaluation Unit I(J)/LG 2.

He flew briefly against Poland, then as a *Staffelkapitän* against France and England. In early August 1940 he was appointed *Kommandeur*. Flying from Calais–Marck, his score reached twenty-one on 13 September, when he was awarded the *Ritterkreuz*. By the end of the Battle of Britain, he had claimed four more victories.

Ihlefeld's next venture was in the Balkans, where on 6 April he suffered the ignominy of being shot down over Yugoslavia and taken prisoner. Fortunately for him, he was soon released by the advancing ground forces to continue the assault on Greece. The following month saw I(J)/LG 2 operating against Crete, although little air opposition was encountered in the latter.

His tally now thirty-six, gained in Channel operations against England in 1941 as well as in the Balkans, Ihlefeld next led I (J) /LG 2 to Romania. Four victories in the East brought him the *Eichenlaub* on 27 June. He continued to score well, and on 22 April 1942, he became the fifth pilot to reach one hundred, receiving the *Schwerter* two days later.

In the following month he left I/JG 77, as I(J)/LG 2 had now been re-designated, to become *Kommodore* of JG 52. With his score in the East at sixty-seven, he returned to the West to command the fighter training unit JG 103. In July 1943 he set up JGr Nord 25, one of two special units to intercept Mosquitos. Unsuccessful, both were disbanded after four months.*

Ihlefeld was then appointed *Kommodore* of JG 11 on home defence, claiming another nineteen victories, fifteen of them Viermots. His final appointment, in 1945, was *Kommodore* of JG 1, tasked with working up on

---

* The other was JGr Süd (Ost), later JGr 50, under Hermann Graf.

the He 162 jet fighter.

In all, Herbert Ihlefeld flew more than 1,000 sorties and claimed 130 victories, seven in Spain, fifty-six against the West the rest in the East.

Hans-Joachim Jabs

A native of Lübeck, 'Achim' Jabs was remarkable for his dual success as both *Zerstörer* and *Nachtjagd Experte*. He joined the Luftwaffe in December 1936. on completion of his training, he became a Bf 109 pilot. But not for long. Göring's 'Ironsides' were considered the elite, and Jabs's outstanding flying ability caused him to be transferred to II/ZG 76 in March 1940.

This was the famous Haifisch (Shark) Gruppe, which painted shark mouths on its aircraft long before the American Volunteer Group in China did so. With seven victories over France, four French and three British, Jabs was one of the most successful Haifisch pilots. Over England in August and September 1940, he added another twelve, which brought him the *Ritterkreuz* on 1 October. At this point he was the leading *Zerstörer* pilot; a remarkable performance against the faster and more agile Hurricanes and spitfires.

Although II/ZG 76 remained in the West, no further victories came his way. Then in September 1941 he was remustered to night fighting, claiming two night victories with III/NJG 3. Then in November he replaced the promoted Egmont zur Lippe-Weissenfeld as *Staffelkapitän* of 5/NJG 2. Shortly after, this *Gruppe* became IV/NJG 1, commanded by Werner Streib, 5/NJG 2 becoming 11/NJG 1. Almost at once, 'Achim' started to add to his score.

In February 1943, the Viermots of the USAAF were starting to make their presence felt. In an act of supreme folly, the heavily laden Bf 110 night-fighters, burdened with black boxes and draggy radar antennae, were ordered to intercept in daylight. On 4 February, Jabs led eight Bf 110s into battle. They downed three B-17s, of which Jabs claimed one, but all eight night-fighters were damaged, and two force-landed.

Meanwhile Jabs was doing well at night. On the night of 19/20 February he accounted for three stirlings in one sortie. Then on 26 February he led twelve Messerschmitts against a force of American Liberators in daylight. One of his aircraft failed to return. Ludwig Becker, *Staffelkapitän* of 12/NJG 1, a leading night *Experte* with forty-four victories to his credit, was killed. Becker, a leading night-fighter tactician, was awarded the *Eichenlaub* posthumously, but the loss to the *Nachtjagd-flieger* was enormous. The idiocy of sending out highly trained specialists in daylight was finally exposed, and the error was not repeated.

When on 1 August 1943, Helmut Lent was appointed *Kommodore* of NJG 3, Jabs replaced him as *Kommandeur* of IV/NJG 1. Whereas most *Nachtjagdflieger* used *Schräge Musik*, Jabs had it removed from his aircraft to obtain a slight increase in performance.

Appointed *Kommodore* of NJG 1 in March 1944, Jabs was awarded the *Eichenlaub* on the 24th. While he survived the war, it was a near thing. on 29 April 1944, returning to his base in Arnhem in daylight, he was bounced by eight Spitfires. Although it was a mismatch, a hard turn in the cumbersome night fighter forced them to overshoot. He then turned into them for a head-on pass and shot one down. As he dived for his base he once again forced them to overshoot, shooting down another as it went by. By now badly hit, he slammed his aircraft onto the ground and legged it as it stopped rolling.

His last victories were two Lancasters at night on 21 February 1945. His unexceptional war total was fifty, twenty-two by day including one Viermot, and twenty-eight by night. But given his skill with the unwieldy Bf 110, he might easily have become the leading *Zerstörer* pilot of the war. Post-war he became a businessman.

REFERENCES

Aders, Gebhard, *History of the German Night Fighter Force 1917–1945*, Janes, London, 1979.

Anon., *The Rise and Fall of the German Air Force, 1933–1945*, Arms & Armour Press, London, 1983.

Bekker, Cajus D., *The Luftwaffe War Diaries*, Macdonald, London, 1967.

Bickers, Richard Townshend, *Von Richthofen, the Legend Evaluated*, Airlife, Shrewsbury, 1996.

Buchner, Hermann, *Stormbird*, Hikoki Publications, Aldershot, 2000.

Caldwell, Donald L, *JG 26, Top Guns of the Luftwaffe*, Ballantine Books, New York, 1993.

Constable, Trevor J. and Raymond F. Toliver, *Fighter Aces of the Luftwaffe*, Aero Publishers, California, 1977.

Constable, Trevor J. and Raymond F. Toliver, *The Blond Knight of Germany*, Arthur Barker, London, 1970.

Crankshaw, Edward, *Gestapo*, Putnam & Co, London, 1956.

Faber, Harold (ed.), *Luftwaffe: an Analysis by Former Luftwaffe Generals*, Times Books, New York, 1977; Sidgwick & Jackson, London, 1979.

Galland, Adolf, *The First and the Last; the German Fighter Force in WW2*, Methuen, London, 1955.

Hinchliffe, Peter, *The Lent Papers, Helmut Lent*, Cerberus Publishing, Bristol, 2003.

Hooton, E.R., *Phoenix Triumphant*, Arms & Armour, London, 1994.

Hooton, E.R., *Eagle in Flames*, Arms & Armour, London, 1997.

Johnen, W., *Duel under the Sea*, W. Kimber, London, 1957.

Knoke, Heinz, *I Flew for the Führer*, Evans, London, 1953.

Morgan, Hugh and John Weal, *German Jet Aces of World War 2*, Osprey, London, 1998.

Obermaier, Ernst, *Die Ritterkreuzträger der Luftwaffe; Jagdflieger 1939–1945*, Verlag Dieter Hoffman, Mainz, 1966.

Parry, Simon W, *Intruders over Britain*, Air Research Publications, London, 1992.

Price, Alfred, *Battle over the Reich*, Ian Allan, London, 1973.

Price, Alfred, *Instruments of Darkness*, Macdonald & Janes, London, 1977.

Price, Alfred, *The Last Year of the Luftwaffe*, Arms & Armour, London, 1991.

Price, Alfred, *The Luftwaffe Data Book*, Greenhill Books, London, 1997.

Richthofen, Manfred von, *The Red Baron*, translated by Peter Kilduff, edited by Stanley M.Ulanoff, Bailey Brothers & Swinfen Ltd, London, 1974.

Scutts, Jerry, *JG 54, Jagdgeschwader 54 Grünherz Aces of the Eastern Front*, Airlife, Shrewsbury, 1992.

Shores, Christopher, *Duel for the Sky*, Blandford Press, Poole, Dorset, 1985.

Sims, Edward H., *The Fighter Pilots*, Cassell, London, 1967.

Spick, Mike, *The Ace Factor*, Airlife, Shrewsbury, 1988.

Spick, Mike, *Luftwaffe Fighter Aces, the Jagdflieger and their Combat Tactics and Techniques*, Greenhill Books, London, 1996.

Spick, Mike, *The Complete Fighter Ace, All the World's Fighter Aces, 1914–2000*, Greenhill Books, London, 1999.

Steinhoff, Johannes, *The Straits of Messina; Diary of a Fighter Commander*, André Deutsch, London, 1971.

Steinhoff, Johannes, *The Last Chance*, Hutchinson, London, 1977.

Townsend, Peter, *Duel of Eagles*, Weidenfeld & Nicolson, London, 1969.

Weal, John, *Focke-Wulf FW 190 Aces of the Russian Front*, Osprey, London, 1995.

Weal, John, *Focke-Wulf FW 190 Aces of the Western Front*, Osprey, London, 1996.

Ziegler, Mano, *Rocket Fighter*, Arms & Armour, London, 1976 (original edition *Raketenjäger Me 163*, Motorbuch, Stuttgart, 1961).

INDEX

Adameit, Horst 159
Andres, Ernst 181
Augenstein, Hans-Heinz 181

Baagoe, Sophus 115
Bahr, Günther 180
Balthasar, Wilhelm 85, 89, 91, 92, 96, 122, 200
Bär, Heinz 'Pritzl' 87, 124, 147, 148, 178, 186–7, 188, 189, 219–20
Barkhorn, Gerhard 156, 159, 188, 196–7
Baro, Dr 143
Bartels, Heinrich 153
Batz, Wilhelm 157
Becker, Karl-Heinz 182
Becker, Ludwig 130, 131, 133, 134, 135, 141, 233
Becker, Martin 'Tino' 141–2, 143, 180
Beckh, Freidrich 124
Beerenbrock, Franz-Josef 211–12
Belser, Helmut 125
Berres, Heinz-Edgar 148
Bertram, Otto 89
Beyer, Franz 151
Bitsch, Emil 151
Bob, Hans-Ekkehard 188
Boelcke, Oswald 21–2, 24, 88
Borchers, Walter 181
Borris, Karl 154, 227–8
Böwing-Treuding, Wolfgang 156
Braham, Bob (RAF) 141
Bretnütz, Heinz 'Pietsch' 121
Brunner, Albert 156
Brustellin, Hans-Heinrich 40

Buchner, Hermann 187, 230–1
Burbridge, Branse & Bill Skelton (RAF) 224
Bühligen, Kurt 113, 147, 148, 153
Bülow-Bothkamp, Harry von 89
Bundrock, Kurt 134

Cramon-Taubadel, Hans-Jürgen von 88
Crüger, Arved 209

Dahl, Walther 178
Denk, Gustav 156
Dickfeld, Adolf 147, 148
Dittmar, Heini, Test Pilot 169, 171
Döbrich, Hans 156
Dörr, Franz 82
Dowding, H C T 'Stuffy' (RAF) 177
Drewer, Martin 143
Driver, Kenneth (SAAF) 118
Duke, Neville (RAF) 119

Ebeling, Heinz 89
Ebener, Kurt 152
Eder, Georg-Peter 153, 168, 187, 230
Ehrler, Heinrich 156, 231–2
Eisenbach Riedesel, Volprecht Freiherr von und zu 186
Ettel, Wolf 149

Falck, Woltgang 81, 83, 129, 131, 214
Fözö, Josef, 'Joschko' 123
Francsi, Gustav 143
Frank, Hans-Dieter 141
Franzisket, Ludwig 116, 117, 118, 119

Frey, Hugo 137
Friebel, Herbert 82
Friedrich, Gerhard 181
Fuchs, Robert 160

Galland, Adolf 40, 42, 45, 46, 59, 82, 84,
    85, 88, 89, 91, 92, 96, 113, 119, 121,
    137, 149, 152, 168, 173, 174, 178–80,
    185, 187, 188, 189, 198–201, 202, 203,
    205, 208, 214, 220
Galland, Wilhelm-Ferdinand 'Wutz' 150
Gänsler, Wilhelm 143, 211, 213
Geiger, August 141
Gentzen, Hannes 81, 84
Geyer, Horst 166
Gildner, Paul 133
Glunz, Adolf 'Addi' 150
Göbbels, Josef 210
Gollob, Gordon Mc 83, 122, 123, 124,
    178, 179, 185, 198
Goltzsch, Kurt 150
Göring, Hermann-Wilhelm 18, 26–31, 33,
    35, 37, 38, 42, 46, 84, 87, 88, 122, 126,
    131, 136, 151, 153, 168, 172–3, 176-
    179, 185, 200, 226, 231, 233
Grabmann, Walter 77
Graf, Hermann 124, 178, 188, 210–11,
    222, 229, 232
Grasser, Hartmann 147
Groth, Erich 90
Grünberg, Hans 'Specker' 188

Haas, Friedrich 183
Haase, Horst 153
Hackl, Anton 'Toni' 147
Hager, Johannes 180
Haiböck, Josef 157
Handke, Erich 143
Handrick, Gotthard 88
Harder, Jürgen 148, 184
Hartmann, Erich 156, 158, 188, 193–6,
    206, 211, 216, 223
Heckmann, Alfred 188
Held, Alfred 82
Herget, Willi 188, 224–5
Hermann, Haus-Joachim 'Hajo' 140

Hißbach, Heinz-Horst 142
Hitler, Adolf, 'Der Gröfaz' 17, 28, 41,
    94–5, 129, 166, 172, 174, 175, 177, 179
Hoffmann, Gerhard 158, 183
Hoffmann, Heinrich 121
Hofmann, Wilhelm 154, 184
Hohagen, Erich 168, 187, 188, 223–4
Höhn, Carola 209
Homuth, Gerhard 116, 117, 119
Hrabak, Dietrich 156, 225
Hrdlicka, Franz 184
Huppertz, Herbert 152
Huy, Wolf-Dietrich 115

Ibel, Max 40, 89
Ihlefeld, Herbert 115, 191, 202–3

Jabs, Hans-Joachim 'Achim' 90, 233–4
Janke, Johannes 40
Jennewein, Josef, 'Pepi' 229–30
Jeschonnek, Hans 35, 36, 37
Johanssen, Karl-Ludwig 180`
Johnen, Wilhelm 180–1
Joppien, Hermann-Friedrich 92, 113, 123
Josten, Günther 158
Junk, Werner 39, 40

Kageneck, Erbo Graf von 118
Kaiser, Herbert 148
Kaldrack, Rolf (Schlitzohr) 90
Kammbuber, Josef 130, 133
Kelb, Fritz 191
Keller, Lothar 121
Kempf, Karl 152
Kesselring, Albert 29, 34
Kirschner, Joachim 156
Kittel, Otto 156, 158, 183, 198
Knacke, Reinhold 133–4, 141
Köhler, Armin 228–9
Kolbow, Hans 121
Körner, Friedrich 116
Korts, Berthold 195
Köster, Alfons 133, 134, 181
Krahl, Karl-Heinz 118
Kramer, Darren (USAAF) 217
Kroschiniski, Hans-Joachim 183

Krupinski, Walter (Graf Punski) 159, 188, 205, 206–7
Kubisch, Walter 134, 141, 142
Kümmritz, Herbert 215

Lacey, Jim (Ginger) (RAF) 224
Lambert, August 158
Lang, Emil 'Bully' 152, 217–18, 229
Lau, Fritz 82
Leie, Erich 113, 183
Lemke, Siegried 'Wumm' 153–4
Lemke, Wilhelm 156–7
Lent, Helmut 75, 77, 83, 131, 133, 134, 141, 142, 211, 212, 215, 216, 234
Liebherr, Hans 224
Lipfert, Helmut 158–95
Lippert, Wolfgang 118
Lippe-Weisenfeld, Egmont Prinz zur 133, 214, 215–16, 233
Lörzer, Bruno 25
Lützow, Günther 'Franzl' 44, 88, 89, 113, 122, 178, 179, 188, 189, 201–2, 213, 220

Machold, Werner 89, 92
Malan, 'Sailor' (RAF) 199
Maltzahn, Günther 'Henri' Freiherr von 88, 89, 118, 201, 203–4, 208, 213
Marseille, Hans-Joachim 'Jochen' 87, 116, 117, 119, 125, 205–6, 216
Mason, 'Imshi' (RAF) 119
Mayer, Egon 'Connie' 113, 134, 135, 137, 150–1
Mayer, Hans-Karl 89
Mayerl, Maximilian 156
Meimberg, Julius 154
Methfessel, Werner 81, 84
Mettig, Martin 89
Meurer, Manfred 141, 212
Michalski, Gerhard 119
Mietusch, Klaus 115, 153
Milch, Erhard 26-27, 31, 32, 33, 34, 35, 37, 38, 176
Mölders, Werner 'Vati' 44, 57, 59, 83, 85, 88, 89, 91, 96, 113, 120, 121, 122, 123, 198–201, 202, 226
Moritz, Wilhelm 137

Müller, Friedrich-Karl 'Nasen' 140
Müncheberg, Joachim 'Jochen' 90, 92, 115, 147, 148, 208–10, 228
Mütherich, Hubert 'Hubs' 121

Nacke, Heinz 90
Naumann, Johannes, 'Focke' 154
Neubert, Frank 75
Neumann, Eduard 'Edu' 115, 148, 178, 205
Nowotny, Walter 'Nowi' 156, 157, 167, 168, 220–1

Obleser, Friedrich 198
Oesan, Walter 'Gulle' 59, 89, 92, 113, 122, 124, 151, 183, 226
Olejnik, Robert 171
Opitz, Rudolf, test pilot 170, 171
Ostermann, Max-Hellmuth 115
Osterkamp, 'Onkel' Theo 87, 88, 90, 94, 96, 199, 203, 217
Ostheimer, Friedrich 215
Overclaiming, discussion of 50

Pelz, Dietrich 185
Pflanz, Rudi 113
Philipp, Hans 'Fips' 124, 136
Pöhs, Josef 'Joschi' 169, 171
Priller, Josef 'Pips' 46, 149, 179, 220

Quast, Werner 'Quax' 150

Radusch, Günther 45, 142, 212
Raht, Gerhard 180
Rall, Günther 120, 188, 197–8
Redlich, Karl-Heinz 116, 117, 119
Reinert, Ernst-Wilhelm 147
Reinhard, Wilhelm 27
Restemeyer, Werner 87
Richthofen, Manfred Freiherr von, the Red Baron legend 18–24, 27, 29, 30, 32, 36, 46, 48, 57, 88, 91, 121, 193
Richthofen, Lothar von 22–4
Richthofen, Wolfram von 36
Rödel, Gustav 45, 84, 119, 148, 178, 199
Rökker, Heinz 143, 212

Rossmann, Edmund 'Paule' 194
Rübell, Günther 148
Rubensdörffer, Walter 88
Rudorffer, Erich 113, 147, 148, 187, 218, 219, 220
Rumpelhardt, Fritz 143, 211, 213
Rupp, Friedrich 82

Sachsenberg, Heinz 188
Sayn-Wittgenstein, Heinrich Prinz von 133, 141, 212, 214, 215
Schäfer, Fritz, test pilot 162–3
Schall, Franz 168
Schallmoser, Edward, 'the Jet Rammer' 188
Scheel, Günther 156
Scheib, Gerhard 141
Schellmann, Wolfgang 82, 89, 121
Scheiß, Franz 148
Schleich, Eduard Ritter von 25
Schlichting, Joachim 44
Schlief, Hptm 77
Schmid, Johann 113
Schmid, Josef 'Beppo' 38
Schmidt, Erich 121, 123
Schmidt, Winfried 123
Schmitt, Rudolf 191
Schnaufer, Heinz-Wolfgang 143, 180, 211, 213
Schnell, Siegfried 'Wumm' 113
Schnörrer, Karl 'Quax' 167
Schoenebeck, Carl-August Freiherr von 39
Schönert, Rudolf 134, 252
Schöpfel, Gerhard 149
Schroer, Werner 116, 119, 148
Schuck, Walter 158
Schulte, Helmuth 82
Schulz, Otto 119, 147–8
Schwaiger, Franz 151
Semrau, Paul 133, 181
Simsch, Siegfried 152
Sinner, Rudolf 187
Sochatzy, Kurt 121, 123
Späte, Wolfgang 169–70, 172
Sperrle, Hugo 35–6
Stahlschmidt, Hans-Arnold 'Fifi' 116, 119

Staub, Josef 134
Streib, Werner 130, 131, 133, 134, 139, 212, 213–14, 233
Steinbatz, Leopold, 'Poldi' 124, 222
Steinhoff, Johannes 'Macky' 9–12, 83, 147, 148, 155, 168, 174, 178, 179, 184, 187, 188, 189, 196, 204, 206, 220, 223–4
Strelow, Hans 125, 216–17
Strüning, Heinz 133
Stumpf, Hans-Jürgen 34–5
Sturm, Heinrich 158

Tangermann, Kurt 160
Tegtmeier, Fritz 157
Teumer, Alfred 167
Thierfelder, Werner 166
Tietzen, Horst 'Jacob' 89, 225–6
Trautloft, Hannes 40, 46, 57, 89, 178, 201, 202–3, 213
Troitsch, Hans 82

Ubben, Kurt 'Kuddel' 115, 151, 153
Udet, Ernst 'Udlinger' 21, 24, 25, 28, 32–4, 36, 37, 121

Vieck, Carl 88
Vogt, Gerhard 154

Wachowiak, Friedrich 152
Wagner, Edmund 121
Waldmann, Hans-Peter 'Dackel' 158
Weber, Joachim 187
Weber, Karl-Heinz 152
Weiß Robert 'Bazi' 153
Weißenberger, Theodor, 124, 156, 168, 187, 231
Welter, Kurt 182, 226
Wever, Walther 31–2, 35
Wick, Helmut 89, 91, 200, 201
Wilcke, Wolf-Dietrich 120
Wörndl, Alois 171
Wübke, Waldemar 'Hein' 189
Wurmheller, Josef 'Sepp' 113, 152

Ziegler, Mano, test pilot 171
Zweigart, Eugen-Ludwig 152